CHRIST AND THE LAW IN PAUL

BY

BRICE L. MARTIN

Wipf and Stock Publishers
EUGENE, OREGON

Wipf and Stock Publishers
199 West 8th Avenue, Suite 3
Eugene, Oregon 97401

Christ and the Law in Paul
By Martin, Brice L.

ISBN: 1-57910-762-1
Publication date: September, 2001
Previously published by E. J. Brill, 1989.

TABLE OF CONTENTS

PREFACE

The following work is an expansion, up-dating, and rethinking of the Pauline part of my doctoral dissertation, *Matthew and Paul on Christ and the Law: Compatible or Incompatible Theologies?*, McMaster University, 1977. The work also contains material that was published in two short articles: "Paul on Christ and the Law," JETS 26 (1983) 271-283; and "Some Reflections on the Identity of *egō* in Romans 7:14-25," SJT 34 (1981), 39-47. I am especially indebted to all who have written on this topic before me. They have labored and I have entered into their labors. I am grateful to my wife, Erma, and my two children, Anna and David, who put up with me during the long hours it took me to write this book. I am thankful also for my trusty Kaypro II computer; without it I do not think I would ever have had the courage to write. Above all I am thankful to Paul, who inspired by God, has written to us of God's matchless grace, and of our new life in Christ.

The Scriptural quotations are from the RSV.

This reprint is the same text as the 1989 edition. I, however, no longer have access to the original printer and word processor so the formatting is different but the pagination is the same; the page breaks are usually within a few lines of the original. I should have stated on pp 2 and 68, as I did on pp 134, 141, and 154, that there is some telic force to *telos* in Rom 10:4; for the believer Christ brings the enslavement, condemnation, and death which came through the law to their *appointed* end.

In the footsteps of E. P. Sanders many have continued to claim that Paul's concern is to have Jew and Gentile equal and that to see Paul as presenting Judaism as a religion of works righteousness distorts Judaism. This view does not recognize that for Paul the human plight is much deeper and more profound than it is in contemporary Judaism, and that the required solution is much greater. For Paul salvation can only come through Christ (see chs 3 and 4). This starting point in large measure accounts for a different presentation of Judaism. From his Christian standpoint Paul states what Judaism is really up to; this at various points does not necessarily correlate with what contemporary Jews self-consciously believed (see § 3.2.3.2 p 89 below).

Further support for my view that there is at least an implicit distinction between the 'moral' law and the 'ceremonial' law (see § 2.2 pp. 32-34 below) can be found in the comments of Greg Bahnsen (pp 110-113) and Walter Kaiser (pp 188-190) in *The Law, The Gospel, and the Modern Christian*. ed. Wayne G. Strickland. Grand Rapids: Zondervan, 1993. I have learned much from Frank Thielman, *A Contextual Approach: Paul and the Law* (Downers Grove, Ill. 1994) on how Paul actually appeals to the Mosaic law for guidance even in letters such as 1 and 2 Thessalonians where the term *nomos* does not appear (pp. 69-79; 256-258). I also appreciate Thielman's extensive comments on the role of the Spirit in the eschatological age to empower us to obey the law (*From Plight to Solution*. Leiden: Brill, 1989, pp 36, 41-44, 86-91, 102, 108, 116-121); cf. § 5.4.5 pp. 147f below and Ezekiel 36:26-27. In the same work Thielman claims that Paul presents his argument *from plight to solution*; I agree but I also believe Paul thought through his view *from solution to plight*. Once he received the gospel, he had to rethink the role of the law in light of his new view that salvation can only come through Christ.

Readers are invited to send comments to bricelmartin@hotmail.com.

Arthur, Ontario, Canada,
August 20, 2001

ABBREVIATIONS

AB	*Anchor Bible*
BAGD	Bauer, Walter. *A Greek-English Lexicon of the New Testament and other Early Christian Literature*. Translated and adapted by William F. Arndt and F. Wilbur Gingrich. 2nd ed revised and augmented by F. Wilbur Gingrich and Fredrich W. Danker. Chicago: University of Chicago Press, 1979.
BBB	*Bonner Biblische Beiträge*
BDF	Blass, F. and Debrunner A. *A Greek Grammar of The New Testament and Other Early Christian Literature*. Chicago: Universtity of Chicago Press, 1961.
BEvT	*Beiträge zur evangelischen Theologie*
Bib	*Biblica*
BibLeb	*Bibel Und Leben*
BJRL	*Bulletin of the John Rylands Library*
BNTC	*Black's New Testament Commentaries*
BZ	*Biblische Zeitschrift*
BZNW	*Beihefte zur Zeitschrift für die neutestamentliche Wissenschaft*
CBQ	*Catholic Biblical Quarterly*
CD	*Church Dogmatics*
CGTC	*Cambridge Greek Testament Commentary*
EKKNT	*Evangelisch-katholischer Kommentar zum Neuen Testament*
EvT	*Evangelische Theologie*
ExpT	*Expository Times*
FRLANT	*Forschungen zur Religion und Literatur des Alten und Neuen Testaments*
FS	*Festschrift*
HeyJ	*Heythrop Journal*
HNT	*Handbuch zum Neuen Testament*
HNTC	*Harper's New Testament Commentaries*
HTKNT	*Herder's theologischer Kommentar zum Neuen Testament*
HTR	*Harvard Theological Review*
IB	*Interpreter's Bible*
ICC	*International Critical Commentary*
Int	*Interpretation*
JBL	*Journal of Biblical Literature*
JETS	*Journal of the Evangelical Theological Society*
JSNT	*Journal for the Study of the New Testament*
JSOT	*Journal for the Study of the Old Testament*
KD	*Kerygma und Dogma*
KEK	*Kritisch-exegetischer Kommentar über das Neue Testament*

LSJ	Liddell, H. G. and Scott, R. *A Greek-English Lexicon.* Revised and augmented by H. Stuart-Jones and R. McKenzie. 9th ed. Oxford: Clarendon, 1940.
MTZ	*Münchener theologische Zeitschrift*
NCB	*New Century Bible*
NICNT	*New International Commentary on the New Testament*
NIDNTT	Brown, Colin (ed). *The New International Dictionary of New Testament Theology.* 3 Vols. Translated, with additions and Corrections, from the German *Theologisches Begriffslexicon zum Neuen Testament.* (eds. Lothar Coenen, Erich Beyreuther, and Hans Bietenard. Grand Rapids: Zondervan, 1975, 1976, 1978.
NIGTC	*New International Greek Testament Commentary*
NovT	*Novum Testamentum*
NRT	*La nouvelle revue theologique*
NTS	*New Testament Studies*
SBL	*Society of Biblical Literature*
SBT	*Studies in Biblical Theology*
SE	*Studia Evangelica*
SJT	*Scottish Journal of Theology*
SNTSMS	*Society for New Testament Studies Monograph Series*
SWJT	*South West Journal of Theology*
SR	*Studies in Religion/Sciences religieuses*
ST	*Studia Theologica*
TDNT	Kittel, Gerhard, and Friedrich, Gerhard, eds. *Theological Dictionary of the New Testament.* Translated by Geoffrey W. Bromiley 10 vols. Grand Rapids: Eerdmans, 1964-1976.
TDOT	Botterweck, G Johannes, and Ringgren Helmer. *Theological Dictionary of The Old Testament.* 5 Vols. Grand Rapids: Eerdmans, 1974-1986.
TGl	*Theologie und Glaube*
THKNT	*Theologischer Handkommentar zum Neuen Testament*
TLZ	*Theologische Literaturzeitung*
TNTC	*The Tyndale New Testament Commentaries*
TQ	*Theologische Quartalschrift*
TynBul	*Tyndale Bulletin*
TZ	*Theologische Zeitschrift*
VD	*Verbum Domini*
WMANT	*Wissenschaftliche Monographien zum Alten und Neuen Testament*
WUNT	*Wissenschaftliche Untersuchungen zum Neuen Testament*
WTJ	*Westminster Theological Journal*
ZNW	*Zeitschrift für die neutestamentliche Wissenschaft*
ZTK	*Zeitschrift für Theologie und Kirche*

INTRODUCTION

"Circumcised on the eighth day, of the people of Israel, of the tribe of Benjamin, a Hebrew born of Hebrews, as to the law a Pharisee ... as to righteousness under the law blameless" (Phil 3:5-6), catches something of the pride that Paul as a Jew once had in Judaism and its law (Torah). But how does Paul as a Christian view the status of the law now that Christ has come? To this question a quite considerable variety of sometimes mutually exclusive nuanced answers have been given. The answers have ranged from Luther, who denied the *usus normativus* to Lutheranism, which affirmed it; from Calvin who claimed that Christ abrogated the ceremonial law but not the moral law, to the modern view that the law is indivisible; from Albert Schweitzer, who saw the law as belonging to the natural world and the rule of angels, to C. E. B. Cranfield, who believes that Christ is the ultimate goal and innermost meaning of the law.

In the present situation there are manifold points of view on the law as well. Some argue that Christ is the goal of the law (*nomos*), and others that he terminates it, and still others that he does both. Some claim that Paul's view of the law is flatly contradictory while others hold that his view changed and developed, and still others that his statements depend on the circumstances in which he is writing. There is a divergence of opinion on such questions as the origin and purpose of the law, divisions within it, and its validity as a way of life for the Christian.[1]

Recent monographs - i.e., by C Thomas Rhyne (1981), Robert Badenas (1985), Heikki Räisänen (1983), E. P. Sanders (1983), and Hans Hübner (1984) - illustrate the point. Rhyne and Badenas challenge the view that Christ abrogated the law; they believe that he is the goal of the law in the sense that it bears witness to him. Räisänen sees Paul's view as hopelessly contradictory.

---

[1] On the history of research from the latter part of the nineteenth century to the mid-1960's see Otto Kuss, "Nomos bei Paulus," MTZ 17 (1966) 173-227, 177-210. He summarizes the views of Adolph Zahn (1876), Robert Tiling (1878), Fleishauer (1883), Eduard Grafe (1884, 1893), J. Ph. Glock (1885), Samuel Cler (1886), Helmut Witt (1888, 1889), Ernst Kühl (1892, 1894), Friedrich Sieffert (1869), R. Zehnpfund (1897), Paul Feine (1899), Oswald Schulz (1902), Chr. A. Bugge (1903), H. A. A. Kennedy (1917), John F. Walvoord (1937), Peter Bläser (1941), Christian Maurer (1941), Walter Gutbrod (1942), Hans Dieter Wendland (1952), Ragnar Bring (1959), P. G. Verweijs (1960), Andrew John Bandstra (1964), Irene Beck (1964, 1965), and C. E. B Cranfield (1964). In addition, 203-210, Kuss summarizes the work of the Jewish scholars Moritz Löwy (1903, 1904), Joseph Klausner (1950), and Hans- Joachim Schoeps (1959). Andrea van Dülmen, *Die Theologie Des Gesetzes by Paulus* (Stuttgart: Verlag Katholisches Bibelwerk, 1968), 231-257 summarizes the work of Christian Maurer (1941), Peter Bläser (1941), Hans- Joachim Schoeps (1959), Rudolf Bultmann (1961), and Heinrich Schlier (1962).

For a thorough bibliography on the law see Heikki Räisänen, *Paul and the Law* (WUNT 29; Tübingen: Mohr [Siebeck], 1983), 270-297.

Sanders challenges the traditional view that Paul is against "works of law"; in Paul as in Judaism one must do "works of law" to stay saved. Hübner claims that Paul almost completely changed his mind between the writing of Galatians and Romans; in Romans the Torah is not abrogated, Christ is the end of a misused law.

Part of the reason for this divergence of opinion is that Paul says a wide variety of seemingly contradictory things about the law. On the one hand he can say that the law is holy, just, and good (Rom 7:12), and is summed up in the love commandment (Gal 5:14; Rom 13:8-10); yet it brings a curse (Gal 3:13), wrath (Rom 4:15), sin, and death (1 Cor 15:56; Rom 7:7-25). On the one hand we are to fulfill its just requirement (Rom 8:4) and on the other we have died to it and are discharged from it (Rom 7:4-6).

In this inquiry we shall consider the main issues on the law that scholarship has raised, and that arise from an attentive reading of Paul's epistles. Our main task will be to discover the question that Paul is asking and answering and the key which explains his varied negative and positive statements on the law.

This work is divided into five chapters. Chapter one surveys the data on the law in the Pauline letters. Chapter two considers some issues that arise from an attentive reading of the data. Chapter three analyzes the basic problem that Paul has with the law, while chapter four gives the solution. Chapter five considers both the key assertion that Christ is the *telos* of the law and some implications that follow from a proper understanding of that assertion.

My contribution here will be to relate the negative and positive statements on the law to the believer's participation in the death and resurrection of Jesus, and to show that Christ is the *telos* of the law in Rom 10:4 in the sense that for the believer he ends the enslavement, condemnation, and death which the law has brought.

CHAPTER ONE

THE DATA

Of the thirteen books in the Pauline corpus the word *nomos* occurs in only six of them. It does not occur in 1 or 2 Thessalonians, 2 Corinthians, Philemon, Colossians, 2 Timothy, or Titus, yet the concept of the law is present in 2 Corinthians and Colossians. *Nomos* occurs 119 times and in all but three cases (Eph 2:15; 1 Tim 1:8, 9) in books which are indisputably Pauline. Of the remaining 116 times it occurs 3 times in Philippians, 9 times in 1 Corinthians, but 33 times in Galatians, and 74 times in Romans. Although a statistical counting of words could be misleading as an indicator of the relative importance of a concept, in the case of Paul and the law it accurately indicates that the major statements about the law are given in Galatians and Romans.

My consideration of the law in the disputed Pauline literature (Colossians, Ephesians, 1 Timothy)[1] will be confined to the footnotes.[2] These books would contribute little to an overall understanding of Paul's view of the law and can be correlated with the other statements about the law in the Pauline literature.[3]

---

[1] Colossians is frequently viewed as Pauline, Ephesians somewhat less so, and the Pastorals less still. Two scholars who regard each of these books as Pauline are Donald Guthrie, *New Testament Introduction: The Pauline Epistles* (Chicago: Inter-Varsity, 1963) 99-128, 167-71, 198-236; and John A. T. Robinson, *Redating The New Testament* (London: SCM, 1976) 61-85. For a defense of the Pauline authorship of Colossians see Werner Georg Kümmel, *Introduction to the New Testament* (London: SCM, 1966) 240-44. For a defense of the Pauline authorship of Ephesians see Barth, *Ephesians* I, 36-50. For a defense of the Pauline authorship of the Pastoral Epistles see Donald Guthrie, *The Pastoral Epistles* (London: Tyndale Press, 1957) 12-52; and J. N. D. Kelly, *A Commentary on The Pastoral Epistles* (BNTC; London: A & C Black, 1963). For a defense of all thirteen letters as Pauline see: Donald Guthrie, *The Pauline Epistles*; and Robinson, *Redating*, 31-85.

[2] In Col 2:14 God has "canceled the bond (*to ... cheirographon*) which stood against us with its legal demands" (*tois dogmasin*). At 2:8, 20 the Christian has died to "the elemental spirits of the universe" (*ta stoicheia tou kosmou*) which are opposed to Christ. In each of these passages there is an exegetical tradition which links them with the law of Moses. See Räisänen, *Law*, 203-207; and Herold Weiss, "The Law in the Epistle to the Colossians," CBQ 34 (1972), 294-314, 294-305 for a summary of views. Colossians is also opposed to imposing presumably Jewish regulations (of food, drink, festivals, new moon and Sabbath) on Christians (2:16-17).

In Ephesians 2:15 Christ has abolished the law of commandments contained in ordinances (*ton nomon tōn entolōn en dogmasin katargēsas*) yet at 6:2-3 the fifth commandment of the decalogue, the commandment to honor Father and mother is binding for the Christian. On the meaning of this text see Markus Barth, *Ephesians* (2 Vols. AB; New York: Doubleday, 1974) I, 287-291.

At 1 Tim 1:8, 9 the law is good if it is used lawfully (*kalos ho nomos ean tis autō̧ nomimōs chrētai*). The law is not laid down for the just but for the lawless (*anomois*).

[3] Räisänen, *Law*, 205, has radical views on the law yet acknowledges that the law in Colossians is indistinguishable from the authentic Pauline letters.

I shall consider the data on the law in Paul's letters in the chronological order in which, so far as I can tell, Paul wrote his letters, namely: Galatians, 1 Corinthians, 2 Corinthians, Romans, and Philippians.[4]

1.1 GALATIANS

Galatians[5] reflects Paul's sense of the urgency of his readers' situation. They stood in danger of no longer adhering to the gospel as he had preached it because "false teachers" had come in to "trouble" (*tarassontes*), "unsettle" (*anastatountes*), and "bewitch" (*ebaskanen*) them (Gal 1:7; 3:1; 5:12). The danger lay in perverting (*metastrepsai*) the gospel of Christ (Gal 1:7). The tone is set by the amazement and anathema in 1:6-9 instead of the customary thanksgiving.

In 1:10-12 Paul alludes to the charge of the false teachers who are leading his converts astray (cf 4:17). They seem to say that he has accommodated his gospel to the caprice of men and has watered it down. He has no gospel but the gospel of Jerusalem, no authority but the authority that Jerusalem has given him.

---

[4] See below 53-55 for considerations that Paul's treatment of the law progresses from Galatians to Corinthians to Romans. The order of the letters is disputed, however; it is frequently argued that Galatians comes after 1 and 2 Corinthians and/or that Philippians is from the same period. In any case Galatians and 1 and 2 Corinthians were written before Romans.

[5] There is a question whether "Galatians" (3:1; cf 1:3) refers to people who are ethnically Galatian or who belong to the Roman province of Galatia (1:3; cf 3:1). If it is the latter it could refer to non-ethnic Galatians who live in the southern part of the province of Galatia. It is in non-ethnic south Galatia where, according to Acts, Paul on his first missionary journey founded the churches of Antioch, Iconium, Lystra, and Derbe (Acts chs 13, 14). If they are ethnic north Galatians then they would not have been Paul's converts until he "went throughout the Phrygian and Galatic region" (Acts 16:6) (after the council of Jerusalem) or until after he traversed "the Galatic region and Phrygia" (Acts 18:23) (between his Corinthian and Ephesian ministries).

Until the eighteenth century it was universally agreed that Paul wrote to churches in North Galatia. This was particularly understandable since after AD 137, and AD 297 South Galatia no longer belonged to the province of Galatia. The north Galatian view was vigorously maintained by Lightfoot (1865). William Ramsey (1893, 1899) was a prominent advocate for the "South Galatian" view. He argued that none of the main Roman roads goes through North Galatia, and that the southern side of the Anatolian plateau was more important than the northern under the earlier Roman empire. The fuller development of the Northern Empire was not until AD 292. In the contemporary scene, German scholarship tends to favor the North Galatian view, while British scholarship tends to favor the South Galatian view. Another argument for the early south Galatian view is that Paul does not appeal to the decision of the Council of Jerusalem when it would have been his advantage to do so in Gal 2:1-10 (where he claims that his view agrees with the Jerusalem apostles). A problem with this view, though, is that 1 and 2 Thessalonians do not seem to be as advanced theologically as Galatians, and do not indicate that the law is an issue. For a thorough and balanced statement of the evidence see F. F. Bruce, *Commentary on Galatians* (NIGTC: Grand Rapids: Eerdmans, 1982) 3-18; 43-56. Bruce favors the south Galatian view. I tend to favor it too. In any case Galatians clearly precedes Romans.

His gospel disagrees with Jerusalem. Jerusalem upholds circumcision and the Torah, but he repudiates circumcision and the Torah and dishonors God by accommodating it to the favor of men.

In response Paul claims that neither his apostolic authority nor his gospel is derived from man (*para anthrōpou*) nor accommodated to man (*kata anthrōpon*) (1:11, 12), but it has come directly through a revelation of Jesus Christ (1:12). In 1:13-2:14 Paul argues from personal history. 1:13-24 emphasizes his minimal contact with the Jerusalem church and 2:1-10 emphasizes his agreement with it. Peter's refusal to eat with Gentile Christians was hypocritical (2:11-14). The Galatians' experience agrees with Paul's gospel (3:1-5) as does the scriptural example of Abraham (3:6-14). 2:15-21 is a systematic summary of his gospel. His statements on the law begin at 2:15 and continue throughout the remainder of the letter.

The false teachers apparently said that to be saved, one need not only have faith in Christ, but must also obey the law of Moses.[6] Paul on other hand urges that salvation only comes through faith. In Gal 2:16 he three times states that a man is justified not "by works of the law" (*ex ergōn nomou*); but through "faith" (*pistis, pisteuō*). In this verse he uses three different expressions for faith: *dia pisteōs Iēsou Christou*, *ek pisteōs Christou*, and *eis Christon Iēsoun episteusamen*. It is also by "hearing with faith" (*ex akoēs pisteōs*) and not "by works of the law" (*ex ergōn nomou*) that one receives the Spirit (3:2, 5). Those who strive for salvation *ex ergōn nomou* are under a curse, because as Deut 27:26 LXX says, "Cursed be everyone who does not abide by all things written in the book of the law, and do them" (3:10). A man is not justified before God "by the law" (*en nomǭ*), because Hab 2:4 says that it is the one who is righteous by faith that will live (*ho dikaios ek pisteōs zēsetai*, 3:11); the law does not rest on faith (*ho de nomos ouk estin ek pisteōs*, 3:12). That Christ had to die indicates that no one could be justified by the law; if justification (*dikaiosynē*) were to come through the law (*dia nomou*) then Christ would have died in vain (2:21).

As a Christian, Paul could say, "I through the law (*dia nomou*) died to the law (*nomǭ*), that I might live to God" (*theǭ*) (2:19). To the Galatians he could say, Christ redeemed us from the curse of the law (*ek tēs kataras tou nomou*), having become "a curse for us" (*hyper hēmōn katara*, 3:13). In Gal 3:15-18 the law, which could not bring salvation, is contrasted with the promises which were given to Abraham and to his offspring (Christ). Since the law only comes 430 years after the promise, it no more nullifies the promise than a second party, by adding a codicil, could nullify a man's will. God gave the inheritance to Abraham by promise (*di epangelias*); it does not, then, come by means of law

[6] This seems to be the same issue that is dealt with at the council of Jerusalem in Acts 15:1 where the men had come down from Judea and were teaching the brethren "Unless you are circumcised according to the custom of Moses, you cannot be saved."

(*ek nomou*). This inheritance is nothing other than salvation. What, then, had been the point of the law (*ti oun ho nomos*; 3:19)? The answer is that the law was added because of transgressions *(tōn parabaseōn charin*) until the offspring (= Christ; cf v 16) should come to whom the promise had been made.

If the law adds nothing to the promise of the inheritance of salvation, is it ranged against the promise (*ho oun nomos kata tōn epangeliōn [tou theou]*)? The answer is an emphatic no (*mē genoito*)! The law would be against the promise only if it pretended to compete with it by offering "life." True if a law were given which could "make alive" (*zōopoiēsai*) then "righteousness" (*dikaiosynē*) would indeed be by the law (*ek nomou*, 3:21). But this is of course contrary to fact. No code of law can breath life into its subjects. Until faith came, argues Paul, "we were confined under the law" (*hypo nomon ephrouroumetha*). The law was our custodian (*paidagōgos*) until Christ came (*eis Christon*), so that we might be justified by faith. But since faith had now come we were no longer under a custodian, but free (3:23-25).

If Gentile Christians were to adopt the prescriptions of the law, they would return to bondage to "the elemental spirits of the universe" (*ta stoicheia tou kosmou*, 4:3). This statement presents the Mosaic economy in the harshest light. When God sent his Son it was "to redeem those who were under the law" (*hina tous hypo nomon exagorasę̄*, 4:5). Having been set free from all claim to the law, why should the Galatians wish to be under it? It was in order that we should stay free that Christ freed us; we are to "stand fast, therefore, and not submit again to a yoke of slavery" (5:1).

Since the Galatians had been set free, they were not to submit to circumcision. If they were to do so Christ would be of no advantage to them; they, on the other hand, would be obligated to keep the whole law (*holon ton nomon poiēsai*, 5:2-4). But the circumcised *de facto* do not "keep the law" (*nomon phylassousin*, 6:13).

Being set free did not mean that the Galatians were to use their freedom "as an opportunity for the flesh" (*eis aphormēn tę̄ sarki*). They were, rather, to serve one another through love (*dia tēs agapēs*, 5:13). The command of love epitomized the law in "the single word" of Lev 19:18, "you shall love your neighbor as yourself." This was possible for one controlled by the Spirit as opposed to the flesh (5:16-25). There is no law (*nomos*) or legal condemnation against the one who manifests the fruit of the Spirit (5:22). The lives of the Galatians were to be a fulfillment of "the law of Christ" (*ton nomon tou Christou*, 6:2).

The Epistle to the Galatians sketches numerous themes central to Paul's view of Christ and the law, but it leaves several of these relatively unfinished, and, consequently, somewhat paradoxical (i.e., the law given "because of transgressions," the impotence of "the flesh," the reduction of the Mosaic regime to the level of service to *stoicheia* or elemental spirits of the universe).

1.2 1 CORINTHIANS

While in Galatians Paul's converts have succumbed to a false understanding of the gospel, in the Corinthian letters they have been plagued with immoral behavior. 1 and 2 Corinthians were written during Paul's Ephesian ministry (cf Acts 19:1-20:1). 1 Corinthians is occasioned by shocking news about the behavior of his converts at Corinth. By the time he writes 2 Corinthians 1-9 they have repented.[7]

In 1 Corinthians the law appears only in a relatively minor role. It is interesting, however, that at one point (9:8-9) Paul claims that the itinerant Christian missionary, like himself, has been guaranteed financial support not by human authority (*kata anthrōpon*) but by the law; for "it is written in the law of Moses 'you shall not muzzle an ox when it is treading out the grain'" (Deut 25:4). The real scope of this law was not revealed until now.

At 14:21 Paul quotes from Isa 28:11-12 to support his view that speaking in tongues is a sign, not for believers, but for unbelievers. He introduces this quotation with "in the law it is written" (*en tǭ nomǭ gegraptai*). At 14:34 Paul derives from "the law says," (*ho nomos legei*) his prescription that women should keep silent in the church. At 7:19 he claims neither circumcision (*peritomē*) counts for anything nor uncircumcision (*akrobystia*), but "keeping the commandments of God" (*tērēsis entolōn theou*).

These are statements in 1 Corinthians where Paul views the law positively. At 9:20-21, however, he mixes together both positive and negative statements. He states that to those under the law (*tois hypo nomon*) he became as one under the law (*hōs hypo nomon*) even though he himself is not under the law (*mē ōn autos hypo nomon*) that he might win those under the law (*tous hypo nomon*). To those outside the law (*tois anomois*) he became as one outside the law (*hōs anomos*). But he is not without law toward God (*mē ōn anomos theou*), for he is "under the law of Christ" (*ennomos Christou*).

In one passage, however, the law is understood merely negatively, and is referred to in a way which is reminiscent of the whole elaborate scheme of thought that we find in Romans. In 1 Cor 15:56 he states that "the sting of death is sin, and the power of sin is the law." This assertion was not necessary to Paul's immediate point; if it nevertheless appears here, it is an index to the importance he attaches to his distinctive vision of the economy of salvation.

---

[7] On the complexities of Paul's relationship with the Church at Corinth and the question of the integrity of 1 and 2 Corinthians see C. K. Barrett, *The First Epistle to the Corinthians* (2nd ed. BNTC; London: Black, 1971) 1-16; C. K. Barrett, *The Second Epistle to the Corinthians* (BNTC; London: Black, 1973) 1-21; and F. F. Bruce, *1 and 2 Corinthians*. NCB; London: Oliphants, 1971, 18-25; 164-174.

1.3 2 CORINTHIANS

The relevant passage on the law in 2 Corinthians is 3:1-18. Paul tells his readers that they are a letter from Christ (*epistolē Christou*) written, not with ink on tablets of stone (*en plaxin lithinais*), but written with the Spirit (*pneumati*) of the living God *on tablets of human hearts (en plaxin kardias sarkinais*, 3:3). God has qualified him and his readers to be ministers of a new covenant (*diakonous kainēs diathēkēs*) not in the written code (*to ... gramma*) which kills (*apoktennei*) but in the Spirit (*to ... pneuma*) which gives life (*zǭopoiei*, 3:6).

The Mosaic economy was the dispensation of death (*hē diakonia tou thanatou*, 3:7) and condemnation (*tēs katakriseōs*, 3:9) carved in letters of stone. Yet it had come in such splendor (*en doxę̄*) that the Israelites could not look at Moses' face because of its brightness, albeit a brightness that was fading (3:7). The dispensation of the Spirit (*hē diakonia tou pneumatos*) and righteousness (*tēs dikaiosynēs*), however, is attended with far greater splendor (*mallon perisseuei ... doxę̄*, 3:8-9). Because of the surpassing splendor of the latter, the former, in comparison, has no splendor (*ou dedoxastai*, 3:10). The old dispensation, which faded away (*to katargoumenon*), came with splendor (*dia doxēs*); the new dispensation, which remains (*to menon*), came with much more splendor (*pollǭ mallon ... en doxę̄*, 3:11).

1.4 Romans

Paul wrote Romans in Corinth (cf 16:1; 16:23; 1 Cor 1:14) at the end of his third missionary journey on his way to Jerusalem with the collection (cf 15:25-26) in about AD 57.[8]

Romans has more similarities with Galatians than with any other letter, yet it represents several changes of motif, and above all offers a fuller expression of Paul's views; here we find a more systematic expression of his "gospel" and of his treatment of the law.

It is puzzling why Paul should write his most comprehensive, reflective, and detailed epistle to a church which has not visited and which neither he nor any of his lieutenants has founded. The church at Rome, moreover, does not seem to have the serious problems which are encountered in the churches of Galatia

---

[8] It is so dated by F. F. Bruce, "The Romans Debate-Continued," BJRL 64 (1982) 334-359, 336, and Robinson *Redating*, 55. It is dated in the winter/spring of AD 57/58 by William Sanday, and Arthur C. Headlam, *A Critical and Exegetical Commentary on the Epistle to the Romans* (ICC; 5th ed. Edinburgh: T. & T. Clark, 1902) xiii; and by Matthew Black, *Romans* (NCB; London: Oliphants, 1973) 20. But C. E. B. Cranfield, *A Critical and Exegetical Commentary on the Epistle to the Romans* (2 Vols. ICC; 6th ed; Edinburgh: T. & T. Clark, 1975, 1979) I, 14, dates it one year earlier in the winter/spring of AD 55/56.

and Corinth. He thanks God for their world renowned faith (1:8) and claims that what he has written to them is a "reminder" (15:14, 15). He gives no indication that it is anything they lacked or misunderstood. When he finally comes to them, it will not be to instruct them but to strengthen and encourage them (1:11, 12), to be encouraged by them (1:12), and to have fruit (*karpos*) among them as among the rest of the Gentiles (1:13).

Romans has been viewed as being independent both of Paul's present circumstances and of the circumstances of the Church of Rome,[9] or as being determined by either his present circumstances[10] or the circumstances of the

---

[9] According to the traditional view the content of Romans is not an index to the situation of the church at Rome or the situation that Paul faces in his ministry. Until comparatively recent times scholarship more or less followed Melanchthon in his description of Romans as a compendium of Christian Doctrine (*Christianae religionis compendium*). See Karl P. Donfried (ed), *The Romans Debate* (Minneapolis: Augsburg, 1977]) xi. Karl Barth, *The Epistle to The Romans* (1933; r.p. New York: Oxford University Press, 1977), and Anders Nygren, *Commentary on Romans* (Philadelphia: Fortress, 1949) are two modern representatives of those who expound Romans independently of the historical question.

T. W. Manson and Robert Jewett are examples of those who see Romans as a circular letter and thus independent of a situation at Rome or a situation Paul faces in his ministry. T. W. Manson, "St. Paul's Letter to the Romans - And Others," r.p. in *The Romans Debate* [ed. K. P. Donfried; Minneapolis: Augsburg, 1977] 1-16; Robert Jewett, *Paul's Anthropological Terms: A Study of Their Use in Conflict Settings* (Leiden: Brill, 1971) 41-48.

Günther Bornkamm believes that Romans is Paul's "last will and testament." Romans can be explained by past controversies, not by present or future ones. It contains many of the themes of the earlier letters of Galatians, Corinthians, and Philippians. Like them it is polemical; the polemic, however, is general and is directed not against this or that group but against the Jew and his understanding of salvation. Behind Romans stands the external history of Paul's ministry and the internal history of his theological thinking. More so than his other letters Romans is an in depth discussion of Paul's message and theology about what is "eternally and universally valid." Günther Bornkamm, "The Letter to the Romans as Paul's Last Will and Testament," r.p. in *The Romans Debate* (ed. Karl P. Donfried. Minneapolis: Augsburg, 1977), 23-31.

Robert Karris has a somewhat similar view. Rom 14:1-15:13 is general Pauline paraenesis and represents solutions to problems which occurred in his former missionary work. There is little evidence that there were opposing parties of "the weak" (= Jewish Christians) and "the strong" (= Gentile Christians) in Rome. The treatment of this question in Rom 14:1-15:13 is rather a theoretical development of the actual treatment of 1 Cor 8-10. In this section as in 1-11 Paul uses OT quotations to support and confirm his principles (cf 14:11; 15:3; 9-12). Robert J. Karris, "Romans 14:1-15:13 and the Occasion of Romans," r.p. in *The Romans Debate* (ed. K. P. Donfried; Minneapolis: Augsburg, 1977) 75-99, 77-98.

[10] Some scholars see Romans in light of Paul's present and future plans. C. H. Dodd, *The Epistle of Paul to the Romans* (r.p. London: Fontana Books, 1959), 18-19, for example, reads Romans in light of Paul's future missionary plans in Rome and Spain (15:24; 1:10-13). His evangelism in the east having been completed, he wants to start a mission in Spain. For this work he would like to have Rome as a suitable base of operations. But Paul is not sure of his welcome in Rome since in some Christian circles he is a *persona non grata*. He, therefore, presents them "with a comprehensive and reasoned statement of the fundamentals of Christianity as he understood it, which is at the same time an *apologia* for the principles and methods of this Gentile mission." Stanley Kent Stowers, *The*

Church at Rome.[11] There is also a question of whether Romans is addressed mainly to Jews or Gentiles, or to Jewish or Gentile Christians.

Diatribe and Paul's Letter to the Romans (Chico. CA: Scholars Press, 1981), 182, believes that Romans is explained by Paul's desire to preach the gospel in Rome (1:15). In Romans Paul preaches the gospel. Romans is a "self-introduction of Paul as a teacher and preacher of the gospel."

Jacob Jervell is an example of those who view Romans in light of Paul's impending visit to Jerusalem. The main content of Rom 1-11 is the defense which Paul plans to give before the church in Jerusalem. He would like Rome's support in view of a possible confrontation at Jerusalem from unbelieving Jews and from Jewish Christians (15:30-33). Should Jerusalem not recognize him the unity of the church would be destroyed. The collection is the sign of the Gentiles recognition of and respect for the mother church at Jerusalem. Paul regards himself as *the* apostle to the Gentiles; in his presentation of the collection to Jerusalem he would like to represent all of Gentile Christianity including Rome the center of the Gentile world. Jacob Jervell, "The Letter to Jerusalem," in *The Romans Debate* (ed. K. P. Donfried; Minneapolis: Augsburg, 1977) 61-74, 64-68, 73-4.

Somewhat similar to Jervell are Drane, Sanders, and Hübner. John W. Drane, "Why did Paul write Romans?" in *Pauline Studies: Essays Presented to F. F. Bruce on his 70th Birthday* (eds. Donald A. Hagner and Murray J. Harris. Grand Rapids: Eerdmans, 1980), 209-227, 223; E. P. Sanders, *Paul and Palestinian Judaism: A Comparison of Patterns of Religion* (Philadelphia: Fortress, 1977), 488; E. P. Sanders, *Paul, the Law, and the Jewish People* (Philadelphia: Fortress, 1983), 30-31; Hans Hübner, *Law in Paul's Thought* (ed. John Riches. Edinburgh: T. & T. Clark, 1984) 64-65.

[11] Donfried claims that since Paul wrote every other letter to address a specific situation of the recipients, we should make the same assumption in Romans. G. Klein believes that Paul did not write Romans because of what he wants from them but because of what he can give to them. The church at Rome lacked an apostolic foundation and Paul wrote Romans to give them one. But most scholars see conflict within the church at Rome. Minear detects five separate groups of "the weak" (Jewish Christians) and "the strong" (Gentile Christians) whom Paul addresses in various parts of his letter. W. S. Campbell believes that the liberal-minded Gentile Christian majority (the strong of faith) were unwilling to have fellowship with the conservative Jewish Christian minority (the weak of faith). To resolve this situation Paul stresses the equality of Jew and Gentile in sin (3:20) and in the Gospel (10:12). Karl P. Donfried, "False Presuppositions in the Study of Romans," r.p. in *The Romans Debate* (ed. Karl P. Donfried. Minneapolis: Augsburg, 1977) 120-148, 122; Günter Klein, "Paul's Purpose in Writing The Epistle To The Romans," r.p. in *The Romans Debate* (ed. Karl P. Donfried. Minneapolis: Augsburg, 1977) 32-49; Paul S. Minear, *The Obedience of Faith* (SBT 2nd Series 19; London: SCM, 1971); W. S. Campbell, "Why Did Paul Write Romans?" ExpT 85 (1974), 264-269, 268-9.

Others such as F. F. Bruce and J. C. Beker believe that the occasion of Romans is explained by the situation in the church at Rome and by Paul's forthcoming visits to Jerusalem, Rome, and Spain (see also Käsemann). According to Beker, Paul wants support from Rome for his Spanish mission but even more importantly he wants Rome on his side when he presents the collection to Jerusalem. Aware of conflicts between Jews and Gentiles within the church at Rome, Paul warns the Gentile majority against looking down on the Jewish minority (15:1; 14:15; 11:13, 20-21). But the fundamental problem is that Jewish Christianity does not understand the basic equality of Jew and Gentile and the role of the Gentiles in salvation history. Romans is basically a "dialogue with Jews" and asserts the oneness of Jew and Gentile within the people of God but in a manner that preserves the salvation-historical priority of Israel. Bruce, *Romans Debate*, 334-359; J. Christiaan Beker, *Paul the Apostle: The Triumph of God in Life and Thought* (Philadelphia: Fortress, 1980), 71-93; Ernst Käsemann, *Commentary On Romans* (Grand Rapids: Eerdmans, 1980), 402-406.

My own view is that Paul had a number of reasons for writing Romans.[12] Romans can be explained in part by Paul's intended visit to Spain.[13] To obtain Rome's support he tells them what his gospel is and assures them that he is not an antinomian (see 3:8; 6:1f). To be welcomed as a preacher of the gospel in Rome he preaches the gospel in Romans.

Romans can be explained in part by the situation at Rome.[14] Originally the Roman Church was made up exclusively of Jewish Christians, but by the time Paul writes Romans the Church would most likely be predominantly Gentile.[15] There may have been tension between the two groups. This could be the explanation for the warning to the Gentiles in 11:17-22,[16] and the treatment of "the weak" and "the strong" in chs 14-15.[17]

Romans can be explained in part by Paul's impending visit to Jerusalem. According to Acts Paul has been careful throughout his ministry to maintain contact with Jerusalem (Acts 9:26; 11:30; 15:2; 18:22; 19:21) and to make sure that his gospel agrees with Jerusalem's (Acts 15; cf Gal 2).[18] He makes it clear that the gospel has gone to the Jew first (1:16; chs 9-11) and that Gentile Christianity has a spiritual indebtedness to Jerusalem (Rom 15:25-27). He may

---

[12] Most of the views expressed in the preceding three footnotes are correct in what they affirm but incorrect in what they deny.

[13] Bruce *Romans Debate*, 350-51 has noted that Paul's earlier evangelistic work had a base in either Antioch, Corinth, or Ephesus.

[14] After a thorough examination of the textual question Harry Gamble Jr., *The Textual History of the Letter to the Romans* (Grand Rapids: Eerdmans, 1977), has shown that the omission of *en Rhōmę̄* (1:7, 15) in some texts is not original, and that Romans 16 (the greetings chapter) was written to Rome. Since, therefore, Paul knows so many Christians at Rome it is likely that he has some idea of what is going on there.

[15] As in Acts Gentile God fearers would have come into the primitive community via the synagogue. The edict of Claudius to expel all the Jews in Rome in AD 49 meant that the church at Rome had become almost exclusively Gentile. The edict seems to have been lifted after Claudius' death in AD 54, and by the time Paul writes Romans in AD 57 many Jews would have returned to Rome. See Bruce, *Romans Debate*, 337-42; Compare Priscilla's and Aquila's movement from Rome to Corinth to Rome during this period (Acts 18:2; 1 Cor 16:19; Rom 16:3); compare also the number of Jewish names in Rom 16.

[16] At 11:17-22 the Gentile is reminded that he is a wild olive branch grafted into the olive tree, because the Jew, the natural olive branch, has been cut off. He is reminded too that he does not support the root (the Jew) but the root supports him.

[17] The problem of "weak" and "strong" in chs 14-15 is better explained in terms of a Jewish-Gentile problem than as a development of the question of meat sacrificed to idols in 1 Cor 8-10. Romans is largely about the relationship of Jews and Gentiles and their place in salvation history (see 1:17; 2:9, 10; chs 9-11; 15:1-13). In Romans 14 the problem is not only about "food" but also about "days" (14:5, 6). The words *koinon* ("unclean") (14:14) and *katharon* ("clean") (14:20) indicate Jewish food laws. In Romans Paul says nothing about food sacrificed to idols. A major portion of Romans is devoted to the relationship of Jew and Greek (Rom 1:16; 2:9, 10; Chs 9-11; 15:7-13).

[18] See Bruce, *Romans Debate*, 352.

have written to Rome for their support for his trip to Jerusalem.[19] He reminds his readers that he has received a special grace from God to be the apostle to the Gentiles (1:5; 15:15, 16).

Romans can be explained in part by the impending danger that Paul faces in Jerusalem (15:31). One motive in light of the danger may have been to write what is in some sense a "last will and testament" to Rome so that in the event of his death the great church at the center of the Empire would have a record of what his gospel is. Although we have no evidence for this Paul might have had one version of this last will and testament sent to Rome and another version kept for his defense in Jerusalem.

Romans is not a compendium of Christian doctrine or a dogmatics in outline but it does give a systematic exposition of "the gospel of God" (1:1).[20] To expound his view of the gospel he employs the style of the diatribe and sets up a Jewish interlocutor based on his past history as a Jew and on his past experience with Jews.[21]

---

[19] Bruce, *Romans Debate*, 353-355, observes that Paul sees the Scriptures being fulfilled both in his role of taking the gospel from Jerusalem (Rom 11:26-27f; cf Isa 59:20-21; Ps 14:7; 53:6; Rom 15:19), and of having the Gentiles bring gifts to Jerusalem (cf Isa 60:5-7; 66:20; Rom cf 15; esp 15:16).

[20] F. F. Bruce indicates that the theme of Romans is "the Gospel" and Leon Morris has claimed that it is "God." I believe that combining the two views hits it precisely. Throughout Romans the gospel is initiated by God and all the glory belongs to God. F. F. Bruce, *The Epistle of Paul To The Romans* (TNTC; London: Tyndale, 1963) 67-68; cf 9-10; 31-40; Leon Morris, "The Theme of Romans," in *Apostolic History and The Gospel: Biblical and Historical Essays presented to F. F. Bruce on His 60th Birthday* (eds. W. W. Gasque and Ralph P. Martin. Exeter: Paternoster, 1970) 249-263.

[21] The classic statement on the diatribe from the standpoint of NT studies was given in Rudolf Bultmann's 1910 doctoral dissertation. Rudolf Bultmann, *Der Stil der paulinischen Predigt und die Kynischstoische Diatribe* (FRLANT; Göttingen: Vandenhoeck & Ruprecht, 1910); see Stowers, *Diatribe*, 125. The evidence has been reexamined by Stanley Kent Stowers (*Diatribe*). In contrast to earlier scholarship he concludes that the main thrust of the diatribe is dialogical, not polemical. By rendering an indictment and not a polemic it exposes error in order to lead to the truth. Growing out of the philosophical school situation, it features an address to an imaginary interlocutor, and deals with objections and false conclusions from him. These grow out of the internal logic of the argumentation, but also reflect the teacher's typical experiences of objections and false conclusions from his students (ibid., esp 2-3; 76-77; 115-116; 153, 177-8; 180).

Rom 2:1-5; 2:17-24; 9:19-21; 11:17-24; and 14:4, 10 employ the style of the diatribe. But unlike the diatribe Romans has a specifically Christian content and appeals to the OT scriptures. It, furthermore, uses objections and false conclusions much more consistently (Stowers, *Diatribe*, 79-85, 153, 177-179).

The dialogue in Romans is based on Paul's past experiences as a teacher of Jews and Gentiles. It allows him to deal indirectly with the pedagogical needs of the Church of Rome (Stowers, *Diatribe*, 152, 177, 178, 181). Objections and false conclusions occur when there is a major turn in the discourse or a new section of the argument (Rom 3:1; 6:1; 7:7; 9:14; and 11:1), and when there is the possibility of false inference or the need to censure known belief; they react to either indictment (3:1-9; 11:1, 11, 19) or protreptic (positive development) (3:31; 6:1, 15; 7:7, 13; 9:14, 19) (Stowers, *Diatribe*, 148-151).

I cannot follow Stowers, however, when he claims that the content of Romans is appropriate only

Not only the occasion and purpose of Romans has caused much debate, but its structure has as well. It was generally agreed that 12:1 begins the paraenetic section and that 8:39 concludes the doctrinal section, but until relatively recently Rom 9-11 was not viewed as having a necessary or integral place in the letter.[22] More recent scholarship has observed, though, how crucially important the question of Israel is in Paul's thought. It has even been argued that Rom 9-11 is the climax of the letter.[23]

The theme of Romans is stated in 1:16-17. Salvation is granted to those who believe. The scriptural proof, *ho de dikaios ek pisteōs zēsetai* (1:17 = Hab 2:4), neatly sums up 1-8. The dynamic thrust of Rom 5-8 is future salvation (*zēsetai*)[24] and in Rom 1-4 it is righteousness by faith (*ho de dikaios ek pisteōs*) rather than works (*ho de dikaios ex ergōn*).[25]

Rom 1:18-3:20 shows that neither Gentile nor Jew can be saved by works; all are under the power of sin (3:9), all are guilty before God (3:19-20), all are under the wrath of God. In 3:21-26 Paul states his thesis that we are righteous by faith on the basis of what God has done in Christ. 3:27-31 states some conclusions of this thesis, and 4:1-25 provides the scriptural support.[26] Believing that he has proved his point that justification is received by faith and not obtained by works, he draws out some of its implications in 5:1-11.[27]

---

for insiders and not for outsiders (Stowers, *Diatribe*, 182-183). The objections and false conclusions in Rom 1-7 are much more appropriate to an unbelieving Jew who is being led to the truth than to someone who is already a Christian. The addressees of Rom 16 are neither prospective nor former "students" (cf Stowers, *Diatribe*, 183). Stowers does not take seriously that Romans is a "reminder" of something his readers already know (15:15) and that they are perfectly able to instruct themselves (15:14) (Stowers, *Diatribe*, 181). He overlooks the fact that Paul wants to have "fruit" or converts (1:13). He seems to overlook his other insights that in Romans Paul "preaches the gospel" (Stowers, *Diatribe*, 182). He preaches the gospel in part so that the Romans will know what his gospel is.

[22] e.g., Dodd, *Romans*, 148; Sanday and Headlam, *Romans*, 225. For discussion of this problem see Beker, *Paul*, 63-64; and Käsemann, *Romans*, 253-256; et. al.

[23] e.g., Beker, *Paul*, 87.

[24] Feuillet observes that death-life is the fundamental antithesis in Rom 5-8 and that the term sanctification occurs only twice (6:19, 22). A. Feuillet, "La Citation d'Habacuc II.4 et les huit premier Chapitres de L'Épître aux Romains," NTS 6 (1959-60), 52-80, 56.

[25] See Nygren, *Romans*, 65-91; followed by N. A. Dahl, "Two Notes on Romans 5," ST 5 (1951), 37-48, 39; and Ulrich Luz, "Zum Aufbau von Röm. 1-8," TZ 25 (1969), 161-181, 166; et. al.

[26] cf Käsemann, *Romans*, 91, 102, 105.

[27] Traditionally in protestant circles Romans 1-8 has been divided into "justification" (Rom 1-4[5]) and "sanctification" (Rom 5[6]-8) with much stress placed on justification. However since the late nineteenth century some German scholars (e.g., Wernle, Wrede, Lüdemann, Schweitzer) downplayed the importance of the "justification" language of Rom 5[6]-8). There was no general agreement in either group as to where the division occurs, whether at the end of 4:25, 5:11, or 5:21 (see Beker, *Paul*, 66f, 377; Dahl, *Notes*, 39-40; and Luz, *Aufbau*, 177-178 for summary, discussion, and survey of views).

Dahl, *Notes*, 37-39 has helped us resolve the problem, by observing that 5:1-11 has several

5:12-8:39 gives a more profound analysis of the plight of mankind and its solution. Outside of Christ the problem is death (5:12-21), sin (6:1-23), law (7:1-25), and flesh (7:14, 18, 25; 8:1-13). But because of God's action in Christ there has been a reversal. For those in Christ there is life (5:12-21), righteousness (6:15-23), and Spirit (Rom 7:6; 8:4-30).[28]

Chs 9-11 elucidate the salvation-historical priority of Israel; they develop the statement that the gospel is "to the Jew first and also to the Greek" (*Ioudaiǭ te prōton kai Hellēni*) (1:17). 12:1-15:13 is paraenetic. 12:1-13:14 is general exhortation, and 14:1-15:13 deals with the relations between Jewish and Gentile Christians.[29]

A presupposition of "righteousness through faith" is the unrighteousness of the man without faith. In 1:18-32 Paul accordingly depicts mankind's bondage to sin. No one, neither Jew nor Greek, merits salvation. All are subject to the final condemnation of God.

All who have sinned "without the law" (*anomōs = Gentiles*) will also perish "without the law" (*anomos*), and all who have sinned under the law (*en nomǭ = Jews*) will be judged by the law (*dia nomou*, 2:12). It is not the "hearers of the law" (*hoi akroatai nomou*) who are "righteous" (*dikaioi*) before God; it is the doers (*hoi poiētai nomou*) of the law who "will be justified" (*dikaiōthēsontai*, 2:13).

When Gentiles who have not the law (*ethnē ta mē nomon echonta*) do by nature what the law requires (*ta tou nomou*), they are a law to themselves (*heautois eisin nomos*). Even though they do not have the law (*nomon mē echontes*) they show that what the law requires (*to ergon tou nomou*) is written on their hearts (2:14-15).

The Jew, on the other hand, relies on the law, is instructed in the law (*katēchoumenos ek tou nomou*, 2:18), "boasts in the law" (*en nomǭ kauchasai*, 2:23), and has in the law "the embodiment of knowledge and truth" (*tēn morphōsin tēs gnōseōs kai tēs alētheias en tǭ nomǭ*, 2:20). Yet he dishonors God because he breaks the law (*dia tēs parabaseōs tou nomou*, 2:23). Since the Jew does not keep the law (*nomon prassēs*), his circumcision (*peritomē*) is no longer of value (*ōphelei*), in fact, it has become uncircumcision (*akrobystia*, 2:25).

---

themes which are developed more fully in Rom 8. E.g., compare "glory" (*doxa*) (5:2; 8:18; cf 8:30), "hope" (*elpis*) (5:2, 4, 5; 8:20, 24); "love" (*agapē*) (5:5, 8; 8:35, 39), and "Spirit" (*pneuma*) (5:5; 8:5-6, 9-11, 13-16, 23, 26-27; cf 7:6; 8:2, 4). Another key observation is that in 5:1-11 Paul changes from the second and third person to the first person, from an argumentative style to a confessional style (see Dahl, *Notes*, 40 et. al.).

[28] For a discussion of various views, and the complexities of the structure and argument of Rom 5-8, see Luz, *Aufbau*, 166, 169-191.

[29] cf Käsemann, *Romans*, 323.

Not only does one's circumcision become uncircumcision if he breaks the law, but one's uncircumcision becomes circumcision if he keeps the law. The man who is uncircumcised (*akrobystia*) but "keeps the precepts of the law" (*ta dikaiōmata tou nomou phylassę̄*) will have his uncircumcision (*hē akrobystia autou*) regarded as circumcision (*eis peritomēn logisthēsetai*, 2:26). The physically uncircumcised person (*hē ek physeōs akrobystia*) who "keeps the law" (*ton nomon telousa*) will condemn those who have the written code and circumcision but "break the law" (2:27). Being a true Jew and having real circumcision is not outward but inward (2:28, 29).

Paul's conclusion is that all men, both Jews and Greeks, are "under the power of sin" (*hyph' hamartian*, 3:9); the scriptures testify to this (3:10-18).

The law, then, far from saving anyone, makes him accountable to God. What the law says (*hosa ho nomos legei*), it says to those who are "under the law" (*en tǭ nomǭ*) so that "every mouth may be stopped, and the whole world may be held accountable to God" (3:19). No one is justified "by works of the law" (*ex ergōn nomou*) because through the law (*dia ... nomou*) one receives only the knowledge of sin (3:20).

Thus far Paul has been intent on showing that the need of redemption is universal, with the accent on the thesis that the Jews are no exception. Now (3:21-4:25) he presents what he calls the manifestation of "the righteousness of God" (3:21), the concrete reality by which the universal need of redemption is met, namely, Christ's propitiatory death (3:24-25). This was the "redemption" (*apolytrōsis*, 3:24) by which Jew and Gentile alike could enter into appropriate righteousness "as a gift" (*dōrean*). The result (3:27-31) was, first, to exclude absolutely and totally the religious "boast" (*kauchēsis*), which for Paul was the cardinal sin of the religious man, and, second, to make the Gentiles candidates for salvation. Did this overthrow the law (i.e., the scripture)? On the contrary, it supported and established it. In the following chapter (4:1-25) Abraham provided the extended illustration and proof that such had always been God's style of operation; his being reckoned righteous "by faith," moreover, belonged to a single, consistent plan of salvation. Abraham was justified by faith in the promise, but "we" (cf 4:24, *di' hēmas*) by faith in its fulfillment (4:24f).

In 3:21-31 the righteousness of God is manifested and the justification of man is accomplished *chōris (ergōn) nomou* (3:21, 28). Boasting is thus excluded, not *dia (nomou) tōn ergōn* but *dia nomou pisteōs* (3:27). In this process to which the law (*ho nomos*) and the prophets bear witness, the law (*nomos*) is not overthrown (*katargeō*) but upheld (*histanō*, 3:31).

In 4:13-16 the law brings transgression and wrath (4:15). The promise to Abraham and his descendants does not come *dia nomou* (4:13); it comes to all who share the faith of Abraham and not only to "the adherents of the law" (*hoi ek nomou, to ek tou nomou* 4:14, 16).

In Rom 5-8 Paul is concerned with the completion of God's saving act. Righteousness accepted in faith as a gift (chs. 1-4) (i.e., reconciliation to God by the death of Christ, 3:24-25; 5:10) is so stunning an act of God that the follow-up of full and final salvation is *a fortiori* secure (5:10). What stands in the way of full and final salvation? The bondage of man! The treatment of salvation, then, entails the breaking of man's bondage to sin and death, and to their instrument, the law. This works out in detail as an account: (a) not of the universality of sin (chs. 1-3), but of its source and origin, the sin of Adam (5:12-21); (b) of the break with sin (6:1-23) which participation in Christ's death makes actual as well as imperative (6:4); and (c) of the freedom from the law (7:4-6) and of the situation in which the law, "holy and just and good" (*hagia kai dikaia kai agathē*), could do nothing but condemn (7:7-25). Only then could Paul sketch the triumphant completion of the work of salvation (8:1-39).

Paul's distinctive treatment of the law had been announced in 3:19-20; 5:20; and 6:14-15 (passages which prepared for the treatment in Rom 7). He points out that the law could do nothing but make men conscious of sin (3:20), that the law came on the scene "to increase the trespass" (5:20), and that the dominion of sin over man depended on his living "under law" (*hypo nomon*, 6:14-15).

In Rom 7:1-3, by use of the marriage analogy, Paul argues that by death to the law, the Christian is free from the law. He has died to the law through the body of Christ (*ethanatōthēte to nomō̧ dia tou sōmatos tou Christou*) so that he may belong to another (*eis to genesthai hymas heterō̧*, 7:4). Discharged from the law (*katērgēthēmen apo tou nomou*) he can now serve in "the new life of the Spirit" (*kainotēti pneumatos*, 7:6).

If one's sinful passions are aroused by the law (7:5), and if one has died to sin (6:2, 11) and to the law (7:4), the natural question arises: "Is the law sin (*ho nomos hamartia*; 7:7)?" The answer is an emphatic no (*mē genoito*, 7:7)! Without the law (*ei mē dia nomou*) "I" (*egō*) would never know sin. If the law (*ho nomos*) had not said "You shall not covet," "I" would never have known what it is to covet (7:7). But sin, finding opportunity (*aphormēn*) in the commandment (*dia tēs entolēs*) works all kinds of covetousness. Apart from the law (*chōris gar nomou*) sin lies dead (7:8).

The "I" (*egō*) of Rom 7 was alive once "apart from the law" (*chōris nomon*); but when the commandment (*tēs entolēs*) came, sin revived (*hē hamartia anezēsen*) and "I" died (7:9). The commandment which promised life proved to be death to "me" (7:10). Sin, finding opportunity (*aphormēn*), deceived and killed "me" (*egō*, 7:11). The law (*ho ... nomos*) and the commandment (*hē entolē*) are holy, just, and good (7:12). It was not the law (*to ... agathon*), but sin (*hē hamartia*) which brought death to "me" (*egō*, 7:13). The law is spiritual (*ho nomos pneumatikos estin*) but "I" (*egō*) am carnal, sold under sin (*egō de sarkinos eimi pepramenos hypo tēn hamartian*, 7:14). "I," by doing the evil that "I" do not want, agree that the law is good (*symphēmi tō̧ nomō̧ hoti kalos*, 7:16).

"I" find a law (*ton nomon*) that when "I" wish to do right, evil lies close at hand (7:21). "I" delight in "the law of God" (*tǭ nomǭ tou theou*) in my inmost self (*kata ton esō anthrōpon*, 7:22), but see in my members "another law" (*heteron nomon*) at war with the law of my mind (*tǭ nomǭ tou noos mou*) taking me captive to "the law of sin" (*tǭ nomǭ tēs hamartias*) which dwells in my members (7:23). "I (of) myself (*autos egō*) serve the law of God (*nomǭ theou*) with my mind, but with my flesh I serve the law of sin" (*nomǭ hamartias*, 7:25).

Rom 8 resumes the argument of 7:6. The Christian has died to the law and is freed from the law; he serves in the newness of the Spirit (7:4-6). The law of the Spirit of life in Christ Jesus (*ho ... nomos tou pneumatos tēs zōēs en Christǭ Iēsou*) has freed him from the law of sin and death (*apo tou nomou tēs hamartias kai tou thanatou*, 8:2). What the law could not do (*to ... adynaton tou nomou*) because it was weak through the flesh (*en hǭ ēsthenei dia tēs sarkos*), God has done. He sent "his own son in the likeness of sinful flesh, and for sin he condemned sin in the flesh," so that "the just requirement of the law" (*to dikaiōma tou nomou*) might be fulfilled in us, who walk not "according to the flesh" (*kata sarka*) but "according to the Spirit" (*kata pneuma*, 8:3-4). The one whose mind is set on the flesh does not, and cannot, submit to God's law (*tǭ... nomǭ tou theou*, 8:7).

Following this systematic exposition of the gospel, Paul asks why Israel has not entered into messianic salvation. It is ironic that Israel had strained after a law promising righteousness, but "did not succeed in fulfilling that law" (*eis nomon ouk ephthasen*, 9:31). Since Israel was ignorant of the righteousness that comes from God (*tēn tou theou dikaiosynēn*) and sought to establish its own (*tēn idian zētountes stēsai*) it did not submit to the righteousness of God (*tę̄ dikaiosynē tou theou*, 10:3). Christ, however, is the *telos* of the law, unto righteousness (*eis dikaiosynēn*) for all who believe (*panti tǭ pisteuonti*) (10:4). But the one "who practices (*ho poiēsas*) the righteousness which is based on the law (*tēn dikaiosynēn tēn ek [tou] nomou*) shall live by it" (*en autois*) (10:5).

In the paraenetic section of Romans, love is the pivotal concept. It leads the list of the exhortations in 12:9-21. At 13:8, Paul exhorts that Christians should owe no one anything except to love one another, "for he who loves his neighbor has fulfilled the law" (*ho gar agapōn ton heteron nomon peplērōken*). The specific commandments from the Decalogue, not to commit adultery, kill, steal, or covet, or any other are summed up in the sentence "You shall love your neighbor as yourself" (*Agapēseis ton plēsion sou hōs seauton*, 13:9 = Lev 19:18 LXX). Since love does not wrong a neighbor, it is the fulfilling of the law (*plērōma ... nomou*, 13:10).

1.5 PHILIPPIANS

When Paul writes Philippians he is in prison (1:7, 13, 14, 17). This could be in Rome (cf Acts 28:14-31), Caesarea (cf Acts 23:33-26:32), or elsewhere (cf 2 Cor 11:23; 6:5). If he is in Rome or Caesarea, Philippians is written after Romans.[30]

Phil 3:1-11 is a particularly significant passage. A sort of "testament," it features an autobiographical passage which shows the importance the law had had for Paul before his conversion to Christ. This existential aspect of Paul's stance towards the law gives a special bite to his warnings against Judaizers. Look out for dogs (*kynas*), evildoers (*kakous ergatas*), and for those who mutilate the flesh (*tēn katatomēn*, 3:2), for, says Paul, we in contrast to them are the true circumcision (*hē peritomē*). We worship God in spirit (*hoi pneumati theou latreuontes*), and glory in Christ Jesus (*kauchōmenoi en Christǭ Iēsou*), and put no confidence in the flesh (*kai ouk en sarki pepoithotes*, 3:3). Though he himself does not put confidence in the flesh, he could do so more than anyone, for he was "circumcised on the eighth day, of the people of Israel, of the tribe of Benjamin, a Hebrew born of Hebrews; as to the law a Pharisee (*kata nomon Pharisaios*), as to zeal (*zēlos*) a persecutor of the church, as to righteousness under the law blameless" (*kata dikaiosynēn tēn en nomǭ genomenos amemptos*, 3:6).

At one time he considered all these things as "gain" (*kerdos*, plural *kerdē*), but now he considers them and everything else whatever, as loss (*zēmian*) for the

[30] The traditional view is that he is writing from Rome. The difficulty is that there are so many journeys and communications between Rome and Philippi (cf 4:14, 18; 2:19, 25, 26), and that Paul intends to visit Philippi (cf Phil 1:26; 2:24). By then his mission in the east would be completed and his focus would be on Spain (Rom 15:24-28).

In this century a number of scholars have *posited* an Ephesian imprisonment (cf 1 Cor 6:5; 11:23). The problem is that there is no direct evidence for this even though we learn of his many troubles in Ephesus and Asia (Acts 19:23-20:1; 1 Cor 15:32; 16:9; 2 Cor 1:8f). There is, also, no reference to his major effort of a collection for the poor in which Macedonia placed such a prominent part (2 Cor 8:1-5; 9:1-4; Rom 15:26f).

It could be one of his many imprisonments but these probably would have been of brief duration. This imprisonment seems to be of extended duration (cf 1:13f; 2:25-30) and based on a capital charge (2:17).

I tend to favor the Caesarean view. It would fit well with a visit to Philippi on Paul's journey to Spain. It is compatible with the reference to the praetorian guard (1:13). It explains why there is no reference to the collection, and it agrees with a prison term of extended duration based on a serious charge. If he did not write from Caesarea the best alternative seems to be Rome. For discussion of the evidence see Guthrie, *The Pauline Epistles*, 144-154; Kümmel, *Introduction*, 229-235; Robinson, *Redating*, 57-61; and Bo Reicke "Caesarea, Rome, and the Captivity Epistles," in *Apostolic History and the Gospel* (FS F. F. Bruce. eds. W. W. Gasque and Ralph P. Martin. Exeter: Paternoster, 1970) 277-286, 282-286. Robinson favors Caesarea, Kümmel favors either Caesarea or Rome, and Guthrie and Reicke favor Rome. In any case our understanding of Paul's view of the law is affected little.

sake of Christ (3:7-9). He has "suffered the loss" (*ezēmiōthēn*) of all things and has counted them as "refuse" (*skybala*) in order that he may "gain" (*kerdēsō*) Christ. He has done this to "be found in him (*en autō̧* = Christ), not having a righteousness of ... [his] own based on law (*mē echōn emēn dikaiosynēn tēn ek nomou*), but that which is *dia pisteōs Christou*, the righteousness from God that depends on faith" (*tēn ek theou dikaiosynēn epi tȩ̄ pistei*, 3:9).

1.6 Positive and Negative Aspects of the Law

The most striking feature about our survey of the data is the remarkably positive and negative ways in which Paul speaks about the law. The positive and negative points may be summed up as follows:

1.6.1 Positive Aspects

The law is of no mere human authority (cf 1 Cor 9:8) but is "the law of God" (Rom 7:22, 25; 8:7). Given by God (Rom 9:4; cf 3:2), and written by God (*gegraptai*, 1 Cor 9:9; 14:21; cf 14:34) it contains the will of God (Rom 2:17, 18), bears witness to the righteousness of God (Rom 3:21), and is in accord with the promises of God (Gal 3:21).

The law is "holy," "good," and "of the Spirit" (Rom 7:12, 14, 16); its essence is love (Rom 13:8-10; Gal 5:14) its embodiment is "knowledge" and "truth" (Rom 2:20). Through faith rather than works it is established (*histanomen*), not destroyed (*katargoumen*) (Rom 3:31). Its "just requirement" (*dikaiōma*) is fulfilled by the one who walks "according to the Spirit" (*kata pneuma*) rather than "according to the flesh" (*kata sarka*) (Rom 8:4).

1.6.2 Negative Aspects

The law brings a curse (Gal 3:13), wrath (Rom 4;15), sin (Rom 7:7f), and death (Rom 7:9-11; 2 Cor 3:6-9; cf Rom 5:12-21). The law gives sin its "opportunity" (*aphormē*, Rom 7:8, 11) and its power (1 Cor 15:56), and allows sin to be charged against us (Rom 5:13). It produces transgressions (Rom 4;15; cf Gal 3:19), makes the trespass increase (Rom 5:20), enslaves (Gal 3:23; 4:5, 21-31; Rom 6:14f; 7:4-6, 23-25), and condemns to death (2 Cor 3:9; Rom 2:12; cf Rom 8:1, 3; Col. 2;14). It so stands at the root of sin and death that it is called the law of sin (and death) (Rom 7:23, 25; 8:7).

To live *en nomō̧* (Gal 3:11; 5:4), *ek (tou) nomou* (Rom 4;14, 16; 10:5; Gal 3:18, 21; Phil 3:9), *dia nomou* (Rom 3;20; 4:13; Gal 2:21), or *hypo nomon* (Rom 6:14f; Gal 4:21; 5:18) is fatal.

For the Christian the law is in some sense over and done with. For him Christ has redeemed him from the curse of the law (Gal 3:13); he has died to the law (Rom 7:4, 6; Gal 2:19), is freed from the law (Rom 7:6), and is no longer under the law (Rom 6:14f).

We cannot confine exclusively positive statements or exclusively negative statements to a particular letter, for all the major letters have both positive and negative statements. In Galatians the statements are predominately negative but 5:14 is positive. In 1 Corinthians the statements are predominantly positive but 15:56 is negative. In Romans there is a more balanced mixture of both positive and negative statements.

How can these positive and negative features be explained? Can the negative or positive statements on *nomos* refer to something other than the law? Can the negative statements be confined to a particular part of the law? Does Paul make negative statements about the law because he is against boasting in the law? Has Paul's view developed from letter to letter? Does he change his mind about the law from letter to letter? Do his statements on the law depend on the circumstances of the letter? Are his statements flatly contradictory? Is the law valid or invalid for the believer? In what sense is it valid or invalid?

We shall consider this type of issue in the next chapter.

CHAPTER TWO

ISSUES RAISED BY THE DATA

The following issues deal with questions that arise from a careful reading of the text and which have been raised by biblical scholarship.

2.1 THE USAGE OF NOMOS

Three points concerning Paul's use of *nomos* will be made: (1) no importance can be placed on the presence or absence of the definite article; (2) *nomos* can refer to the OT as a whole or limited to various parts within it; and (3) normally *nomos* refers to the OT or Jewish law.

2.1.1 THE ARTHROUS AND ANARTHROUS USE OF NOMOS

In the last century in particular, certain scholars argued that *nomos* without the definite article refers to law in general and not specifically to the Mosaic law.[1] But this distinction has been refuted by Eduard Grafe and Peter Bläser.[2] Grafe observes that the equation of the two forms is seen in the usage of *hypo nomon* (Gal 3:23) and *ho nomos* (Gal 3:24), and in Rom 2:23-27 where what the Jew breaks is nomos (vv 23, 25) and what the uncircumcised person keeps is *ho nomos* (vv 26-7).[3] George E. Howard also observes that in such passages as Rom 2:17; 13:8; Gal 6:13; and Phil 3:5 the contexts require that *nomos* refer to the law of Moses.[4] I might add that at several places it appears in the same verse both with and without the definite article, with no apparent difference in meaning.[5] Gutbrod notes that in the LXX there is no discernible difference in meaning if the article is absent.[6]

---

[1] In Britain this position was held by J. B. Lightfoot, *The Epistle of Saint Paul to the Galatians* ([1865] r.p. Grand Rapids: Zondervan, 1957), 118; and E. H. Gifford, *The Epistle of Paul to The Romans* (London: Murray, 1886), 41-48. On the continent it was held, according to P. Peter Bläser, *Das Gesetz bei Paulus* (Münster: Aschendorff, 1941), 2-5, by C. Holstein and G. Volkmar.

[2] Bläser, *Gesetz*, 1-31; Eduard Grafe, *Die Paulinische Lehre von Gesetz nach den vier Hauptbriefen* (Leipzig: Mohr [Siebeck], 1893), 2-11. See also Räisänen, *Law*, 16-18.

[3] Grafe, *Gesetz*, 5-6.

[4] George E. Howard, "Christ the End of the Law. The Meaning of Romans 10:4ff.," JBL 88 (1969) 331-337, 331 n 2. Howard also points out that the anarthrous use of *nomos* refers to the Mosaic law in the Apocrypha (1 Macc 4:12; Sir 19:20, 24; 21:11; Bar 4:12), Philo (de Ebriet 17, 25, 135; de Sobriet 21; de Congr. Quer. Erudit Gratia 169; de Somn 214), Josephus (Antiq 3, 237; 12, 256; 16, 43), and the NT (Heb 8:4; 10:8; Jas 2:11; 4:11).

[5] I.e., at Rom 2:14, 23, 27; 7:1, 2, 7; Gal 4:21.

[6] Walter Gutbrod, "nomos," TDNT IV 1036-1085, 1047. The examples he cites include Bar 4:12; 1 Macc 4:42; and esp Sir 19:20, 24; 21:11.

2.1.2 NOMOS AND VARIOUS ASPECTS OF THE OLD TESTAMENT

Nomos in Paul can refer to the OT as a whole, the Pentateuch, the Mosaic legislation, the Decalogue, the OT prophets, and perhaps the creation narratives. *Ho nomos legei* (1 Cor 14:34) probably refers to the creation narratives of Gen 1:26-31 and 2:21-24 (on which Paul has based the argument of 11:3-16) rather than to Gen 3:16.[7] *Tǭ nomǭ gegraptai* (1 Cor 14:21) refers to Isa 28:11-12. The commandments *ou klepseis* and *ouk epithymēseis* in Rom 13:9 are references to the Decalogue. The Mosaic legislation is explicitly referred to in 1 Cor 9:9 (*en gar tǭ Mōüseōs nomǭ gegraptai* and in Gal 3:17 (*ho meta tetrakosia kai triakonta etē gegonōs nomos*), and is probably referred to in Rom 5:13a and 5:20. In the phrase *tou nomou kai tōn prophētōn* (Rom 3:21), *tou nomou* refers to the Pentateuch; but in the clause *hosa ho nomos legei* (Rom 3:19), the reference is to the whole of the OT, to the whole catena of quotations adduced in Rom 3:10-18 from the Psalms and Isaiah.

Contrary to the opinion of some, Paul's use of *nomos* in these texts is similar to its use in the LXX and elsewhere in the NT and to the use of *tôrâh* in the OT and in Rabbinic literature.[8] In the OT the older prophets use *tôrâh* for the word of God which comes to them. This word can include legal, cultic, or political material. In Lev and Num *tôrâh* is a term for the regulation of specific cultic or ritual practices. In a later period *tôrâh* is a term for cultic direction of the priest (Hag 2:11; Mal 2:6-9). But in the wisdom literature it can be instruction given by a teacher of wisdom (Prov 13:14; 28:4, 7, 9).[9]

Tôrâh in the Deuteronomic writings can be the Decalogue (Deut 4:44) or Deut itself (Deut 27:3, 8).[10] Deut is called "the book of this law" (Deut 28:61;

---

[7] Bruce, *Corinthians*, 136.

[8] C. H. Dodd, *The Bible and the Greeks* (London: Hodder & Stoughton, 1935), 33-34, argued that frequently the LXX mistranslated *tôrâh* by *nomos* because *nomos* has a legalistic connotation and *tôrâh* generally means instruction. He claimed that Philo, Hellenistic Judaism, and Paul picked up on this misunderstanding, and, therefore, misunderstood the meaning of *tôrâh* in the OT. In this assessment he was followed by H. J. Schoeps, *Paul: The Theology of the Apostle in the Light of Jewish History* (London: Lutterworth, 1961), 29, 213; and Samuel Sandmel, *The Genius of Paul: A Study in History* (r.p. Philadelphia: Fortress, 1979), 46-47; et. al. For refutation see Stephen Westerholm, "Torah, *nomos*, and law: A question of 'Meaning'," SR 15 (1986) 327-336; Adele Reinhartz, "The Meaning of *nomos* in Philo's *Exposition of The Law*," SR 15 (1986), 337-345; and Alan F. Segal, "Torah and *nomos* in Recent Scholarly Discussion," SR 13 (1984), 19-27. Segal (ibid., 21) notes that it is amazing how much of the ammunition to defeat this position had already been given by H. Kleinknecht, "nomos," TDNT IV, 1022-1035, though it is presented there without any reference to its importance.

[9] Hans-Helmut Esser, "Nomos," NIDNTT I, 440; cf Gutbrod, "nomos," TDNT IV, 1045; George Foot Moore, *Judaism in The First Centuries of The Christian Era: The Age of the Tannaim* (3 Vols. Cambridge: Harvard University Press. 1927, 1930), 263-265.

[10] Gutbrod, "nomos," TDNT IV, 1046.

cf 29:20; 30:10; 31:26; cf Josh 1:8; 2 Ki 22:8, 11).[11] In the Chronicler and the later psalms the content of the *tôrâh* is extended to include the whole of the Pentateuch (e.g., 1 Chron 16:40; 22:12; 2 Chron 23:18; 30:16; 34:14; Ezr 7:6 etc).[12]

In Rabbinic Judaism *tôrâh* can refer to the decalogue, the Pentateuch, the OT, or the oral tradition. Parts of the Pentateuch which have no legal character are called *tôrâh*. Other parts of the OT can be called *tôrâh* because they agree with the Pentateuch.[13] For the rabbis *tôrâh* functioned something like "a canon within the canon."[14] The prime authority was the Pentateuch, the other OT writings were authoritative *tôrâh* because they agreed with it. To give credence to the Oral Torah at some point the fiction was invented that all Torah, written and oral was revealed to Moses at Sinai.[15]

In the LXX *nomos* sometimes refers to the Pentateuch. It has this meaning in the phrase *hoi nomoi kai hoi prophētai* (e.g., 2 Macc 15:9; Sir Prol 1:1ff, 24; cf Zech 7:12). Other expressions with reference to the OT law include *to biblion tou nomou* (1 Esdr 9:39),[16] *ho nomos kyriou* (1 Esdr 1:31 etc), *ho nomos tou theou* (3 Macc 7:10, 12), and *ho nomos Mōüseōs* (1 Esdr 8:3; Tob 6:13 BA 7:13 BA).[17]

In the New Testament apart from Paul it can reasonably be argued that all the references refer to Biblical or Jewish law. In the synoptic Gospels *nomos* occurs only in Matthew (eight times) and Luke (nine times). The phrases "the law of Moses" (Lk 2:22) and "the law of Moses and the prophets" (Lk 24:44) are each used once, but "the law and the Prophets" is found five times (Matt 5:17; 7:12; 11:13; 22:36; Lk 16:16). In each case the law clearly refers to the Pentateuch. In the expressions, "the law of the Lord" (Lk 2:23, 24, 39; 10:26)

---

[11] Esser, "Nomos," NIDNTT I, 440.

[12] Gutbrod, "nomos," TDNT IV, 1046.

[13] Gutbrod, "nomos," TDNT IV, 1054.

[14] Esser, "Nomos," NIDNTT I, 442.

[15] See Moore, *Judaism* I, 258; Gutbrod, "nomos," TDNT IV, 1055-6. Shammai is the first to distinguish explicitly between the written *tôrâh* and the Oral *tôrâh*. See Ephraim E. Urbach, *The Sages: Their Concepts and Beliefs* (2 Vols. trans Israel Abrahams. Jerusalem: Magnes, 1975) 290. Moore observes that the authenticity of the oral law could be assured only if it was delivered by Moses and transmitted by uninterrupted and worthy transmission (Moore, *Judaism* I, 290). But the oral Torah actually consists of the tradition of the fathers, the enactments, and the decrees (see Urbach I *Sages*, 293). These grew out of the necessity of new laws and precedents for changing times and situations (see Moore *Judaism* I, 258-60). There had, however, always been an oral tradition. Moore notes, for example, that the priests' knowledge of the details of the ritual is constantly assumed in the Pentateuch. Only after the destruction of the temple in AD 70 was the whole elaborate temple ritual written down (Moore, *Judaism* I, 251).

[16] Gutbrod, "nomos," TDNT IV, 1047.

[17] Gutbrod, "nomos," TDNT IV, 1048.

and "the law" (Matt 5:18; 12:5; 22:36; Lk 2:27; 10:26; 16:17), the Pentateuch is at least included.[18]

Nomos occurs fourteen times in John's Gospel. The law is frequently associated with Moses (1:17; 1:45; 7:19, 23). It can refer to the Pentateuch (1:45) or other parts of the OT, since citations from the OT outside of the Pentateuch are from the law (*nomos*) (10:34; 12:34; 15:25).[19]

Acts, like Luke, refers to the Pentateuch with the phrases "the law and the prophets" (13:15; 24:14) and "the law of Moses" (13:39; 15:5; 28:23). "The law" at 7:53 could conceivably be limited to the decalogue, but elsewhere in Acts (Acts 6:13; 18:13; 21:20, 24, 28; 22:12; 23:3) it at least includes the Pentateuch. There are, furthermore, expressions which seem to include extra-biblical Jewish laws: namely, "the law of the Jews" (Acts 25:8), "your own [Jewish] law" (Acts 18:15), "their law" (23:29), and "the law of our Fathers" (Acts 22:3).

At Hebrews 8:10 and 10:16 we have the plural *nomous* in a quotation from Jeremiah 31:33 and the stress is clearly on God's moral laws; these laws do not seem to be limited to the Pentateuch. The phrase "the law of Moses" (10:28) is a reference to the Pentateuch and also has a moral connotation. But elsewhere in Hebrews (i.e. 7:5, 12, 19, 28; 8:4; 9:19, 22; 10:1, 8) *nomos* refers to the cultic and priestly aspects of the Pentateuch.[20]

The law in James is always in the context of moral law. "The law" at 2:9, 10, 11; cf 4:11 as a minimum includes the decalogue and the love commandment from Lev 19:18. In context "the law of liberty" (*nomos eleutherias*) (1:25;; 2:12) and "the royal law" *nomos basilikos* (2:8) should be understood in a similar manner. "The royal law" would seem to refer to Yahweh as the king who gave the law.[21]

2.1.3 ERGŌN NOMOU

To discover the exact nuance of *ergōn nomou* in Paul is difficult.[22] *Erga nomou* has always been regarded as an objective genitive. Gaston,[23] however, makes the somewhat startling suggestion that *erga nomou* is a subjective genitive. He observes that Lohmeyer believed the only natural grammatical

---

[18] Cf Gutbrod, "nomos," TDNT IV, 1059-60.

[19] Dodd, *Greeks*, 38.

[20] cf Gutbrod, "nomos," TDNT IV, 1078.

[21] cf Dodd, *Greeks*, 39.

[22] For a recent discussion see Joseph B. Tyson, "'Works of Law' in Galatians," JBL 92 (1973), 423-431. He is heavily dependent on the classic discussion of Ernst Lohmeyer, "Gesetzeswerke," ZNW 28 (1929), 177-209 r.p. in *Probleme paulinischer Theologie* (Darmstadt: Wissenschaftliche Buchgesellshaft, 1954, 33-74.

[23] Lloyd Gaston, "Works of Law as a Subjective Genitive," SR 13 (1984) 39-46.

possibility is "the works worked by the law" but that it obviously must mean "works which the law prescribes," yet, according to Gaston, he could not demonstrate in forty pages that it does mean what it must mean.[24]

Gaston argues that the law is a positive power which works disastrous consequences (Rom 3:20; 5:13; 20; 7:8-11), and that the only text in Paul both with the noun *nomos* and a verb with the stem *erg-* is Rom 4:15: "the law works (*katergazetai*) wrath." At Rom 2:14 the Gentiles by idolatrous sinning show they have "the work of the law" (i.e. wrath and sin) written on their hearts.[25] The rules of grammar must take precedence over theological presuppositions.[26]

Against Gaston I would argue: (1) The phrase "works of law" seems to be used interchangeably with "works" where the works obviously refer to our works used in a negative way (Rom 4:2, 6; 9:32; 11:6). (2) It is not the law which works disastrous consequences but sin as a personified power works disastrous consequences by means of the law (e.g., Rom 7:9-11). (3) It is not only bad things that come by means of the law but also good things. At Rom 3:20 it may be God who brings about knowledge of sin by means of the law; and it may be better to be exposed to my sinful condition than not to be exposed to it. In some texts it is not a curse but a privilege to have the Torah (Rom 3:2; 9:4; see 2:17f; 7:14a). (4) In Rom 2:14 it is more natural to think of the good effect of the "work of the law" (i.e., knowledge of God's will, or knowledge of the requirement of the law) than its evil effect (i.e., wrath and sin). (5) True the rules of grammar must take precedence over theological presuppositions, but context must take first importance.

"Works of law" are, then, hardly "works which the law works." If it cannot mean "works which the law prescribes" it could perhaps mean "works which one does by means of the law." Just as sin brings about death by means of the law, and God reveals his will by means of the law, so one can work by means of the law. Tyson argues that Paul does not reject acts of obedience to the Torah but nomistic service. By nomistic service he means circumcision and the food laws.[27] I disagree; there is no difference between obeying the law and doing works of law. The connotation is mainly moral. Paul is against works of law only if one does them to be saved by them.[28]

---

[24] Gaston, *Works*, 40.

[25] Gaston, *Works*, 44-45.

[26] Gaston, *Works*, 46.

[27] Tyson, *Works*, 425-431.

[28] See Ulrich Wilckens, *Rechtfertigung als Freiheit: Paulusstudien* (Neukirchen-Vluyn: Neukirchener Verlag, 1974), 77-109.

2.1.4 DISPUTED PASSAGES

At Rom 3:27 he contrasts the *nomos ergōn* with the *nomos pisteōs*. At Rom 7:21-25 he speaks of a *heteros nomos* (7:23) and contrasts the *ho nomos tou noos mou* (7:23) with the *ho nomos tēs hamartias* (7:23; cf 7:25). At Rom 8:2 he contrasts the *ho nomos tou pneumatos tēs zōēs* with the *ho nomos tēs hamartias kai tou thanatou*. It is generally held that these passages do not refer to the Torah. We shall consider each passage in turn.

2.1.4.1 NOMOS IN ROM 3:27

Traditionally *nomos* in Rom 3:27 and 8:2 had been interpreted as "rule," "order," "norm," "system," "principle," or "way of salvation."[29] But some have noted the similarity of the order of faith with the Torah.[30] While others see the new system as ending the old. The law of faith is antithetical to the Mosaic law.[31]

Gerhard Friedrich and Peter von der Osten-Sacken are two prominent proponents of the view that *nomos pisteōs* refers to the law. According to Friedrich v 27 repeats v 21; "the law of faith" is the way of salvation to which the law and the prophets bear witness.[32] According to Osten-Sacken the law is brought to validity through faith.[33]

Räisänen has argued against this position. He believes that "it is excluded" (*exekleisthē*) (3:27) must be viewed as a divine passive. The boasting is excluded not through the law (against Friedrich), nor through believing men (against Hübner, Osten-Sacken), but through the deed of God in Christ.[34] It is natural that v 27 refers to an historical event perhaps *proetheto* (v 25). He believes further that v 28 authorizes a figurative use of *nomos pisteōs*. When the two *nomoi* are understood in a figurative sense there are fundamental similarities between v 27

---

[29] See Cranfield, *Romans* I ad. loc., 219; Käsemann, *Romans*, 102-03. and Räisänen, *Gesetz*, 101.

[30] Examples of those who regard *nomos pisteōs* in Rom 3:27 as referring to the Torah are Klaus Berger "Abraham in den paulinischen Hauptbriefen," MTZ 17 (1966) 47-89, 64; C. E. B. Cranfield, *Romans* I, 220; Ernst Fuchs, *Die Freiheit des Glaubens. Römer 5-8 ausgelegt* (BEvt, Vol. 14. Munich: Chr. Kaiser Verlag, 1949), 85; G. Friedrich, "Das Gesetz des Glaubens Rom 3.27," TZ 10 (1954), 401-417; Victor Paul Furnish, *Theology and Ethics in Paul* (Nashville & New York; Abingdon, 1968), 160; Ferdinand Hahn, "Gesetzesverständnis im Römer- und Galaterbrief," ZNW 67 (1976) 29-63, 41; 48-49; Hübner, *Law*, 137-140; Otto Michel, *Der Brief an Die Römer* (KEK; 4th ed. Göttingen: Vandenhoeck & Ruprecht, 1966), 111; Peter von der Osten-Sacken, *Römer 8 als Beispiel paulinischer Soteriologie* (FRLANT 112; Göttingen, Vandenhoeck & Ruprecht, 1975), 245-247; C. Thomas Rhyne, *Faith Establishes The Law* (Chico, CA; Scholars Press, 1981), 67-71; Hans Wilhelm Schmidt, *Der Brief des Paulus an die Römer* (THKNT; Berlin: Evangelische, 1963), 73-74; and Ulrich Wilckens, *Der Brief an die Römer* (3 vols. EKKNT; Zurich: Benziger Verlag, 1978, 1980, 1982) I, 245-47.

[31] See Räisänen, *Gesetz*, 102 n 7 for examples.

[32] Friedrich, *Gesetz*, 401-417.

[33] Osten-Sacken, *Römer 8*, 245.

[34] Räisänen, *Gesetz*, 112; similarly Käsemann, *Romans*, 103.

and v 28. *Nomos pisteōs* (v 27) is equivalent to "a man justified by faith" (*dikaiousthai pistei anthrōpon*) (v 28); and *nomos tōn ergōn* is the opposite of *dikaiousthai pistei anthrōpōn chōris ergōn nomou*. He concludes that *nomos pisteōs* is the order of salvation which is established by faith; and *nomos tōn ergōn* is the order which is built on the works of the law. 3:27 does not refer back to v 21 (against Friedrich) but to 3:19b-20.[35]

Räisänen correctly argues that it is neither the Torah nor believing men that exclude boasting. But this does not exclude *nomos pisteōs* as the law viewed from the standpoint of faith, and as a reference back to 3:21. It is not the law which excludes boasting but what the law bears witness to that excludes boasting, namely God's act of salvation in Christ which is appropriated by faith and is described in 3:21-26. The correspondence that Räisänen sees between v 27 and v 28 in no way demands a figurative use of *nomos*. For "justified by works of law" (vv 28, 20) is precisely the law viewed from the standpoint of works, and "justified by faith" (v 28) is precisely the law viewed from the standpoint of faith.

At 3:21-26 the law and the prophets bear witness to the righteousness of God which comes through faith in Jesus Christ. Paul in his preaching of the gospel appeals to Torah texts. In the Torah the gospel is proclaimed. In Rom 3:31 faith establishes the law. C. Thomas Rhyne has shown that Romans 4:1-25 is an exposition of Gen 15:6 and that the law in its role as witness to righteousness by faith is established in the apostolic preaching of justification by faith.[36] Also in the immediately preceding and following context *nomos* refers to the OT law.[37]

2.1.4.2 NOMOS IN ROM 7:21-25

Clearly the *ho nomos tou theou* (7:22) and *nomos theou* (7:25) are references to the Torah. *Nomos*, however, is not immediately obvious as a reference to the Torah in the following passages:[38] *nomos* (7:21), *heteros nomos* (7:23), *ho nomos tou noos* (7:23), *ho nomos tēs hamartias* (7:23), and *nomos hamartias* (7:25)[39]

At 7:14 *egō*'s problem is with the law. At 7:16 he agrees that the law is good (*kalos*); his problem is that he wants to obey the law but is unable to do it. Similarly in 7:18 he wishes to do the good but does not do it, and in 7:19 he does not do the good (*agathon*) that he wants but does the evil (*kakon*) that he hates

---

[35] Räisänen, *Gesetz*, 112; cf Räisänen, *Law*, 50-51.

[36] Rhyne, *Law*, 63-93.

[37] Rhyne, *Law*, 68; Friedrich, *Gesetz*, 404-05.

[38] The references to *nomos* in these passages are usually understood as something like "rule" or "principle."

[39] Cf below 28-31 for the discussion of "the law of Sin and Death."

(cf 7:15). This indicates that the good (7:16, 18, 19) is what the law commands and the evil (7:19) is what the law condemns.

"I delight in the law of God according to the inward man" (7:22) is similar to 7:16 where "I" agree that the law is good. "I myself serve the law of God with my mind (*nous*)" (7:25a) is similar to 7:18, 19 where "I" want to do the good. "With my flesh ... I serve ... the law of sin" (7:25b) is similar to being taken captive to the law of sin which dwells in my members (7:23), and to doing the evil which "I" hate (7:19). "The law of my mind" is equivalent to "the law of God" (7:22, 25a). It is the law which my mind delights in and serves (7:22, 25a); it is the good that "I" wish to do (7:18, 19). The "other law" (7:23) is the opposite of "the law of my mind" and should probably be equated with "the law of sin."[40] "The law of sin" is the opposite of "the law of God" (7:25) and of "the law of my mind" (7:23). "The law of sin which dwells in my members" (7:23) recalls "our sinful passions aroused by the law were at work in our members" (7:5). Sin becomes known (7:7) and manifest (7:13) by means of the law. The law which in itself is holy and good (7:12, 13) provides sin with its base of operations (7:8, 11). "The law of sin" (7:23, 25) is, then, but a concise way of speaking of the relationship between sin and the law in 7:7-13.

Ton nomon in 7:21 may be understood as an accusative of respect. It could be translated "I discover, then, with respect to the law that when I wish to do good, evil lies close at hand."[41] It is what "my" confrontation with the law has been teaching "me" in 7:14-20. This is similar to the earlier statements that through the law comes knowledge of sin (3:20), and "I" had not known sin except by means of the law (7:7). All the references to *nomos* in 7:21-25, therefore, should be understood as a reference to the law.[42]

2.1.4.3 NOMOS IN ROM 8:2

There has been a great divergence of opinion on the meaning of *nomos* in Rom 8:2a. Suggested meanings have been "power,"[43] "rule,"[44] "authority,"[45] "authority and constraint,"[46] "religion,"[47] and "order."[48]

---

[40] See Wilckens, *Römer* II, 367.

[41] Wilckens, *Römer* II 89 notes that most of the Fathers understood *nomos* in v 21 to be a reference to the law of Moses.

[42] Wilckens, *Römer* II 88-97 also believes that *nomos* in each case is a reference to the Torah. cf. Osten-Sacken, *Römer 8*, 209-212.

[43] John Murray, *The Epistle to the Romans* (2 Vols. NICNT; Grand Rapids: Eerdmans, 1958, 1965), 276.

[44] Käsemann, *Romans*, 215-16.

[45] Sanday and Headlam, *Romans*, 190.

[46] Cranfield, *Romans* I, 376.

[47] C. K. Barrett, *The Epistle to the Romans* (HNTC; New York: Harper & Row, 1957), 155.

[48] Nygren, *Romans*, 311-12; Black, *Romans*, 114; Kuss, *Römer* II, 486; van Dülmen, *Gesetzes*,

In the early church, however, some believed that it refers to the law. Werner Keuck notes that Clement of Alexandria and John Chrysostom of the ancient Greek Fathers read Rom 8:2a (*ho nomos tou pneumatos tēs zōēs*) in the light of Rom 7:14a (*ho nomos pneumatikos estin*) and made them both refer to the OT law.[49]

Cranfield considers, but ultimately rejects, this view. He suggests that one might be tempted to take it as "God's law, now established by Christ's work in its true and original character and office as 'spiritual' and 'unto life' ... which has effected the believer's liberation."[50]

Recently, several scholars have argued that *nomos* in Rom 8:2a refers to the law.[51] Paul Meyer sees "the law of sin and death" as a shorthand summation of 7:7-12 where God's law is used by sin to produce death, and "the law of the Spirit of life in Christ Jesus" as the same Divine law brought to fulfillment through the life-giving power which it was unable to provide but which belongs to the Spirit.[52]

Hans Hübner argues that law of the Spirit refers back to 7:14, and that the law of sin and death is the abused law. When the law is transferred from the sphere of the *pneuma* into the death-bringing sphere of *hamartia* it is deprived of its real intentionality. 8:2 confirms 8:4; for those who "walk according to the flesh" the law manifests itself as death-bringing, but for those who "walk according to the spirit," according to the true character of the law, it manifests itself as spiritual and life-giving.[53]

Hans Wilhelm Schmidt believes that to the one "in the flesh" the OT law is falsified as a *nomos ergōn* and is encountered as a *nomos hamartias*. But to the one who is "in Christ" and has received the Spirit, it discloses itself in its true being (cf 7:14).[54]

119-120; Van Dülmen also accepts "aeon," "sphere," and "system of Lordship" (ibid., 120).

49 Werner Keuck, "Das 'Geistliche Gesetz': im Röm: 7, 14a in der Auslegung der griechischen Väter," in *Wort Gottes in der Zeit* (FS Karl Herman Schelkle. [eds.] Helmut Feld and Josef Nolte Düsseldorf: Patmos, 1973) 215-235, 228-9; 231-2.

50 Cranfield, *Romans* I, 376 n 1.

51 Hahn, "Gesetzesverständnis," 46-48; Hans Hübner, "Das Gesetz als elementares Thema einer Biblischen Theologie," KD 22 (1976) 250-76, 270-71; Hübner, *Law*, 144-146; Eduard Lohse, "'Ho nomos tou pneumatos tēs zōēs,' Exegetische Anmerkungen zu Röm 8,2." *Neues Testament und Christliche Existenz* (FS Herbert Braun. ed Hans Dieter Betz and Luise Schottroff; Tübingen: Mohr [Siebeck], 1973) 279-287, 280, 283-287; Schmidt, *Römer*, 136; Paul Meyer, "Romans 10:4 and the End of the Law," in *The Divine Helmsman: Studies on God's Control of Human Events* (ed. J. L. Crenshaw and S. Sandmel. New York: KTAV, 1980) 59-78, 73; Osten-Sacken, *Römer 8*, 210-11; 226-228; and Wilckens, *Römer* II, 123. For a list of others see Osten-Sacken, ibid, 226 n 3.

52 Meyer, *End*, 73, 77 n 24.

53 Hübner, *Law*, 144-45.

54 Schmidt, *Römer*, 136.

Eduard Lohse agrees; for those who read the law from the standpoint of faith, it discloses life, but for those who read it from the standpoint of works, it discloses sin and death. In the preceding verses (7:21-25) the one in the flesh may serve the law of God with his mind but what he really serves is the law of sin (Rom 7:25). The law contains the will of God but because of a disastrous alliance between sin and the law it has become *nomos hamartias* for the unsaved man.[55] In the following verses (8:3-7) Paul clearly refers to the OT law; the gate to freedom is only opened up through the sending of God's son. It is the freedom to fulfill "the just requirement of the law" (*dikaiōma tou nomou*), the just requirement of this holy just and good will of God. The Christian is freed from (*vom*) the law as a way of salvation and for (*zum*) the law as an inner commandment. The *ho nomos tou pneumatos tēs zōēs* is equated with fulfilling the law by love; it occurs where there is living brought about by the Spirit. The word *nomos* has been carefully chosen, the idea of two opposing "rules" or "orders" cannot account for the use of the same word *nomos* in 8:2a and 8:2b.[56]

Räisänen does not agree with Lohse although he concedes that *nomos* is deliberately chosen. He claims rather that *nomos* bears a polemical relation to the law, and that in context it does not consistently refer to the law. At 7:21-25 *nomos* has a range of meanings; only twice, i.e. in the expression "the law of God" (*[ho] nomos [tou] theou*) (vv 22, 25), does it refer to the law. He also believes that the logic of Lohse's position is refuted since the subject of the sentence is *nomos* not Jesus Christ. From Lohse's viewpoint it would be Christ Jesus who frees us from the law of sin and death and brings us into the law of the Spirit of life.[57]

I would criticize Räisänen's view since he is forced to see tension if not outright contradiction in Paul's argument at 8:2-4. He sees a tension between 8:4 where the Christian is to fulfill the just requirement of the law and 8:2 where the power of sin over men is severed through the dominion of the Spirit. He believes that from this change of lordship it follows that the one who is freed from the law does not need to fulfill it; he can do it charismatically. He claims that 7:7-8:3 can be confidently interpreted on the basis of 6:14 (where we are not under the law but under grace) and on the basis of 7:1-6 (where we have died to the law), but in 8:4 (where we are to fulfill the just requirement of the law) Paul speaks in an entirely different language from 7:1-6.[58] In response to Räisänen, if *nomos* refers to the Torah in 8:2 there is no contradiction with 8:4.[59]

---

[55] See Hahn, *Gesetzesverständnis* 46; and Hübner, *Law* 145, who also argue that the Law of God is the same as the law of sin.

[56] Lohse, *Ho nomos*, 283-287.

[57] Räisänen, *Gesetz*, 113-116; cf. Räisänen, *Law*, 52.

[58] Räisänen, *Gesetz*, 116-117.

[59] The tension between the positive and negative statements on the law will be dealt with below 40-41, 43-44, 129-155.

Räisänen's strongest point against *nomos* as a reference to the law is the fact that *nomos* is the subject of the sentence. This objection can be answered. The subject of the sentence may not be *nomos* but the full phrase "the law of the Spirit of life in Christ Jesus."

The *gar* in 8:2 links 8:2a with 8:1; and the *gar* in 8:3 links 8:2b with 8:3a. "No condemnation *in Christ Jesus*" (8:1) correlates with being set free by "the law of the Spirit of life *in Christ Jesus* (8:2a)." Bondage to "the law of sin and death" (8:2) is correlative with "what the law could not do in that it was weak through the flesh" (8:3a), and with condemnation for those outside of Christ (8:1) In the phrase "the law of the Spirit of life in Christ Jesus" there is an interplay between "in Christ Jesus," "law," "spirit," and "life." In the phrase "the law of sin and death" there is an interplay between "law," "sin," and "death." In 7:7-25 and in 8:3-9; 12-13[60] the plight of the one who does not belong to Christ involves an interplay of "flesh," "law," "sin," and "death," and the solution for the one who belongs to Christ in 8:4-13 involves an interplay of being "in Christ Jesus," "law," "spirit," and "life." The person described in 7:7-25 is controlled by the flesh rather than the Spirit; sin gains its base of operations by means of the law and brings forth death. Similarly in 8:4-9, 12, 13 the one who does not belong to Christ does not obey the law and is controlled by the flesh whose aim is death. But the one who belongs to Christ in 8:4-13 is controlled by the Spirit whose aim is life, and by the Spirit is enabled to obey the law.[61] "The law of sin and death" is but a succinct way of expressing the relationship between the law, sin, and death in 7:7-25 and 8:4-9, 12, 13. "The law of the Spirit of life in Christ Jesus"[62] is but a concise way of expressing the relationship of "in Christ Jesus," "law," "Spirit," and "life" in 8:4-13. In Rom 8:2 the new situation ("the law of the Spirit of life in Christ Jesus") has set me free from the old ("the law of sin and death"). The question, then, is what has brought about the new situation of "the law of the Spirit of life in Christ Jesus." The answer in context would seem to be God's action in Christ in 8:3b, God's sending his own Son in the likeness of sinful flesh and as a sin offering condemning sin in the flesh.[63]

---

[60] On 7:7-13 as a reference to the sin of Adam, and 7:14-25 as a reference to the pre-Christian state see below 74-84.

[61] The just requirement of the law can be fulfilled in those who walk *kata pneuma* rather than *kata sarka* (Rom 8:4). The *phronēma* of the flesh is death but the *phronēma* of the Spirit is life and peace (8:6). Only one with the Spirit can be subject to "the law of God" (8:7). The indwelling Spirit will give life. Those who by the Spirit put to death the deeds of the body will live (8:13). In the present, however, the Christian is already "alive to God in Christ Jesus" (6:11).

[62] The phrase may also recall 7:10 where the aim of the commandment is life; and 7:14 where the law is Spiritual.

[63] God's action "through (*dia*) Jesus Christ our Lord" (7:25a) is the solution to the similar plight of 7:23-24. Ulrich Wilckens, "Zur Entwicklung des paulinischen Gesetzesverständnises," NTS 28 (1982), 154-190, 185.

The contrast of *ho ... nomos tou pneumatos tēs zōēs en Christō Iēsou* with *tou nomou tēs hamartias kai tou thanatou* (Rom 8:2) should be understood in light of the contrast between *pneuma* and *gramma* in 2 Cor 3:6 and Rom 7:6 (since Rom 8 continues the thought of 7:6).

At 2 Cor 3:6 *to gramma* is a reference to the Decalogue which was engraved "on tablets of stone" (*en plaxin lithinais*) (3:3), and to the whole Mosaic economy which was the dispensation of death (*hē diakonia tou thanatou*) and condemnation (*katakriseōs*, 3:7, 9). The old dispensation was one of impotence (*adynaton*), condemnation, sin, and death (Rom 8:1-9; 2 Cor 3:6-18.). The written code (*gramma*) kills (2 Cor 3:6) in the sense that it does not empower one to keep the law, but pronounces the death sentence on the law-breaker (cf Gal 3:10 = Deut 27:26 LXX; Rom 7:5, 9-11; Deut 30:17-18.). Yet it came with *doxa* (2 Cor 3:7, 9-11).

At 2 Cor 3:6 *to pneuma* is a reference to Jeremiah's (31:31-34) new covenant (*kainēs diathēkēs*, 3:6) which has now been written "on tablets of human hearts" (*en plaxin kardias sarkinais*, (3:3). It is the dispensation of the Spirit (*hē diakonia tou pneumatos*) and of righteousness (*dikaiosynēs*, 3:8, 9). As such, God's saving righteousness is manifested in it and God gives us new life because of it (cf 2 Cor 3:6 *to ... pneuma zōopoiei*, Rom 8:10ff; 1 Cor 15:45b). The one with God's law written on his heart is no longer enslaved and condemned. He has new life breathed into him; he walks *kata pneuma* rather than *kata sarka* and is thus able to fulfill the *to dikaiōma tou nomou* (Rom 8:4).

2.2 THE MORAL LAW VERSUS THE CEREMONIAL LAW

Calvin argued that Christ is the end of the ceremonial law but not the moral law,[64] now, however, it is the commonly held view that the law is indivisible.[65]

Recently, though, some have argued that Christ abrogates the ceremonial law but not the moral law.[66] C. E. B. Cranfield is a major proponent of this view.

---

[64] See John Calvin, *Institutes of The Christian Religion* (2 Vols. ed. John T. McNeill; Philadelphia: Westminster, 1960) ii. 7. 17.

[65] See for example Gutbrod, "nomos," TDNT IV 1072; F. F. Bruce, "Paul And The Law of Moses," BJRL 57 (1975) 259-279, 266; John Knox, *The Ethic of Jesus in the Teaching of the Church. Its Authority and Its Relevance* (New York: Abingdon, 1961), 99; Robert Banks, *Jesus and The Law in The Synoptic Tradition* (SNTSMS 28; Cambridge: Cambridge University Press, 1975), 109; Leander Keck, *Paul and His Letters* (Philadelphia: Fortress, 1979), 86; Stanislas Lyonnet, "St Paul: Liberty and Law," *The Bridge*, 4 (1962) 229-251, 232; Käsemann, *Romans* 215; Morton Scott Enslin, *The Ethics of Paul* (New York: Harper & Brothers, 1930), 85. For a summary of the discussion see Bläser, *Gesetz*, 38-44, 63-71; Grafe, *Gesetz*, 11-25; Richard N. Longenecker, *Paul: Apostle of Liberty* (New York: Harper & Row, 1964), 119-20.

[66] For example Christoph Haufe, "Die Stellung des Paulus zum Gesetz," TLZ 91 (1966), 171-178; Christoph Haufe, *Die Sittliche Rechtfertigungslehre des Paulus* (Halle [Salle], 1957), 20ff; Jost Eckert, *Die urchristliche Verkündigung im Streit zwischen Paulus und seinem Gegnern nach dem*

He believes that the ceremonial ordinances are no longer obligatory, and the ritual regulations are valid only as a witness to Christ. In the moral and civil realms one must distinguish between those commandments which express the absolute will of God and those which are limited to temporal human conditions.[67]

Others believe that although Paul does not make an explicit distinction between the moral and cultic law he nonetheless makes an implicit distinction.[68] Schrage observes that Paul never cites a ritual law which is valid for Christians, while he does so cite moral laws. Paul factually requires observance of the ethical part of the Bible, even when he does not explicitly cite a law.[69]

Scholars have speculated as to why Paul made the distinction. E. P. Sanders in 1978 argued that Paul seems to exclude the "ceremonial" law - in Jewish terminology, the "commandments between God and man" - while keeping the "commandments (which govern relations) between man and man." He cannot recommend keeping any of the commandments between God and man which he mentions, yet he always condemns transgression of commandments between man and man. This "spiritualization" of the ceremonial laws was not unique to Paul and doubtless had been attempted previously by other Hellenistic Jews.[70]

By 1983 he had a different explanation. Paul he argued has two principle convictions: 1) all are to be saved on the same basis; and 2) he was called to be the apostle to the Gentiles. Putting these principles into practice understandably resulted in deleting circumcision, Sabbath, and food laws from "the whole law" or "the commandments of God."[71] He claims further that with the command to love one's neighbor we only can say he meant a *reduced* law because we can observe the ways in which he reduced it, not because Paul himself admits that he reduced it; Paul still calls it "the whole law."[72] Sanders adds that 1 Cor 7:19

Galaterbrief (Biblische Untersuchung 6. Regensburg: Pustet, 1971), 159; and Hübner, *Law* 84-87.

[67] Cranfield, *Law*, 67.

[68] Roger Mohrlang, *Matthew and Paul: A Comparison of Ethical Perspectives* (SNTSMS 48; Cambridge: Cambridge University Press, 1984), 34; E. P. Sanders, "On the Question of Fulfilling the Law in Paul and Rabbinic Judaism," in *Donum Gentilicium: New Testament Studies in Honour of David Daube* (eds. E. Bammel, C. K. Barrett, and W. D. Davies, 103-26. Oxford: Clarendon, 1978) 103-126, 125; Sanders, *Jewish People*, 101; Heikki Räisänen, "Legalism and Salvation by the Law," in *Die paulinische Literatur und Theologie* (ed. S. Pederson, 63-83. Scandinavische Beiträge. Aarhus: Forlaget Aros, 1980), 80; Räisänen, *Law*, 24-27; Wolfgang Schrage, *Die konkreten Einzelgebote in der paulinischen Paränese: Ein Beitrag zur neutestamentlichen Ethik* (Gutersloh: Mohn, 1961), 231-233; Rudolf Bultmann, *Theology of The New Testament* (2 Vols. New York: Scribner's, 1951, 1955) I, 261. Hans Conzelmann, *An Outline of the Theology of the New Testament* (London: SCM, 1969), 223; Grafe, *Gesetz*, 31.

[69] Schrage, *Einzelgebote*, 231-233.

[70] Sanders, *Fulfilling* 125; cf Sanders, *Palestinian Judaism*, 544.

[71] Sanders, *Jewish People*, 102-3.

[72] Sanders, *Jewish People*, 103.

("Neither circumcision nor uncircumcision counts for anything, but keeping the commandments of God") makes clear the degree to which Paul could change the content of the law, while still saying that it should be kept. Paul may have been hampered from facing in a theoretical way his reduction of "the law" by the general view in Judaism that the law is one, and that all parts were equally ordained by God.[73]

Räisänen agrees that Paul did not consciously reduce the Torah to the moral law yet he did so unconsciously.[74] The distinction between the moral and ceremonial law all started with the rejection, more instinctive than reflective, of certain ritual parts of the law which were neither relevant nor comprehensible from a Gentile perspective. During his work Paul came more and more to internalize the Gentile point of view.[75] According to him, Sanders (1978) view does not exactly hit the situation, for the commandments between God and man include not only the ceremonial law but also idolatry.[76] It is better to speak of ritual laws which "created a social distinction between Jews and other races," namely circumcision, Sabbath and the food laws. He observes that in Galatians the cultic side of the law is prominent, yet in Romans it is basically ignored (for example at 2:2-16, 5:14; 8:4 and 13:8-10).[77] He sees the same kind of unconscious reduction elsewhere in the NT (Colossians, 1 Timothy, James) and early Christian literature (Justin). The first to make the explicit distinction between the moral and ceremonial law is the Epistle of Barnabas.[78]

In general I agree with Schrage and Sanders (1978) than with Sanders (1983) and Räisänen. Paul makes at least an implicit distinction between the moral law and the ceremonial law, but as will be seen the reason is not that they are burdensome to Gentiles. I would add that when Paul refers to those who would be saved he does not differentiate between the halakic and ceremonial aspects of the law. But when an uncircumcised Gentile can obey the precepts of the law (Rom 2:27), the reference must be to the moral, not the ceremonial or halakic, aspects of the law.

We have reasons to believe, then, that Paul makes at least an implicit distinction between the ceremonial law and the moral law. It will be argued below that the man outside of Christ is enslaved not to the ceremonial law but to the moral law. Paul could perfectly obey the ceremonial law without feeling

---

[73] Sanders, *Jewish People*, 103 see Sanders, *Palestinian Judaism* 112; Moore, *Judaism* I, 235.

[74] Räisänen, *Law*, 26.

[75] Räisänen, *Legalism*, 79-80. For a discussion of the problems involved see: Hans Hübner, "Das ganze und das eine Gesetz," KD 21 (1975), 239-256; Hübner, *Law*, 36-42; 83-87.

[76] Räisänen, *Law*, 23.

[77] Räisänen, *Law*, 24-27.

[78] Räisänen, *Law*, 29-33.

enslaved (cf Phil 3:4ff) and he continued to obey when it suited his purpose (cf 1 Cor 9:20ff).

2.3 THE ORIGIN OF THE LAW

In Romans and 1 Corinthians the law clearly originates with God. The law is given by God (Rom 9:4) and written by God (*gegraptai*, 1 Cor 9:9; 14:21; cf 14:34) and is called "the law of God" (7:22, 25; 8:7). Some have argued, though, that in Galatians the law does not originate with God but with the angels.[79] The key text is Gal 3:19. In the process of contrasting the later law which cannot nullify the earlier promise Paul says the law "was ordained by angels through an intermediary. Now an intermediary implies more than one; but God is one" (*diatageis di' angelōn en cheiri mesitou. ho de mesitēs henos ouk estin, ho de theos heis estin*). Even here the view that the Torah did not spring from God is difficult to maintain. The preposition is *dia* not *hypo*;[80] *dia* means not "by" but "through the agency of."[81] The Torah stems ultimately not from the angels but from God. *Diatageis*, *prosetethē*, and *edothē* (vv 19, 21) should be viewed as Divine passives;[82] God gave the law, he added the law after the promise, he ordained it through the agency (*di'*) of angels in the hands of a mediator (Moses). Also at Deut 33:2 (LXX), Josephus (Antiq. XV: 5: 3), Jubilees 1:27-29, Acts 7:53 and in Talmudic passages the presence of angels at the giving of the law is a mark of its excellence.[83] Calvin noted that the authority of the law was greatly confirmed by its having so many witnesses.[84]

---

[79] See Schoeps, *Paul*, 182-3; cf Albrecht Oepke, *Der Brief des Paulus an die Galater* (THKNT; 3rd ed. Berlin: Evangelische, 1957), 80-84, 115; Günter Klein, *Rekonstruktion und Interpretation. Gesammelte Aufsätze zum Neuen Testament* (BEvT; München: Chr. Kaiser Verlag, 1969), 209-210; John W. Drane, *Paul: Libertine or Legalist? A Study in the Theology of the Major Pauline Epistles* (London: SPCK, 1975), 34; Hübner, *Law*, 27-9; 46-7; Albert Schweitzer, *The Mysticism of Paul The Apostle* (New York: Holt, 1931), 70; et. al. Räisänen agrees that in Gal 3:19 the law originates with angels but characteristically in Paul it originates with God (Räisänen, *Law*, 128-33). Albert Schweitzer, *Mysticism*, 69-74 proposed that Paul systematically presupposed that the law was given by evil spiritual powers, the rulers of the old aeon. He also establishes a connection between the angelic law-giver and "the elements of the world" (Gal 4:3, 9). For others who make this connection see Räisänen, *Law*, 131.

[80] Cf Franz Mussner, *Der Galaterbrief* (3rd ed. Freiburg: Herder, 1977), ad. loc., 247.

[81] Donald Guthrie, *Galatians* (NCB; London, Oliphants, 1969), 104; Ernest de Witt Burton, *A Critical and Exegetical Commentary on the Epistle to the Galatians* (ICC; Edinburgh: T. & T. Clark, 1921) ad. loc., 189; Mussner, *Galaterbrief*, ad. loc. 247; H. W. MacGorman, "Problem Passages in Galatians," SWJT 15 (1972) 35-51, 44.

[82] Cf Mussner, *Galaterbrief*, ad. loc. 247.

[83] Cf Lightfoot, *Galatians* ad. loc., 145; Longenecker, *Paul* 146, n 109; and Ragnar Bring, *Commentary on Galatians* (Philadelphia: Muhlenberg, 1961) ad. loc., 82-84.

[84] As cited in Bruce, *Galatians*, ad. loc., 177.

In modern times the mediator has almost universally been understood to be Moses. Many of the ancient church Fathers, however, understood it to be Christ.[85] C. H. Cosgrove has argued that the mediator is so closely associated with angels that it is more easy to think of the angels' mediator than Israel's mediator.[86] But it seems evident that the mediator must be Moses. *En cheiri mesitou* recalls *en cheiri Mōüseōs* in the LXX (Lev 26:46; Num 4:37, 41, 45 etc.) at the giving of the law.[87] Bruce observes that Moses was the Israelites' mediator with God throughout the wilderness wanderings and at Deut 5:5 he says "I stood between (*ana meson*) Yahweh and you."[88]

Three views on the meaning of *ho de mesitēs henos ouk estin* can be excluded:[89] The first view is that of Vanhoye followed by Bruce;[90] Vanhoye thinks of Moses as a mediator of the people of Israel and the angel of the presence who was with Moses in the wilderness as the mediator of the angels. *Ho de mesitēs henos ouk estin* is a general statement. It probably means that a mediator represents more than one party, rather than a mediator represents not merely one person but a party of persons.[91] It is difficult to see how a person is a mediator if he represents only one side of a dispute. Disputes can take place between two individuals; in such a case if he represents only his side of the dispute then a mediator would be of one rather than more than one.[92] This last point eliminates a second view, that of Oepke. He claims that the mediator here

---

[85] See Lightfoot, *Galatians*, ad. loc, 146.

[86] C. H. Cosgrove, "The Mosaic Law Preaches Faith: A Study in Galatians 3," WTJ 41 (1978-79) 146-171, 158.

[87] See Lightfoot, *Galatians* ad. loc. 146; Hans Dieter Betz, *Galatians: A Commentary on Paul's Letter to the Churches in Galatia* (Hermeneia. Philadelphia: Fortress, 1979) ad. loc., 170; cf Mussner, *Galaterbrief*, ad. loc., 248.

[88] For Moses' role as the mediator of the Torah in Judaism see Betz, *Galatians*, 170-1; and Bruce, *Galatians*, 178.

[89] For a survey of views see Ragnar Bring, *Christus und das Gesetz: Die Bedeutung des Gesetzes des Alten Testaments nach Paulus und sein Glauben an Christus* (Leiden: E. J. Brill, 1969), 78-86. Earlier commentators report over 300 different interpretations on this verse; see Betz, *Galatians*, 171 n 78.

[90] A. Vanhoye "Un médiateur des anges en Ga 3, 19-20," Bib 59 (1978), 403-11; Bruce, *Galatians*, ad. loc. 179.

[91] This point seems to exclude the claim of Theodor Zahn, *Der Brief des Paulus an die Galater* (Leipzig: Deichert, 1907), 176-7, that it refers to the Israelites, and the claim of a considerable number of scholars that it refers to the angels: e.g., Eckert, *Verkündigung*, 83; Hübner, *Law*, 26-7, 46; Ulrich Luz, *Das Geschichtsverständnis des Paulus* (BEvT; Munich: Chr. Kaiser Verlag, 1968), 190; Mussner, *Galaterbrief*, ad. loc. 249; Oepke, *Galater*, 84; Albrecht Oepke, "mesitēs, mesiteuō," TDNT IV 598-624, 618-19; Heinrich Schlier *Der Brief an Die Galater* (KEK; Göttingen: Vandenhoeck & Ruprecht, 1965), 161; and Schweitzer, *Mysticism*, 70;

[92] See Herman Ridderbos, *The Epistle of Paul to the Churches of Galatia: The English Text with Introduction Exposition and Notes*. (Grand Rapids: Eerdmans, 1953) ad. loc., 140; Burton, *Galatians* ad. loc. 191.

negotiates between the Israelites and the angels for a mediator usually negotiates between two pluralities.[93] A third view which can be excluded is that of Bring. He believes Moses is the mediator not only for the Jews but also for the Gentiles;[94] there is no hint of such a view in the context of either Galatians or Exodus. It is much more likely that Moses is the mediator who mediates between God and the people of Israel.

The statement *ho de theos heis estin* taken by itself most naturally means that there is one God as opposed to a plurality of gods (see Deut 6:4; 1 Cor 8:6). An alternative possibility might be a reference to *heis ho theos* in Rom 3:30 where it is the same God who is God of both Jews and Gentiles and justifies both in the same way. Bring indeed takes *heis ho theos* in the latter sense and argues that in the previous clause Moses is a mediator not only to the Jews but also to the Gentiles. But either view makes little sense in the context of Gal 3:20 for the mediator of more than one party (3:20) and the one God (3:20b) are mutually exclusive concepts.[95]

The context makes good sense if Moses mediated the law, if an agreement was made between God and the people of Israel on how the law was to be kept. But with reference to the promise, "God is one" in the sense that he acted unilaterally and unconditionally.[96] The natural question would then be, "is the (mediated) law opposed to the (unmediated) promise (= v 21)?" This view seems to pose the least difficulties even though *ho de theos heis estin* is a somewhat odd way of saying this.[97]

2.4 THE PURPOSE OF THE LAW

The original purpose of the law at creation was "life" (*eis zōēn*) (Rom 7:10) but it resulted in "death" (*eis thanaton*) (Rom 7:10). Since the fall of Adam, man has a fallen human nature, is "in the flesh" (*en sarki*), and death has reigned.[98]

The Mosaic law was given later. Its purpose for Paul as we shall see on the basis of Gal 2:21 and 3:21 was not to give righteousness and life.[99] Since the law which was given later cannot nullify the promise which was given earlier, Paul asks why the law was given (*Ti oun ho nomos;*) (Gal 3:19a). He answers, it was added (*prosetethē*) because of transgressions (*tōn parabaseōn charin*). By itself

[93] Oepke "mesitēs, mesiteuō," TDNT IV, 618-19.

[94] Bring, *Gesetz*, 86-93.

[95] See Betz, *Galatians* ad. loc. 171-72; For a critique of Bring's view see Mussner, *Galaterbrief*, ad. loc. 250 n 30.

[96] See Lightfoot, *Galatians*, ad. loc. 147; Guthrie, *Galatians*, ad. loc. 105-6.

[97] Cf Bruce, *Galatians*, ad. loc. 178.

[98] See below 69-108.

[99] See below 72-100.

charin may indicate either the goal (e.g., Titus 1:5; 11; Jude 16) or the reason (e.g., 1 Jn 3:12; Lk 7:47).[100]

If *charin* means "purpose" or "goal" the idea is that the law was added to provoke transgressions or to make them increase. This is the common view and is based on texts such as Gal 3:13; 3:23; Rom 3:20; 4:15; 5:20; 7:5; 7:7-25; 1 Cor 15:56.[101] If *charin* is causal the idea could be that the law is introduced to prevent transgressions.[102] The main support for this interpretation is the meaning of *paidagōgos* in Gal 3:24. Lull[103] and Longenecker[104] provide a convincing survey of the evidence from the Graeco-Roman and Jewish worlds, and conclude that the *paidagōgos* had a constraining role. Lull states that his job was to teach self-restraint to the unbridled passions of minors and to protect them from all sorts of moral and physical dangers.[105] Longenecker says that the role of the *paidagōgos* was to carry out the father's directives in supervising and disciplining his sons.[106]

This conclusion is somewhat compatible with Gal 4:1-7 where those under the law are compared to children who are heirs. They are no better than slaves but are under "guardians and trustees" (*epitropous ... kai oikonomous*). It could conceivably be compatible with 3:23 where those under the law are likened to being in jail. But it hardly agrees with the statements that the law brings a "curse" (Gal 3:13) or that "law came in to increase the trespass" (*hina pleonasę̄ to paraptōma*) (Rom 5:20).

Certainly for Paul the law does not result in the restraint of sin but in its increase (Rom 4:15; 5:20; 7:5; 7:7-25). I believe a distinction can be made here between the ostensible intention and the real intention. We normally make laws and accept them so that they will prevent crime rather than increase it, even though they may have the opposite effect. The same is true in salvation history. Israel accepts the law so that sin will be prevented. But the real intention of God would correspond to the actual result, the increase of sin.

The real purpose in the giving of the law is thus a negative one as opposed to the positive purpose of the original commandment which was given to Adam. It is given not to bring life (Gal 3:21) but to make sin exceedingly sinful, to show man that he cannot save himself by means of the law, and to show man his need

---

100 BAGD 877; Burton, *Galatians* ad. loc. 158.

101 see e.g., C. E. B. Cranfield, "St. Paul and the Law," SJT 17 (1964) 42-68, 46-47; Betz, *Galatians*, 163-167; Bruce, *Galatians*, 182-3; Schoeps, *Paul*, 174.

102 David J. Lull, "'The Law was our Pedagogue': A Study in Galatians 3:19-25," JBL 105 (1986) 481-498, 483 n 10 notes that this view is found among the earliest commentaries on Galatians.

103 Lull, *Pedagogue*, 486-96.

104 Richard N. Longenecker, "The Pedagogical Nature of the Law in Galatians 3:19-4:7," JETS 25 (1982) 53-61, 53-56.

105 Lull, *Pedagogue*, 489-94.

106 Longenecker, *Pedagogical Nature*, 55.

for a savior. Man "in the flesh" is unable to obey the law (Rom 7:14-25; 8:3) and, consequently, unable to be saved. He is under a curse (Gal 3:13) and under the wrath of God (Rom 4:15); he is enslaved (Rom 7:4-6;23, 25; Gal 3:23 etc) and condemned to death (Rom 5:12-21; Rom 7:5; 7-25; 2 Cor 3 etc). The law is the catalyst that makes sin increase (Rom 7:5, 7-11, 5:20; 1 Cor 15:56). The law is given until Christ comes to rescue man from his situation (Gal 3:19b; 3:22, 23; cf Rom 5:12-21; Gal 2:21).[107]

2.5 CONTRADICTIONS IN PAUL'S VIEW OF THE LAW?

Two recent interpreters who take the view that Paul makes truly self-contradictory statements about the law are Heikki Räisänen and E. P. Sanders.[108]

2.5.1 E. P. SANDERS

In 1977 E. P. Sanders stated that Paul is a coherent but unsystematic thinker.[109] But by 1983, in part under the influence of Räisänen, he has to some extent changed his mind. He now believes that Romans 1:18-2:29, 5:12-21, and 7:7-25 are internally inconsistent and each contradicts the other and the conclusions of Romans 3 do not follow from the arguments of Romans 2. Romans 1:18-2:29 is internally inconsistent for it argues for universal sinfulness yet at certain points some can obey the law perfectly well; righteousness by the law is a real possibility.[110]

The conclusions in Rom 3 that all are condemned do not naturally follow from Rom 2. The offer of salvation on the basis of fulfilling the law is held out repeatedly (2:7, 10, 13, 14f, 25-28) as a real possibility. The conclusion which follows naturally from ch 2 is repent and obey the law from the bottom of your heart, so that you will be a true Jew.[111]

In Romans 2 the same law judges everyone; but at 5:12-14 during the period from Adam to Moses, sin led to death even without the law. Paul then inconsistently says that law is required for sin to be counted, but that it was counted anyway. Transgression led to condemnation even between Adam and

---

[107] On the negative purpose of the law cf Christain Maurer, *Die Gesetzeslehre des Paulus nach ihrem Ursprung und in ihrer Entfaltung dargelegt* (Zollikon-Zurich: Evangelischer Verlag, 1941), 88; Bultmann, *Theology* I, 263, 267; Räisänen, *Law*, 150-155 etc.

[108] For a list of people who have seen self contradiction in Paul's view of the law and/or his theology generally see Räisänen, *Law*, 11-15.

[109] Sanders, *Palestinian Judaism*, 433, 518-24. Here he explicitly agrees with Bultmann, Conzelmann, Bornkamm, Käsemann, Whiteley, Kümmel, and Schweitzer (ibid 518 n 1).

[110] Sanders, *Jewish People*, 35-6, 125, 129.

[111] Sanders, *Jewish People*, 128-9, 134 n 43. cf Ferdinand Hahn, *Gesetzesverständnis*, 36-37.

Moses (5:14, 18). Rom 1:18-29 and 5:12-21 do not, like Rom 7, argue that no one can obey the law, but that sin is universal.[112]

In Roman 7:5, 7-12 the law is aligned with death, sin, and flesh, but at 7:13 Paul recoils because it potentially denies that God acted for the good. Now it is not God's fault, nor the law's, but sin's. He attributes responsibility for transgression first to sin's use of the law and then to the sin which pervades what is fleshly and prevents it from obeying God's law. In recoiling from attributing transgression and thus condemnation to the law (7:13), he retracts the normal positive connection between sin, God's will, and the law. Paul then overstates both human inability and Christian ability to fulfill the law. The fleshly human is incapable of doing anything which the law commands (7:15-23).[113]

Only Christians are able to fulfill the requirement of the law, and they do so perfectly, while those in the flesh cannot submit to God's law and cannot please God by submitting to his law (8:3-8). This extreme position contradicts his experience both as Pharisee and as apostle (Gal 2:15f; Phil 3; 1 Cor passim). There are further difficulties. The law is God's law (7:25), it was given for life (7:10), yet God failed for he had to launch a rescue operation apart from law (8:3), he had to redeem his own failure by sending his Son. God, moreover, gave the law to be obeyed, but humans are entirely unable to do so; therefore he had to launch a second effort. This dilemma is partly responsible for the passion and anguish of Romans 7.[114]

It is not his treatment of the law but his conclusion, that all are condemned that all can be saved by God through Christ, which is consistent. Each of Paul's statements can be understood as coming from the application of his central convictions to diverse problems. Paul's most extreme negative statements can be understood if we think of them arising organically at the end of a chain of thought which begins with the assertion that righteousness is by faith and not by law. Each step arises from the preceding one and is progressively more negative, from "the law does not righteous," to "the law produces transgression," to "the law itself is one of the powers to which Christians must die along with sin and the flesh." In Romans 7 Paul attempts to pull back.[115]

Against Sanders, Paul's conclusions in Romans 3 do not contradict Romans 2.[116] In Romans 2 his Jewish opponents would agree with him; God "will render

---

[112] Sanders, *Jewish People*, 35-6, 125.

[113] Sanders, *Jewish People*, 79-80.

[114] Sanders, *Jewish People*, 80.

[115] Sanders, *Jewish People*, 81, 84, 85, 86; cf *Palestinian Judaism* 474.

[116] See below 90-93. Until otherwise proven it must be presumed, especially from a thinker of the reputation of Paul, that there is unity in the text. Bernard J. F. Lonergan, *Method in Theology* (New York: Herder and Herder, 1972), 160, reminds us how we can easily demonstrate the absurdities of an ancient author if he is speaking of "P" and we are thinking of "Q," if he is not talking about the thing that we think he is talking about.

to everyman according to his works" (2:6); those who do good receive eternal life (2:7; 10) and those who do evil are judged (2:8, 9); "God shows no partiality" (2:11); it is not the hearers of the law but the doers of the law who will be justified (2:13). Paul is employing the well known rhetorical principle of reversal. He sets up his interlocutor.[117] His point is that no one does good, no one obeys the law, no one is justified, all are under the power of sin (Rom 3:9-20). Romans 2 shows the need for the gospel of God's grace in Romans 3:21-4:25.

Rom 1:18-3:20 claims that no one obeys the law whereas Rom 7:14-25 argues further that no one can obey the law. Romans 5:12-21 does not explicitly say, but correlates with the view, that no one can obey the law. It will be argued below that at 5:12-14 there was law between Adam and Moses, and that death does not occur apart from the law.[118]

In Rom 8:2-4 God did not have to redeem his own failure by sending his Son, Paul could quite consistently say that God planned it that way from the beginning.

There is no contradiction to say that the law originates with God and expresses His will, and to say that it is aligned with sin and death. The law could be aligned with sin in the sense that people are under its power; when they receive the law they are unable to obey it, and so are exposed to their sinful condition. The law could be aligned with death in that disobedience to the law brings the sentence of death.

Paul, it seems to me, no where states that Christians obey the law perfectly. If they obeyed the law perfectly there would be no need for Pauline exhortation, the point is that the Christian does sin, but by the power of the Spirit he is able not to sin. The non Christian does not have the Spirit, is in the flesh, under the power of sin, and has no choice but to sin.

2.5.2 HEIKKI RÄISÄNEN

Räisänen is much more radical than Sanders in his claim that Paul makes truly self-contradictory statements on the law. The following are some examples of what he believes are contradictions or tensions. *Edothē* in Gal 3:21 indicates that God is the law-giver; but at 3:19 the law originates not from God but from the angels.[119] At Gal 5:1 we are set free from the Mosaic law yet at 3:13 "the curse of the law" from which we have been redeemed refers to law in a more

---

[117] We observed above 12-13 that in the doctrinal section of Romans Paul argues from Jewish premises and presents his Jewish interlocutor with a step by step presentation of the gospel.

[118] See below 73-75.

[119] Räisänen, *Law*, 132.

universal sense. But this universal sense of law contradicts the late arrival of the law in 3:15-20.[120]

Paul on the one hand appeals to the law (1 Cor 14:34) and claims that it is established (Rom 3:31), and on the other hand states that it is abolished.[121] The importance of "keeping the commandments of God" (1 Cor 7:19) is at odds not only with the negative statements in Galatians but also with Rom 7:13 (where the *entolē* can only cause death), and with Rom 13:9 (where the many commandments are reduced to the one commandment of love.[122]

The law is a poison which kills (2 Cor 3) and on the other hand is merely an ineffective medicine which is just too weak to prevent man's death (Rom Ch 7; 8:3); it is again *pneumatikos* (7:14) and *eis zōēn* (7:10).[123]

In Rom 2:14-15 and 2:26-7 the Gentile does good, whereas in the rest of Rom 2; 1:18-32 and ch 7 no one obeys the law.[124] At Rom 5:13 sin is not charged up between Adam and Moses because there is no law, but at 5:14 death reigns in the period between Adam and Moses, and at 2:12-14 those *anomos* perish. Until the law sin had been punished because it was sin. Since the law the same punishments are imposed because of "transgression."[125] Rom 5:13-14 assumes that sin was a mighty force since Adam but at 7:7-12 sin was "dead" before the coming of the law.[126] In Rom 5 the power of sin in the world is due to Adam's fall whereas in Rom 7 it is due to the law.[127] In Rom 7 it is only the law with its commandments that brings about actual sinning but at 5:20 transgression and sin are concrete realities already there before the intervention of the law.[128]

Paul understands the relation between the law and sin in different ways. At Rom 3:20 the law *reveals* man as a sinner, but at 5:13, and possibly 4:15, the law is a formal standard which *qualifies* transgressions of it as different from other ways of sinning. At Rom 7:5, 7-11, and 1 Cor 15:56 the law *causes* sin, and at Rom 5:20 *increases* sin.[129]

---

[120] Räisänen, *Law*, 21.

[121] Räisänen, *Law*, 68-9, 72.

[122] Räisänen, *Law*, 68.

[123] Räisänen, *Law*, 152-3; cf 45.

[124] Räisänen, *Law*, 102-103, 110; Heikki Räisänen, "Paul's Theological Difficulties with the Law," *Studia Biblica III: Papers on Paul and Other New Testament Authors* (ed. E. A. Livingstone. JSNT Supplement Series 3; Sheffield: JSOT, 1980) 301-320, 309.

[125] Räisänen, *Law*, 145-6.

[126] Räisänen, *Law*, 147.

[127] Räisänen, *Law*, 177

[128] Räisänen, *Law*, 144.

[129] Räisänen, *Law*, 147.

To be free from the law both Christ and we need to die, yet the law was designed to hold sway for only a limited period.[130]

Räisänen takes issue with J. C. O'Neil and the Dutch conjectural school of the nineteenth century. Their mistake was believing that Paul had to be a logical thinker and therefore that the tensions and contradictions in Paul had to be interpolations.[131] Räisänen is also against those such as Drane and Hübner who explain the tensions and contradictions in terms of development, since letters like Galatians and Romans are internally inconsistent.[132]

He, rejects any attempt to explain these features in terms of the harmonizing of Cranfield, the redactional approach of Käsemann, or the dialectical approach of Conzelmann. Cranfield practices patent harmonizing. Käsemann believes that Paul's real view of the law is radical; where he seems to make conservative statements about the law he is reinterpreting traditional Jewish Christian statements. The dialectical approach is vague and has an apologetic ring.[133]

Räisänen further argues that the tension cannot be resolved by other expedients. It cannot be solved by claiming that the law was never intended as a way of salvation, nor by holding that the law is annulled as a way of salvation but remains in force as an expression of God's will (for in 2 Cor 3:6 the law is a "killing" letter), nor by positing various distinctions within the law with the intention of telling in what sense the law is still in force (for the reduction of the law to the love command annihilates the meaning of the Decalogue as such).[134]

The contradictions and tensions are constant and not merely peripheral; they center around his assertion that the law is abolished and yet is normative. Paul's problem is that he does not consider the intention of the law in its own right, but *a priori* deduces his position from his Christological insights. Paul's conflicting statements can also be explained by his historical and psychological conditioning. They are pointers to his cognitive dissonance with his own Pharisaic background, and are evidence of a mechanism of secondary rationalization.[135]

I would make the following points against Räisänen: Paul does not say that the law originated with the angels but that the law was mediated through angels

---

[130] Räisänen, *Law*, 59.

[131] Räisänen, *Law*, 6; Räisänen, *Difficulties*, 303.

[132] Räisänen, *Law*, 9, 82-3; Räisänen, *Difficulties*, 302.

[133] Räisänen, *Law*, 4; Räisänen, *Difficulties*, 302-303.

[134] Räisänen, *Law*, 82-3.

[135] Räisänen, *Law*, 11-12, 69, 83, 154, 200-01. To some extent Paul shares his difficulties in determining the purpose of the law with other Christian writers, but the tension between a positive and a negative intention is peculiar to him (Räisänen, *Law*, 200). Räisänen does not regard either Ephesians or Colossians as Pauline but believes that the same tension exists in these two letters as well (Räisänen, *Law*, 83-84, 199, 205. 227).

(Gal 3:19).[136] It is not evident that the general sense of law contradicts the later arrival of the Mosaic law. Paul understands the relation between law and sin in *different* but not *mutually exclusive* ways. Paul does not say that the law is too weak to prevent man's death but it is too weak to give man life (Rom 8:3); it is not self-contradictory to say that it kills (2 Cor 3:). The law would hold sway forever had not God sent his son to set us free from it. Although we are set free from the law Paul does not state that the law is abolished.[137]

"Keeping the commandments of God" (1 Cor 7:19) does not contradict Rom 13:9. There the law is not reduced to the love commandment but is summed up (*anakephalaioutai*) in it (Rom 13:9); it does not mean that the individual commandments need not be kept but that love is the underlying principle behind the commandments. The "commandment" (*entolē*) (Rom 7:7ff) causes death not because it is good or from God but because it brought death at the fall. The problem with the Gentile doing good (Rom 2:14-15; 2:26-27) is resolved if the situation is hypothetical.[138] I will argue later that Rom 5:13 does not contradict 5:12 and 5:14. Law did come with Adam and there was a law between Adam and Moses; between Adam and Moses sin was charged up and death reigned.[139]

Several of Räisänen's problems are solved if Rom 7:7-11 refers to the fall of Adam in the Genesis story. Sin was not dead before the coming of the Mosaic law but before the commandment which came to Adam. At Rom 7 transgression and sinful acts are not there before the law because Adam had not yet sinned, whereas they are there before the intervention of the Mosaic law. In Rom 7:10 the law which was given to Adam was for the purpose of life (*eis zōēn*) but it brought death owing to the sin of Adam. Because of the fallenness of man this law which was originally designed for life (*eis zōēn*) (7:10) brings death.

Räisänen does not seem to realize what it takes to have views that are truly contradictory. A contradiction might be verbal but not real. Statements are contradictory if they are both affirmed and denied simultaneously and in the same respect. Statements uprooted from their contexts might be only apparently contradictory.[140]

It should also give us pause when he says that not only Paul but also the rest of the NT has the similar contradiction that the law is both abolished and normative. Räisänen's problem with Paul and the law, as will become evident below, is that he does not understand the question that Paul was asking or answering. Paul's negative and positive statements do not stem from his

[136] See above 35-36.

[137] See below 129-141, 144, 146-153

[138] See below 91-93.

[139] See below 73-78.

[140] See Brice L. Martin, "Some Reflections on the Unity of the New Testament," SR 8 (1979) 143-152, 150.

cognitive dissonance with his Pharisaic background but from his fundamental conviction that the death of Christ was necessary.[141]

2.6 DEVELOPMENT IN PAUL'S VIEW OF THE LAW?

Our survey of the data reveals that from letter to letter Paul does not say the same thing about the law. Consequently, scholars have argued whether the differences are due to the varied circumstances of Paul's writings or to a fundamental development in his thinking.[142]

Hans Hübner notes that as long ago as 1850 Albrecht Ritschl noticed differences in the treatment of the law between Galatians and Romans. He held that the dominant interest in Galatians is ceremonial and in Romans ethical.[143] By 1869, however, Friedrich Sieffert was speaking in terms of development; in Galatians the dominant theme is *eleutheria,* while in Romans it is *dikaiosynē theou,* a concept with much more positive links to the OT.[144] In 1893 Carl Clemen, following Bruno Bauer, dated Romans before Galatians. The relatively more positive position of Romans develops into the relatively more negative position of Galatians.[145] In 1897 Sieffert reacted to Clemen; Romans comes later and is more comprehensive. The law now comes from God, it is seen in terms of inward moral content rather than of outward national expression.[146]

Three more recent scholars who argue for development in Paul are John W. Drane, Hans Hübner, and Ulrich Wilckens.[147] Three who do not see a basic development in Paul are Heikki Räisänen, E. P. Sanders, and W. D. Davies.

---

[141] See below 84-108, 121-123.

[142] See Hübner, *Law*, 1-7 for a history of the discussion. Otto Kuss, *Nomos*, 177-210 gives a historical survey of the exegetical discussion of the Law since the latter part of the 19th century.

[143] Hübner, *Law*, pp 1-2; see Albrecht Ritschl, *Die Entstehung der altkatholischen Kirche: Eine kirchen- und dogmengeschichte Monographie* (Bonn, 1850).

[144] Hübner, *Law*, 2-3; see Friedrich Sieffert, "Bemerkungen zum paulinischen Lehrbegriff, namentlich über das Verhaltnis des Galaterbriefs zum Römerbrief," JDTh, 14 (1869), 250-275.

[145] Hübner, *Law*, 3; see Carl Clemen, *Die Chronologie der paulinischen Briefe aufs neue untersucht* (Halle, 1893); Friedrich Sieffert, "Die Entwicklungslinie der paulinischen Gesetzeslehre nach der vier Hauptschriften des Apostels," *Theologische Studien* (Göttingen, 1897).

[146] Hübner, *Law*, 3-4; see Sieffert, *Entwicklungslinie*.

[147] Other scholars, who do not argue for a full fledged development in Paul, nevertheless observe significant differences between Galatians and Romans; e.g., E. Bammel, "Nomos Christou," in *Studia Evangelica* III. (ed. F. L. Cross. Berlin; Akademie Verlag, 1964) 120-128, 127-28; Betz, *Galatians*, esp 149, 169, 274-5; 433; and Georg Eichholz, *Die Theologie des Paulus im Umriss* (Neukirchen, Neukirchener Verlag, 1972), 247.

2.6.1 JOHN W. DRANE

According to Drane Romans is the synthesis of Galatians (thesis) and 1 Corinthians (antithesis). In Galatians (3:19) the Torah originates with the angels whereas in Romans (7:22, 25: 8:7) it originates with God. In Romans, in contrast to Galatians, the law is given to show man's disobedience to God and God's gracious action to man. Gal 3:19 - "The law ... was added because of transgressions" - is a cryptic completely negative statement about the law's function whereas at Rom 5:20-1, where the "law came in to increase the trespass," the ultimate saving purpose of God is to overcome sin. In Romans 5:20-1 law is the means by which conscious wrongdoing could be shown up as defiance of God's will; this is God's gracious action.

To produce Christian character Galatians relies on the Spirit whereas 1 Cor relies on the law (1 Cor 7:10ff; 19). Galatians is opposed by 1 Cor 7:19 where what matters is "keeping the commandments of God," that is keeping the Mosaic law. But at 2 Cor 3:6 "the written code kills ... the Spirit gives life." This text sounds much more like Galatians than 1 Corinthians but it has the closest similarities with Romans.

1 Corinthians lays down quite specific moral rules which substantially modify the principle of Christian freedom in Galatians. Galatians and 1 Corinthians are polar opposites. 2 Corinthians moves towards a synthesis. Romans is the final synthesis.[148]

2.6.2 HANS HÜBNER

Hübner believes that Paul changes his mind between the writing of Galatians and Romans. The following are some of the points he makes. Romans, in contrast to Gal 5:3, does not say that the law must be obeyed perfectly. Romans affirms that circumcision does have force in conjunction with faith (Rom 4) or with obedience to the law (Rom 2:25-29), but in Gal 5:4 the intention to have oneself circumcised means a fundamental falling from grace. Rom 9:4-5 evaluates Israel's history positively and in Rom 9-11 the history of Israel remains in force even though Israel is unbelieving, but in Galatians law and promise are contrasted with each other as mutually exclusive principles of salvation.[149]

He agrees with Wilckens that in Galatians Paul is engaging in polemics but in Romans he is entering into dialogue, he has taken his opponents seriously and reflected upon their views. He speculates that the antinomian passages of Galatians refer to embittered Jewish Christians, especially the most conservative

---

[148] Drane, *Paul*, 34, 62-68, 131, 135, 161; John W. Drane, "Tradition, Law and Ethics in Pauline Theology," NovT 16 (1974), 167-178.

[149] Hübner, *Law*, 52-59.

ones, who in turn made life difficult for moderates like James. Galatians is in accord with Paul's, but not Jerusalem's, understanding of the agreement at the Jerusalem council. James persuades Paul to reject part of Galatians and to bring his views more in line with Jerusalem. Failing to do this the collection might not be accepted. When Paul writes Romans he is on his way to Jerusalem; Jerusalem is the covert destination of Romans. He perhaps wrote them a letter similar to Romans to make his mediating theology known prior to his arrival.[150] Paul does not view this change in position as being untrue to himself. Justification by faith is what is really important to him, and his view of it has not changed. He has, however, had to rethink his theology with respect to the history of Israel; this results in a completely new view of the Torah.[151]

Galatians does not yet say that sin is known through the law (cf Rom 3:20, 7:7); it is, rather, the function of the law to call forth sinful deeds (*parabaseis*) and to provoke sin (*hamartia*). The law is denigrated as an angelic law. But in Romans the law does not cause sin; there, the law is the law of God, holy, just, good (7:12), and spiritual (7:14).[152] By claiming that in Romans the law does not cause sin, Hübner is forced to deal with Rom 3:20; 4:15; 7:7-12; 5:20 and 11:32, texts which at first sight seem to be fatal to his hypothesis that the relation between law and sin is consecutive not final. At 11:32 "consign to disobedience" means "afflict with disobedience."[153]

The motif of glorying or boasting is absent from the polemical part of Galatians, and is mentioned only in the last chapter (6: 4, 13, 14). Gal 6:4 reads "Let each test his own work, and then his reason to boast will be in himself alone and not in his neighbor." This text permits a Christian to glory or boast on the basis of his life's work at the judgment. But in Romans boasting is disqualified in principle. Paul is not there denouncing a self-glorying by *works* of the law but the opposite; he denounces those who boast that they posses the law but do not produce the works of the law. The boasting in God in ch 5 is a complete reversal of egocentric boasting.[154]

In Romans freedom does not have the central emphasis that it has in Galatians.[155] But Romans, in contrast to Galatians, knows of the *dikaiosynē theou*, of righteousness not only as gift but also as power. Romans distinguishes between freedom from the law and freedom from sin. Freedom from the law - the law which sin perverts - means service for the righteous God; it means obedience to the *dikaiosynē theou* which is at the same time obedience to the

[150] Hübner, *Law*, 61-65.

[151] Hübner, *Law*, 65.

[152] Hübner, *Law*, 78, 83.

[153] Hübner, *Law*, 78-82.

[154] Hübner, *Law*, 102-124; esp 102, 114, 124.

[155] Hübner, *Law*, 130, 135.

Mosaic Law freed from its perversions.[156] In Galatians Christ is the end of the Mosaic law, but in Romans Christ is the end of the carnal misuse of the law.[157] Gal 5:14 states that the whole law (*ho pas nomos*) is fulfilled in loving one's neighbor as oneself. At first sight this text agrees with Rom 13:8-10 and makes the Mosaic law valid for the believer; but on closer examination (*ho pas nomos*) refers to the Torah in a critical and ironical sense.[158]

2.6.3 ULRICH WILCKENS

Ulrich Wilckens[159] believes that Paul's thought about the law begins with the "revelation" which he experienced at his conversion (Gal 1:15). The atoning nature of the death and resurrection caused him to do away with the cult of the Torah. Like other Hellenistic leaders at Antioch he concluded that the Church should include Gentiles. The Jerusalem synod accepted this, but the Jewish-Christians would not accept full communion of Jews and Gentiles. Consequently, Paul separated from Antioch and founded his own Gentile mission independent of the law.

In Paul's early letters the law is mentioned only incidentally with reference to conversion. The law becomes a central topic in his letters due to Jewish Christian opposition. In the Corinthian letters Paul has the church opposed to the synagogue of the Torah. In Philippians Paul intensifies his polemic against the demand for circumcision and the Torah by appealing to his own conversion.

In the heated polemical situation of Galatians Paul develops his doctrine of justification by faith alone in opposition to the Jewish view of justification based on works of law. He intensifies the contrast between Israel and the church with the contrast between the legitimate and illegitimate children of Abraham. Paul's writing of Galatians led to a crisis throughout the church concerning his mission. To overcome this crisis Paul wrote Romans. Here he is more conciliatory; he calls the law God's law and brings together Jews and Gentiles under the judgment of God.[160]

---

156 Hübner, *Law*, 125, 135-36.

157 Hübner, *Law*, 149.

158 Hübner, *Law*, 37.

159 Wilckens, *Entwicklung*, 154-190. Ulrich Wilckens, "Statements on the development of Paul's View of the Law," in *Paul and Paulinism: Essays in Honour of C. K. Barrett* ([eds.] M. D. Hooker and S. G. Wilson. London: SPCK: 1982) 17-26.

160 See esp Wilckens, *Statements*, 25-26.

2.6.4 HEIKKI RÄISÄNEN

Räisänen[161] criticizes those such as Peter Stuhlmacher and Hans Conzelmann[162] who claim that Paul's radical view of the law emerged immediately after his conversion. Such a theory he claims does not sufficiently acknowledge that it was Paul alone who drew radical conclusions. It was a conflict over the law that separated Paul from Barnabas after long years of cooperation.[163] Furthermore the law affirming elements especially in Romans are more easily explained through a process of development under the pressure of events. Had it been clear to Paul from the start that "Christ is the end of the law" then one would have expected him to express this more consistently.

Räisänen disagrees with the theories of development of C. H. Buck - G. Taylor, J. W. Drane, and Hans Hübner[164] who hold that the radicalism of Galatians gave way to the more balanced reflection in Romans. These differences cannot be explained in purely chronological terms. The similarities between the letters are equally striking; they suggest that Romans was written fairly soon after Galatians so that not enough time is left for such a remarkable development.[165]

The differences can be accounted for by the different fronts Paul had to face. His thought did develop but it must have taken place during the long years that passed before the writing of the extant letters.[166] Räisänen[167] *speculates* on how this development *might* have taken place: The mixed congregation at Antioch was founded by the Hellenists expelled from Jerusalem. When Paul came to Antioch, he found there a congregation which did not require the circumcision of Gentile converts. God by giving the missionaries power had shown his acceptance of the uncircumcised Gentiles.

But around about AD 48 some Jewish Christians argued that Gentile Christians, to be part of Israel, had to be circumcised. Gal 2:21 shows that the pressure did not cease even though this view was defeated at the Jerusalem council. The men from James represent the same trend. Peter, Barnabas, and others recognized the force of the restorative argument but Paul did not. Over the

---

[161] Räisänen, *Legalism*, 81 n 84.

[162] Peter Stuhlmacher, "'Das Ende des Gesetzes' über Ursprung und Ansatz der paulinische Theologie," ZTK 67 (1970) 14-39; Hans Conzelmann, *History of Primitive Christianity* (Nashville: Abingdon, 1973), 81.

[163] Cf Alfred Loisy, *The Birth of the Christian Religion* (New Hyde Park, NY: University Books, 1962), 136ff.

[164] Räisänen, *Legalism*, 81 n 84; C. H. Buck, and G. Taylor, *Saint Paul: A Study of The Development of His Thought* (New York: Scribner's, 1969); Drane, *Paul*; and Hübner, *Law*.

[165] Udo Borse, *Der Standort des Galaterbriefes* (BBB 41; Cologne: Hanstein, 1972)

[166] Wilhelm Wrede, *Paulus* (Halle 1904), 72- 84.

[167] Räisänen, *Legalism*, 77-9

years Paul had become internally alienated from the ritual aspects of the law. While agreeing with its moral content, and often complying with its other precepts he felt free from it and dead to it (Gal 2:19). He was not under the law (1 Cor 9:20). He could say that all food was clean (Rom 14:14, 20). Among the Galatian Gentiles he had been just as one of them (Gal 4:12). Nothing shows his alienation better than the frivolous remark on circumcision in Gal 5:12 (cf Phil 3:2).

It was Israel and the Scripture which gave Christians, Gentiles as well as Jews, their identity. What was to the restorers an ethical issue, and to the moderate party around James a practical pastoral question, was a soteriological issue to Paul. If for some it was so important to comply with the law, the law for all practical purposes was made the cornerstone of salvation.[168]

Paul distorted the Jewish position to make the attack easier. He became more radical by gathering arguments for a total rejection of the law. That is why we have numerous problems and self contradictions.[169]

2.6.5 E. P. SANDERS

Sanders distances himself from the elaborate theories of development offered by Drane, and Hübner.[170] He believes that the statements about the law in Galatians and Romans are varying attempts to solve the same problem, rather than reflections on the fundamental development of Paul's thought (against Hübner). He notes several variations of the view that the law is seen from different perspectives. The law is seen, a) in connection with sin or in connection with promise (Hahn), b) as a way of salvation or as a norm of life (Schrage), c) as it encounters those in the flesh or those in the Spirit (Osten-Sacken), and d) as a means of the achievement of self-righteousness or as an expression of the will of God to be obeyed in faith (Schrage, Hübner, cf Käsemann). Sanders rejects c) and d). When Paul objects to the "works of the law" he never objects to the intention to achieve merit by them. The flesh/Spirit distinction does not explain Paul's *de facto* changes in the law. If the basic thing "wrong" with the law is that humans are unable to fulfill it, there is no reason to have those in the Spirit, who have been given the ability, fulfill only part of it. In the spirit one should certainly be able to obey the laws governing circumcision, food, and days.[171]

He believes that there is no single unity which adequately accounts for every single statement about the law. Against those who would argue for mere

[168] Räisänen, *Legalism*, 80.

[169] Räisänen, *Legalism*, 81.

[170] Sanders, *Jewish People*, 163 n 15; Beker, *Paul* 94-108.

[171] Sanders, *Jewish People*, 144-147.

inconsistency, he urges that Paul held a limited number of basic convictions which, when applied to different problems, led him to say different things about the law. Even in Romans 2 he was led to make use of material which is contrary to one of his central convictions (salvation by faith in Jesus Christ) by the desire to assert another conviction (the equality of Jew and Gentile). Nevertheless in Romans 2 Paul goes beyond mere inconsistency to true self-contradiction.[172]

Sanders notes that in both Galatians and Romans there are differences in tone and address. He speculates on the reason for the greater explicitness of Romans.[173] Possibly he became aware that some of his statements could be interpreted antinomistically (Rom 13:8; 6:1-2, 15); this would also account for some of the explicitly favorable statements about the law (3:31; 7:7, 12). Possibly Paul became aware of the need to cite specific laws because of the Corinthian difficulties. Hübner argued that Galatians excludes observance of the law while Romans does not. Sanders argues that in both letters important aspects of the law are optional.[174]

Both in 1977 and in 1983 he claimed that for Paul the solution precedes the problem. In 1977 he argued that Paul's reasoning would have been that, since in Christ God acted to save the world, therefore, when God gave the law it could not have been for the purpose of salvation. Its purpose rather was to consign everyone to sin so that everyone could be saved by God's grace in Christ.[175]

But by 1983, under the influence of Räisänen, his reasoning for the solution preceding the problem has shifted.[176] Paul's analysis springs from his conversion/call rather than from an examination of the human condition prior to faith. Philippians 3 shows that Paul had one righteousness and gave it up for a better one.[177]

The Damascus experience must have lead Paul to evaluate his former life, especially if from the beginning he was called to preach to Gentiles. But the formula "righteoused by faith and not by law," occurs first in Galatians; that particular formulation and the arguments which support it could well have originated in the Galatian conflict.[178]

Thus we come to the following train of experience and thought: 1. God revealed his son to Paul and called him to be the apostle to the Gentiles. 2. Christ

---

[172] Sanders, *Jewish People*, 147.

[173] Sanders, *Palestinian Judaism*, 433 n 9 observes that even though the discussion of the law is more developed and nuanced in Romans than in Galatians it does not follow that Paul changed what he thought. More likely the developments are in his presentation and argument.

[174] Sanders, *Jewish People*, 149, 163 n 20.

[175] Sanders, *Palestinian Judaism*, 475; cf 442-447; 475-76.

[176] Sanders, *Jewish People*, 149-54; cf 32-33; 125.

[177] Sanders, *Jewish People*, 151; 164 n 31.

[178] Sanders, *Jewish People*, 164-65 n 31; Cf Luz, *Geschichtsverständnis* 218-20; and Seyoom Kim, *The Origin of Paul's Gospel* (Grand Rapids: Eerdmans, 1982), esp 269-331.

is not only the Jewish messiah, he is Savior and Lord of the universe. 3. If salvation is by Christ and is intended for Gentile as well as Jew, it is not by the Jewish law *in any case*, no matter how well it is done, and it is without regard to one's interior attitude. 4. Salvation is by faith in Christ, and the law does not rest on faith.[179]

With this beginning point it is fairly simple to understand how Paul came to hold the various positions we see in his letters. If righteousness were by the law, Christ's death would not have been necessary. But God sent Christ to save; therefore righteousness is not by the law (Gal 2:21; 3:21). After this absolute rejection of righteousness by the law, and after making an absolute dichotomy between the law and Christ, however, Paul still had to "justify the ways of God to men." He had to explain why God gave the law, and these explanations connect it with sin and lead to his most negative statements about it. But then he also had to offer guidance for behavior.[180]

2.6.6 W. D. DAVIES

W. D. Davies[181] argues that the differing viewpoints in Paul's letters reflect the situation in which Paul is writing rather than any major development in his thinking. In Galatians with his polemic against Judaizers Paul denigrates the law. Obeying the law means being under a curse (3:10) and submitting to the elemental and cosmic spirits (4:3, 9). The coming of Christ frees men from the curse and tutelage of the Law (2:21; 3:13,19; 5:11).

In Corinthians by contrast Paul responds to Gentile enthusiasts; consequently, he calls for restraint and a behavior governed by his own example (1 Cor 4:16; 11:1) or that of Christ himself (2 Cor 8:9). There is a Christian "way" or "law" informed by universal Christian practice (1 Cor 4:17; 11:16; 14:34; 7:19). In 2 Corinthians Christian life is a life of covenant, and covenant includes demand or law (2 Cor 3).

Romans is more conciliatory than Galatians because Paul desired the support of the Christians in Rome. He is careful to recognize that the Law is holy, righteous and good (7:12, 16), spiritual (7:14), rooted in God (7:22. 25; 8:2, 7) designated for life (7:10), authoritative (7:19), and counts as one of the privileges of Israel (9:4). Yet He does consider that Christ is the end of the Law as a means of salvation (10:4). The law was intended to give life (Lev 18:5). but was unable to do so (Rom 3:23). It had the opposite result (4:13; 7:13). Romans

---

[179] Sanders, *Jewish People*, 152.

[180] Sanders, *Jewish People*, 152.

[181] W. D. Davies, "Paul and The Law: Reflections on Pitfalls in Interpretation," *Paul and Paulinism, Essays in Honour of C. K. Barrett* ([eds.] M. D. Hooker and S. G. Wilson. London: SPCK, 1982) 4-16, 8-10.

7 which is probably a defense of the law reveals the problem. The problem is sin, which makes the intrinsically good law serve its own intrinsically evil ends. The law reveals sin (3:20), incites it (7:5) indeed brings sin to life, for apart from the law sin is dead (7:8-9). What was good in itself becomes a power for evil. The law is diverted from its original purpose, not because of connection with the "elemental spirits," but because of the weakness of "the flesh." The power of sin and the weakness of the flesh collude to frustrate the purpose of the good and holy law.[182]

2.6.7 EVALUATION

It is not likely that Paul's basic view of the law develops gradually in a long gestation period before the writing of his extant letters (contra Räisänen) nor is it likely that he fundamentally changed his mind during the writing of his extant letters. His view originates with his conversion (Sanders, 1983; Wilckens[183]) but it also develops logically out of his fundamental starting point that the death and resurrection of Christ is necessary as an atonement for sin,[184] and that salvation does not, and cannot come by means of the law (cf Sanders, 1977). This starting point (contra Sanders) allows us to make the distinction between the law as a way of salvation and as a norm of life, between the law as it encounters those in the flesh and those in the Spirit, between the law as the means of achieving self-righteousness and as an expression of the will of God to be obeyed in faith.

Paul does not retract in his later letters what he has said in his earlier ones (contra Drane[185] and Hübner[186]). The differences between Galatians, Corinthians,

---

[182] See Jervell, *Letter*, 61-74. Wilckens, *Rechtfertigung*, 110-70. contrast Donfried, *False Presuppositions*, 120-148.

[183] See also Ulrich Wilckens, "Die Bekehrung des Paulus als religionsgeschichtliches Problem," ZTK 56 (1959), 273-293, for the position that Paul's view of the law originates with his conversion. For a consideration and rejection of the view that Paul's view of the law stems from a fundamental misunderstanding of Judaism see above 22-23. For a survey of views on the origin of Paul's view of the law see Luz, *Geschichtsverständnis*, 217-220.

[184] The atoning work of Christ is seen throughout Paul's letters. Its importance is seen for example in the tradition he has received (Rom 4:25; 1 Cor 11:23-26; 15:3) and in the *hyper* formula (Rom 5:6-8; 8:32; 14:15; 1 Cor 1:13; 11:24; 15:3; 2 Cor 5:14-15, 21; Gal 1:4; 2:20; 3:13; 1 Thess 5:10; cf Eph 5:2, 25; 1 Tim 2:6; Titus 2:14). See also such passages as Rom 3:24-26; Rom 8:3, and Gal 2:21.

[185] In addition I would also make the following specific points against Drane. Even in Galatians the law is God's law, and according to Gal 5:14 the law is valid for the believer; Not To be "under law" (Gal 5:18) does not mean that the law should not be obeyed. In Galatians too God's purpose was to save, and God's giving of the law is ultimately within his saving purpose. 1 Cor 15:56 shows that in 1 Corinthians not all statements on the law are positive. Galatians is also concerned with morality and is against unbridled freedom (cf 5:13-25).

[186] In addition I would also make the following specific points against Hübner. At Gal 6:4 self-boasting is permitted because the boasting is not with reference to being saved by works of law. In Gal 5:3 Paul is not against circumcision *per se*; he is against it because for them it means an

and Romans can be explained better by the situation in which Paul is writing (so Davies). 1 Corinthians emphasizes the law and moral rules because Paul is there facing an antinomian front whereas Galatians downplays the law because the Galatians are misusing the law; they are attempting to be saved by means of it. Romans is more balanced than Galatians or 1 Corinthians because Paul is not facing a burning ethical question in the Church at Rome. He also may be clearing up any rumors that he is an antinomian. The passage of time and the varied problems Paul meanwhile faced among his churches undoubtedly led him to reflect further on his theology. It should not surprise us, then, that by the time he wrote Romans new themes appear and old ones are more fully developed.

During the Galatian crisis Paul may have in some way clarified his doctrine of justification by faith alone apart from the works of the law in his own thinking, but the basic elements of his position would have been there already (contra Wilckens). The reason Galatians is so polemical is that the issue is so crucial.

The law does become a central topic due to Jewish Christian opposition (so Wilckens), but we do not know that this crisis was caused by the writing of Galatians (contra Wilckens). The crisis may have been caused by the general way Paul conducted himself in his ministry. Due to the crisis evoked by a misunderstanding of his ministry, Paul may be clarifying his position in Romans.

---

attempt to be justified by the law (5:4). Being justified this way would mean that they would have to obey the law perfectly (5:3) and that the death of Christ was unnecessary (Gal 2:21; 3:21). The omission in Romans that the law must be obeyed perfectly may not mean a conscious departure from Galatians; in Romans to be saved apart from Christ the law must be obeyed, and those who break the law will be punished. In Galatians the law and the promise are not mutually exclusive, the point is that the law which comes later does not nullify the promise (Gal 3:21). The law is God's law mediated through the angels. Galatians has more stress on freedom since freedom is threatened in the churches of Galatia. It is more clear in Romans than in Galatians that the law provokes sin and that God is directly involved in the process of making men disobedient (Rom 5:20; 11:32-36). In Romans sin does not pervert the law, it uses the law to get people to sin. Gal 5:14 and Rom 13:8-10 say the same thing; both refer to the Torah, both say that the Torah is valid for the believer.

There is no evidence that James changed Paul's mind. It is possible that Jerusalem is the covert destination of Romans in the sense that during the writing of Romans his forthcoming visit to Jerusalem may have sharpened his thinking on the questions that he would face there. But Romans is also explained well as a letter to the church at Rome. In the intervening years Paul's understanding has deepened but his fundamental stance has not changed. Romans is written to the church at Rome, a church he has not founded, located in a city he has not yet visited. Since the gospel is not being undermined there, the letter is not polemical. Due to the work of Judaizers Paul was suspect in many places probably also at Rome. Here he gives them a full explanation of his gospel and assures them that he is not an antinomian (cf Rom 3:5-8). When he visits them he wants them to accept him and to support his Spanish mission (cf 15:22-30). The Gentile majority at Rome seem to be looking down on the Jewish minority. Paul reminds them that God first brought the gospel to the Jews (1:16; 2:9, 10; 9:4-5); in spite of the present situation God cares deeply about them, and is not yet finished with them (cf chs 9-11; esp 11:17-24). See above 8-14.

The various emphases on the law in Paul's letters can thus be explained mainly by the situation in which he is writing. Romans, however, presents new themes on the law which are absent from Galatians (a major treatment of the law) but anticipated in Corinthians (a minor treatment of the law). This suggests that Paul's thinking on the law developed in the meantime. The developments are an advancement upon (but not an opposition to) earlier positions. The relationship of the law, sin, and death is first mentioned in 1 Cor 15:56, and developed in Rom 7-8. In 2 Cor 3 the mosaic economy is called the dispensation of condemnation (v 9; cf Rom 5:16, 18; 8:1) and death (v 7). We shall consider later how Rom 5:12-21 relates the law to the Adam-Christ typology. This typology is absent from Galatians but present in 1 Cor 15:21-49.[187] Rom 5:12-21 picks up and develops the statement of 1 Cor 15:21 that all die in Adam and all are made alive in Christ. A major theme of Romans is the righteousness of God. This phrase first appears in 2 Cor 5:21; the concept is continued in Philippians (3:9). Romans also gives a more comprehensive and clear statement of themes which are already in Galatians: e.g., the law provokes sin, and God is directly involved in the process of making mankind disobedient (Gal 3:19; Rom 5:20; 11:32-36). The law is summed up in the commandment to love one's neighbor as oneself (Gal 5:14; Rom 13:8-10 = Lev 19:18). In Romans it is more clearly stated that salvation is all of God, that all the glory belongs to God, and that boasting is therefore excluded.

2.7 VIEWS ON THE ONGOING VALIDITY OF THE LAW

It is natural in the history of exegesis that some interpreters have emphasized the positive aspects of the law while other interpreters have emphasized its negative aspects. Some believe that for Paul the law holds as a way of life for the believer, others do not.

2.7.1 THE LAW IS INVALID FOR THE BELIEVER

The cosmological view of Albert Schweitzer, the messianic age view of H. J. Schoeps, and the Spirit and Love view of Ernst Käsemann and F. F. Bruce are examples of those who hold that for Paul the Law is invalid for the believer.[188]

---

[187] See below 72-75, 121-123.

[188] Räisänen, *Law*, 62 lists others from the 19th and 20th centuries who hold that law is abolished. These include Pleiderer, Wernle, Bousset, Grafe, Glock, Kühl, Prat, Knox, Marshall, Schubert, Gronmeyer, and Sandmel.

2.7.1.1 ALBERT SCHWEITZER

Schweitzer believes that the law which belongs to the natural world and the rule of angels has no place in the messianic Kingdom. The world which has already received its death blow is still maintaining itself for the present. Those who are in Christ are filled with death and resurrection forces; for them the supernatural world is already a reality and, consequently, angel dominion and the law have no more validity.[189]

2.7.1.2 H. J. SCHOEPS

H. J. Schoeps stresses the rabbinic background of Paul's thought.[190] The law ceases when the messianic age begins. Sanh. 97a; Ab. Zara. 9a; and Jer. Meg. 70d[191] indicate that the world is to last six thousand years. The first two thousand years is the time of the Tohuwabohu, followed by the two thousand years each of the Mosaic law, and the messianic era. For Paul, the two thousand year era of the Messiah has begun. "Paul deduces from his faith the Messiah has come in the person of Jesus the conclusion 'Christ is the end of the law (Rom 10:4).'"[192]

According to Schoeps, Sabb. 30a; 151b; Nidda 61b; Pes. Rabb. 51b; Jer. Kilaim IX. 3 stress that as soon as man is dead he is freed from obligation to the commands of the law. This is the background for Rom 7:1-6.[193]

Schoeps goes on to note that in Galatians Paul takes the death of Jesus as his starting point, surveys retrospectively the meaning of the law, and concludes that it was a *paidagōgos eis Christon*. Christ is the end of the law because through the atoning efficacy of his blood he has satisfied the requirement of the law; as one who fulfills the Torah, Christ is the *telos nomou*, and in taking its place and in assuming its functions he takes its place of honor and salvation. Hence the law

---

189 Schweitzer, *Mysticism*, 177ff; cf Conzelmann, *Outline*, 223 for a summary.

190 Schoeps, *Paul*, 168-218.

191 These passages are discussed by W. D. Davies, *Torah in The Messianic Age and/or the Age to Come* (JBL Monograph Series. Vol VII; Philadelphia: SBL, 1952), 78ff. That the Torah could at least be altered in the time to come is given further support by Davies: Lev. R. 9:7 (a late passage; ibid., 55-6) says that all sacrifices except thanksgiving would be annulled in the time to come; Yalqut on Prov 9:2 (80-120 A.D.; ibid., 56) states that at that time all festivals but Purim will cease; Midrash Tehallim on Ps. 146:7 (ibid., 57-8) suggests changes in the laws concerning clean and unclean. Davies (ibid., 65) interprets b. Shab. 151b (A.D. 165-200) as an argument that the Torah no longer holds in the messianic age so that questions about reward for observing it, and guilt and punishment for refusing to do so, do not arise.

Longenecker, *Paul*, 132 further notes that the Qumran Literature (1QS 2:19; 8:9; 9:10-11; CD 14:18-19) speaks of the enacting of laws which were to be in force only until the coming of the Messiah.

192 Schoeps, *Paul*, 173, notes that the same assumption was made by the pseudo-messianic groups in later Jewish history. Sabbatai and the Frankists, believing the last age to have dawned with the coming of the Messiah, declared the Mosaic law annulled. It is not that the messianists turn against the law, rather they reject its further validity.

193 Schoeps, *Paul*, 171.

culminates in Christ. The final consequence of the curse of the law for Paul is that only in the interim period up to its termination by the death of Christ did it have regulative significance.[194]

2.7.1.3 ERNST KÄSEMANN

For Käsemann Christ terminates the Torah. He agrees with the usual view that *telos* means "end" in Romans 10:4. Although linguistically possible, Paul does not leave room for the meaning "goal" or both "end" and "goal."[195] The moral and ceremonial law form an indissoluble unity;[196] only when the law is reduced to the moral law can one postulate its ongoing validity in the Church.[197]

The intensification of the Torah which shaped first century Judaism is impossible for Paul even in the form of the internalizing of the law. The presence of the risen Lord in the power of the Spirit takes the place of the Torah of Moses.[198] Romans 8:2-4 characterizes the new life of the Christian as grounded in the act of salvation and standing in the sphere of the Spirit, in which the will of God is actually fulfilled as it could not be under the rule of the law.[199] This does not mean a) that the law as such is restored by the Spirit,[200] or b) that the law is replaced by a Christian variation of natural law.[201]

2.7.1.4 F. F. BRUCE

Bruce, like Käsemann, believes that the Spirit takes the place of the law in the life of the Christian. In the clause "Christ is the end of the law" (Rom 10:4) the word "end" (*telos*) probably means both "goal" and "terminus." Christ is the goal of the law in the sense that the law was a temporary provision introduced by God until Christ came (Gal 3:19, 24), but Christ was also for that reason the terminus of the law. Now that Christ has come there is no more place for law in man's approach to God.[202]

Bruce mentions several views that may be true theologically but which have no place in Pauline exegesis: a) the view of Calvin that the man in Christ is not under the law as a means of salvation yet he remains under it as a rule of life;[203] b) the view of Calvin that Christ is the end of the ceremonial law (including not only the sacrificial cultus but circumcision and the observance of the sacred

---

194 Schoeps, *Paul*, 180-83.

195 Käsemann, *Romans*, 215.

196 See Enslin, *Ethics*, 85.

197 Käsemann, *Romans*, 215.

198 Käsemann, *Romans*, 191, 210.

199 Käsemann, *Romans*, 215, 218.

200 Cranfield, *Law*, 66-67; Fuchs, *Freiheit*, 85; Schmidt, *Römer*, ad. loc.; Lohse, *ho nomos*, 284-87.

201 cf Käsemann, *Romans*, 215.

202 F. F. Bruce, *Paul: Apostle of the Heart Set Free* (Grand Rapids: Eerdmans, 1977), 191.

203 Calvin, *Institutes*, ii. 7. 12-15; see Bruce, *Paul*, 192.

calendar);[204] c) the view of Lutheran orthodoxy that the law is a summons to repentance (the law's second use) and is guidance for the church (the law's third use);[205] d) the view of Karl Barth that Christ is the end of religion;[206] and e) the view of Ernst Fuchs that Christ is the end of history.[207]

The antithesis between law and Spirit is as absolute as the antithesis between works and faith; it is identical with the contrast between legal bondage and spiritual freedom. The obligations of the moral conduct are fostered not by the dictates of the law but by the operation of the free Spirit. The principle of law was so completely opposed to spiritual freedom that it could never be enlisted in the defense of that freedom: nothing was more certainly calculated to kill true freedom. He opposes Robert Jewett's view that the Galatian Christians had been disposed to accept "external" features of the law such as circumcision and the sacred calendar, without appreciating its more ethical emphases; hence Paul's ethical admonition to them. Bruce replies that Paul's understanding of the gospel excluded the principle of law in any form: to be "under law" was compatible with being under the dominion of sin, with living *kata sarka*. The ethical emphases of the law could be effectively satisfied not through submission to the law but through "walking by the Spirit" (5:16). The law belongs to existence in the flesh, and stimulates the very sins it forbids (3:19). The nine virtues which make up the fruit of the Spirit (Gal 5:22) are in a sphere with which law has nothing to do.[208]

For Bruce the law of love in Gal 5:14 has the same construction as the statutes of the decalogue of the Torah in general, but it is a different kind of law. No external force or sanction can compel the loving of a neighbor as oneself; such love must be generated from within - by the Spirit.[209]

2.7.1.5 WALTER GUTBROD

Gutbrod seems to take a mediating position between a fundamental abrogation of the law and a fundamental validity of the law. The Law as a rule of life is insignificant, and the appeal to the OT does not have the weight which the appeal to the OT had in Judaism. Paul uses the Law as *didachē* but only if it confirms what is already known on other grounds (e.g., 1 Cor 9:8f; 14:21f, 34); it is authoritative only if it follows from obedience to Christ in faith (Rom

---

[204] Calvin, *Institutes*, ii. 7. 17; Bruce, *Paul*, 192.

[205] Bruce, *Paul*, 191-2.

[206] Barth, *Romans*, 37, 374.

[207] Ernst Fuchs, "Christus das Ende der Geschichte," EvT 8 (1948/9), 447ff, as cited in Bruce *Paul*, 193.

[208] Bruce, *Galatians*, 151-2, 218, 239, 240, 255. See Robert Jewett, "The Agitators and the Galatian Congregation," NTS 17 (1970-71) 198-212, 209-212.

[209] Bruce, *Galatians*, 243; cf Bruce, *Paul*, 201.

14:1ff; 12:3). No longer whatsoever is not of the law, but whatsoever is not of faith, is sin (Rom 14:23).[210]

Christ is the end of the law from the standpoint of salvation history.[211] Paul's negation of the law derives from his affirmation of what has taken place in Jesus Christ (Phil 3:9; Rom 8:1). Outside of the death of Christ and death with Christ man is still *en kosmǭ* and as a result is delivered up to the law (Col 2:20). Christ succeeds the law (Rom 10:4) in salvation history. The transition has taken place only for the one with faith; it takes place by participation in the death of Christ (Rom 7:11-13; Gal 2:19; Col 2:20).

2.7.2 THE LAW IS VALID FOR THE BELIEVER

Just as there is a diverse conceptuality among those who believe that the law is invalid for the believer, so there is a diverse conceptuality among those who believe that the law is valid for the believer.

For many the question of whether the law is valid for the believer has hinged on Christ as the *telos* of the law in Rom 10:4, Christ as the "termination" of the law, or Christ as the "goal" of the law. Some, however, see Christ as the termination of the law only in a special sense and still view the law as valid for the believer.

Scholars such as C. E. B. Cranfield, George E. Howard, and C. Thomas Rhyne believe that Christ is the goal of the law, but for others like Hans Conzelmann and E. P. Sanders (1977) the law is ended as a means of salvation but not as a way of life. For R. N. Longenecker and G. E. Ladd Christ terminates the law only in its connection with righteousness, but for Hans Hübner Christ is the end of a misused law.

2.7.2.1 C. E. B. CRANFIELD

Cranfield believes that *telos gar nomou Christos* (Rom 10:4) means that the ultimate goal and innermost meaning of the law is not the condemnation of sinners, but Jesus Christ.[212] Christ is the goal of the law because (a) he is the only one who fully obeys the law (Phil 2:8; Rom 5:19), (b) he is the fulfillment, meaning, and substance of the ceremonies contained in the law,[213] (c) he is the

---

[210] Gutbrod, "nomos," TDNT IV 1077. Wolfgang Schrage, *Ethik des Neuen Testament* (Göttingen: Vandenhoeck & Ruprecht, 1982), 195-98, would affirm the validity of the Torah in a stronger way than Gutbrod yet not believe in its complete authority. Before the Torah can be authoritative for the Christian, Christ must first expound what it means. The Torah is valid only insofar as it agrees with the love command.

[211] Gutbrod, "nomos," TDNT IV, 1075-78.

[212] Cranfield, *Law*, 48-53.

[213] In 1 Cor 5:7 (*kai gar to pascha hēmōn etythē Christos*) Christ is represented as the Church's Passover lamb - i.e., as the true and final paschal Lamb to whom the other paschal lambs, sacrificed

only remedy for man's desperate condition which the law brings to light (Gal 3:23f.), (d) the law sets the necessary forensic stage on which Christ's saving work is wrought, and (e) the law bears witness to Christ (cf Rom 3:21) by virtue of the promises it contains.[214]

He attempts to answer the arguments of those who believe that for Paul the law is ended.[215] *Chōris nomou* (Rom 3:21) means "apart from works of law." *Ou ... hypo nomon* (Rom 6:14), "died to the law" (Rom 7:4), and "discharged from the law" (7:6) mean "not under the curse of the law." "The law of sin and death" (*ho nomos tēs hamartias kai tou thanatou*, Rom 8:2 cf 7:23, 25) is not the law itself in its true character, but either the law as perverted by man's sin and turned into a law of sin and death, or the inner necessity of our fallen nature.

2 Cor 3:1-12 contrasts not two covenants themselves but two ministries; the contrast is between expectation and fulfillment.[216] Verse 6, *ou grammatos alla pneumatos*, is a contrast, not between the OT and a spiritual religion, but between the legalistic religion of the Jews of Paul's day and the new religion of the Spirit. In vv 7-11 the point is that if the service which is rendered by Moses in the giving of the law (a service which effects condemnation and death, vv 7, 9) is accompanied with glory, much more must the service rendered by the Spirit (a service which effects righteousness, v 9) be accompanied by glory. In comparison with the second the first splendor is no splendor (3:10). Because of the structure of vv 7-11, *to katargoumenon* refers, not to the glory of Moses' face (as it does in v 13),[217] but to the ministry of Moses at the giving of the law.

---

according to the law, were pointing forward. In Rom 3:25 Christ is represented as a *hilastērion*; the background is sacrifice, probably with the ritual day of atonement (Lev 16) in mind. Also in 1 Cor 11:25 (*touto to potērion hē kainē diathēkē estin en tō emō haimati*) stamps Christ's approaching death with a sacrificial significance (ibid., 51-52.).

[214] In Gal 3:8 it is the Scripture (Gen 12:3) which preached the gospel beforehand (*proeuēngelisato*) to Abraham saying *"Eneulogēthēsontai en soi panta ta ethnē."* In Rom 1:2-3 Paul refers to the "gospel of God which he promised beforehand (*proepēngeilato*) through his prophets in the Holy Scriptures, the gospel concerning his Son ..." (ibid., 50). Cranfield also believes that in Rom 10:6-10 Paul is contrasting a righteous status which men have through faith in Christ with the righteous status which Christ himself has by his obedience. Rom 10:5 (*ho poiēsas anthrōpos zēsetai en autē*, = Lev 18:5) explains the *gar* of Rom 10:4. In accordance with Lev 18:5 Christ has fulfilled the law by perfectly obeying its requirement and has thereby earned eternal life for himself and those who believe on him (ibid., 49-50). Finally it is in Christ that all the promises of God find their yes (2 Cor 1:20).

[215] He had previously concluded (ibid., 49) that *telos* cannot mean "termination" on the basis of such passages as Rom 3:31; 7:12, 14; 8:4; 13:8-10, and his frequent appeals to the Pentateuch.

[216] Ibid., 58.

[217] Cranfield (ibid., 59) argues (cf C. K. Barrett, *From First Adam to Last: A Study in Pauline Theology* (New York: Scribner's, 1962), 52 n 1) that *to katargoumenon* (v 13) is not the whole religious system based on the law; it, rather, is to be read in light of v 7; vv 14-16 suggest, not that the law is done away with, but that only when men turn to Christ can they see the true glory of the law; In Paul's time, when the law is read in the synagogue, its true meaning is veiled to the Jews (ibid., 59).

In Gal 3:15-25 Cranfield admits that Paul, due to the polemical nature of the book and the Galatians false exaltation of the law, is forced in some measure to depreciate the law; he takes issue, however, with G. S. Duncan's interpretation of the details of Gal 3:19.[218] "Was added" means, not that the law was a mere addition in the mainstream of God's purpose, but merely that it was given after the promise. "Because of transgressions" (that is, because it exposes man's sin) is only one use of the law. "Till the offspring should come to whom the promise had been made" refers not to the strictly temporal reign of the law, but to the bare law in a narrow sense, the law as seen apart from Christ. "Ordained of Angels" does not necessarily mean that the law is depreciated because in Acts 7:53 Stephen emphasizes the majesty of the law by referring to the angels' part in its giving.[219 & 220]

2.7.2.2 GEORGE. E. HOWARD

Another somewhat different interpretation, but still interpreting *telos* as goal in Rom 10:4, is that of George E. Howard. He challenges what he believes are three unwarranted assumptions of the view that *telos* here means end. For him *gar ... de* (Rom 10:5-6) does not mean "for ... but," but as in Rom 7:8-9; 10:10; 11:15-16; and Wisdom 6:17ff, it means "for ... and." He maintains that the Jews of Paul's day believed in salvation not by merit, but by grace, and interpreted Lev 18:5 (quoted in Rom 10:5), not in terms of perfection, but in terms of making Yahweh's law the foremost aspect of one's life. Thus Paul is not contrasting two methods of obtaining righteousness, but comparing them. Rom 10:1-13 is dominated by the theme of the inclusion of the Gentiles. In 10:3 the Jews are wrong in seeking to establish their own righteousness to the exclusion of the Gentiles; Christ, rather, is the goal of the law for *all* who believe (10:4). In 10:5, 6 Paul wants to prove that the law's ultimate goal corresponds to the work of Christ in unifying all nations; in 10:5 it is not the *Jew* but the *anthrōpos* (i.e., any man, Jew or Gentile) who practices righteousness; vv 6-10 also explain

---

[218] Cranfield, *Law*, 62; G. S. Duncan, *The Epistle of Paul to the Galatians* (London: Hodder and Stoughton, 1934), 111ff.

[219] Cranfield, *Law* 61-62. At any rate Cranfield, in disagreement with Duncan (*Galatians*. 334-336), believes that the angels of Gal 3:19 are not to be identified with the *stoicheia* of Gal 4:3, 9. If this were the case it would mean that the giving of the law would be the work of the *stoicheia* which are "weak and beggarly" (4:9) and "of the world" (4:3), ibid., 63. In light of Gerhard Delling's article ("stoicheion," TDNT VII, 670-87) this identification is by no means certain. Also it would contradict Rom 9:4-5 where the giving of the law (*hē nomothesia*) is one of the privileges of Israel.

[220] In Col 2:14 the *cheirographon* which stood against us is not the law itself, but quite possibly the law's condemnation of us (Cranfield, *Law*, 64); cf C. F. D. Moule, *The Epistles of Paul The Apostle to the Colossians and to Philemon* (CGTC; Cambridge: Cambridge University Press, 1957) ad. loc., 97-98.

the system of faith in terms of the inclusion of the Gentiles. When it comes to the unification of all nations, both the systems of law and faith coincide.[221]

2.7.2.3 C. THOMAS RHYNE

For Rhyne the starting point for Paul's view of the law is his remark that faith establishes the law (Rom 3:31).[222] Rom 3:31c and the whole of Romans 4 clarifies the possible misconception that the law is abolished through faith.[223] Rom 4:1-25, an exposition of Gen 15:6, shows that the law in its role as witness to righteousness by faith is established in the apostolic preaching of justification by faith.[224]

Romans 10:4 claims that in Christ the law in its promise of righteousness reaches its goal so that God's righteousness may be available to everyone who believes. The text and contexts of Rom 3:31 and 10:4 cohere together; in both the law is viewed as a witness to righteousness by faith.[225] Paul's statement that Christ is the goal of the law (10:4) carries further the statement that faith establishes the law (3:31) by asserting that Christ himself brings the law in its promise of righteousness to its goal, the goal is that righteousness may be available to everyone who believes.[226]

In 10:4 he grounds the assertions he has made in Rom 10:2-3. *Nomos* in 10:4 recalls *nomos dikaiosynēs*, the law which holds forth the promise of righteousness.[227] Paul has already said that faith in Christ, the stone, enables one to attain to the law which promises righteousness (9:32-33). *Christos* stands for the death and resurrection of Jesus through which God's righteousness becomes available to all (3:24-26; 4:25; cf 1 Cor 1:30; 2 Cor 5:21). Correspondingly, faith (*pas ho pisteuōn*) is belief in the crucified and resurrected Lord (9:32-33).[228] Nothing in the preceding statement suggests a negative relationship between Christ and the law. It is only the Jewish notion that the works of the law are a means of attaining to the law and thus to righteousness that is faulted (9:32; cf 10:5).[229]

---

221 Howard, *End*, 331-2.

222 Rhyne, *Law*, 5-24; 117.

223 Rhyne, *Law*, 25-61; 117.

224 Rhyne, *Law*, 63-93; 117-18.

225 Rhyne, *Law*, 95-116; 118.

226 Rhyne, *Law*, 111, 118-9.

227 Rhyne, *Law*, 103.

228 See Franz Mussner, "'Christus (ist) des Gesetzes Ende zur Gerechtigkeit fur jeden, der glaubt' (Rom. 10:4)," in *Paulus - Apostat oder Apostel* (ed. M. Barth, J. Blank, J. Bloch, F. Mussner, and R. J. Zwi Werblowsky. Regensburg: Pustet, 1977) 31-44, 35-37.

229 Rhyne, *Law*, 103; C Thomas Rhyne, "Nomos dikaiosynēs and the meaning of Romans 10:4," CBQ 47 (1985) 486-499, 492.

Paul would agree that Christ ends this false conception of the law for believers but that is not his point.[230] His point has been that the Jews would have attained to the "law of righteousness" if they had believed on Christ (9:31-33). It would be pointless if he now suddenly speaks of Christ as being the "end" rather than the "goal" of the law.[231] At 10:2-3 the Jews, have an undiscerning zeal for God, are wilfully ignorant of God's righteousness, and attempt to establish their own righteousness; they did not recognize that in Christ the law in its promise of righteousness reaches its goal so that God's righteousness might be available to everyone who believes.[232]

Rhyne argues also that the prepositional phrase *eis dikaiosynēn* should be related to the entire statement *telos gar nomou Christos*. The preposition *eis* may be understood as: consecutive ("so that"), final ("in order that") or, referential ("as far as righteousness is concerned"). Notably Paul reiterates in Rom 10:4 those positive connections between the law and Christ/righteousness/faith that he affirms in 9:31-33. The sequence is as follows: (a) One attains to the *law* through faith in *Christ*; (b) the *law* promises (or demands) righteousness; and (c) One attains to the *law* through *faith* alone. 10:5-8 introduces the Scriptural proof with *gar*; Paul thereby grounds his thesis that Christ is the goal of the law so that righteousness may be available to everyone who believes.[233]

Rom 10:5-8 confirms that *Christ* brings the law in its promise of righteousness to its goal. "The word of faith" in (10:6-13) means that the righteousness promised by the law becomes available in Christ. Paul's Torah text (Deut 30:12-14) is interpreted with reference to Christ and faith (10:6-8), and, consequently, as in 3:21-22 the law becomes a witness to righteousness by faith in Christ. Although in 10:5 Paul views the law in the narrower sense of its commandments and prohibitions, in 10:6-8 he views it in its entirety as a witness along with the prophets.[234]

This section argues that the heart of Israel's failure is their refusal to believe (9:32; 10:16), for Paul stresses faith (10:8) over works (10:5). The strong adversative *alla* in 10:8 indicates that v 8 is the center of 10:5-13; 10:9-13 expands 10:8.[235] Therefore the law as a way of salvation excludes the works of the law as a way of salvation (10:5-8; cf Gal 3:12). Like E. P. Sanders, Rhyne argues that the basis for this exclusion is not that the individual is unable to do the righteousness based on the law, but rather in the law Paul hears

[230] Rhyne, *Law*, 103.

[231] Rhyne, *Law*, 104; Rhyne, *Nomos Dikaiosynēs*, 492 cf Osten-Sacken, *Römer 8*, 254-55.

[232] Rhyne, *Law*, 104.

[233] Rhyne, *Law*, 104, 169; Rhyne, *Nomos Dikaiosynēs*, 493; cf Käsemann, *Romans*, 282-83.

[234] Rhyne, *Law*, 110-11, 173; cf Käsemann, *Romans*, p. 273.

[235] Rhyne, *Law*, 110; so Käsemann, *Romans*, 290-91.

righteousness by faith or "the word of faith preached."[236] The universal nature of this assertion is clear in the following verses.

Rom 9:30-10:21 coheres well with, and presupposes, 3:31-4:25. At 3:21 the law witnesses to righteousness by faith; at 9:30-31 "the law of righteousness" is the law which promises righteousness. At 4:3, 9, 22-24, Gen 15:6 witnesses to righteousness by faith, whereas at 10:6-8 the witness is Deut 30:12-14. At both 3:27 and 9:32 Paul describes two contrasting ways in which the law may be viewed.[237]

Both at 3:24-26; 4:25, and at 10:4-10 the righteousness promised by the law becomes effective in Christ. Both 3:31-4:25, 9:30-32, and 10:2-4 establish the law by faith. In 3:31 faith establishes the law. In Rom 10:4 Christ is the goal of the law.[238]

2.7.2.4 ROBERT BADENAS

Badenas strongly holds to the view that the law is valid. He works out his position on Rom 10:4 in a manner which is in many respects similar to Rhyne. Having surveyed the meaning of *telos* in Classical and Hellenistic Greek, the LXX, the Pseudepigrapha, the letter of Aristeas, Philo, Josephus, and the New Testament,[239] he concludes that, although the primary meaning is teleological, *telos* can mean end in the sense of something that has been brought to completion, and occasionally end in the sense of termination.[240]

He argues on this basis that unless there is strong evidence to the contrary *telos* should be understood as goal in 10:4. For him this is confirmed by the athletic imagery of running a race in 9:30-33.[241] Because the Jews did not see Christ as the goal of the law they stumbled over him and kept on running in the wrong direction.[242]

In this context *nomos* basically means divine revelation and not an ethical code.[243] *Nomos* is not disparaged but is put on the side of *dikaiosynē ek pisteōs* (cf 3:21-22, 27; 3:31-4:25; 10:2-10).[244] In the phrase *nomos dikaiosynēs* (9:31)

---

[236] Rhyne, *Law*, 110-11, 173 n 108; Sanders, *Palestinian Judaism*, 483, n 37; Against Bläser, *Gesetz* 180. Van Dülmen, *Gesetzes* 125; Hans-Jürgen van der Minde, *Schrift und Tradition bei Paulus: Ihre Bedeutung und Funktion im Römerbrief* (Paderborner Theologische Studien, Bd. 3 Munich: Verlag Ferdinand Schöningh, 1976), 109; cf Phil 3:6.

[237] Rhyne, *Law*, 114.

[238] Rhyne, *Law*, 115.

[239] Robert Badenas, *Christ the End of the Law: Romans 10:4 in Pauline Perspective* (JSNT Supplement Series 10; Sheffield: JSOT, 1985), 38-79.

[240] Badenas, *End*, 44, 54-59; 62-65.

[241] Badenas, *End*, 102.

[242] Badenas, *End*, 115.

[243] Badenas, *End*, 103.

[244] Badenas, *End*, 105.

the unattained goal is *nomos* not *dikaiosynēs*.[245] The expression refers to the law which promises righteousness in the sense that the Torah bears witness to righteousness by faith (as in 3:21).[246] The phrase *eis nomon ouk ephthanen* in the same verse means that Israel did not recognize from the Scriptures Jesus Christ as the promised Messiah.[247] Since in the verses immediately preceding 10:4 the issue is the Torah and how Israel misunderstood it, and since *telos nomou* is emphatically placed at the beginning of the sentence, 10:4 is a statement about *telos nomou* (defined in reference to *Christos*) and not vice-versa.[248] Rom 10:4 means that the Torah, in its promise of righteousness to whoever believes pointed to Christ.[249]

2.7.2.5 RAGNAR BRING

An exponent of the view, that *telos* in Rom 10:4 means both goal and termination, is Ragnar Bring.[250] Christ is the end of the law in that he puts an end to law-righteousness and the condemnation which the law brings. He is the goal of the law in that all that the law aimed at is summed up in him. The Semitic background for *telos* is the Hebrew *sôp* and *qēs* ("to bring something to a conclusion") and the Aramaic *k^elal* ("summation").[251] Salvation comes as a two act drama; the first act (the law) is a preparation for the second act (Christ). The ultimate goal in each act of the drama of salvation is to bring in the rule of God's righteousness. The first act (the law) fulfills this aim, not by a real expectation that men perform the prescriptions of the law, but in order that all men might be condemned and consigned under the rule of sin.[252] The second act (Christ) does not abolish the prescriptions of the law, but by perfect obedience overcomes the condemnation which is brought in the first act and ushers in life and (the) righteousness (of God); thus the goal of the law[253] is attained.[254]

---

245 Badenas, *End*, 104.

246 Badenas, *End*, 103-104.

247 Badenas, *End*, 105.

248 Badenas, *End*, 112.

249 Badenas, *End*, 116-118.

250 Bring, *Gesetz*, 35-72.

251 Bring, *Gesetz*, 40-42.

252 Bring, *Gesetz*, 41, 48-49, 68-69.

253 Bring, *Gesetz*, 62 believes that in Rom 9:31-33 *nomos* means the same thing as *dikaiosynēs* since God's law is a *nomos dikaiosynēs* (9:31).

254 Ibid., 50, 61, 69-70-71.

Christ as the one who does the law[255] attains the righteousness of God; he attains what the Jews, who pursued a law of righteousness (*diōkōn nomon dikaiosynēs*, 9:31), did not attain.[256] The quotations of Isa 8:14; 28:16 in Rom 9:32-33 refer to Christ; their purpose is to show the relevance of faith in God's helping righteousness.[257]

For Bring, then, "goal," and not "end," gives the primary emphasis of *telos* in Rom 10:4.

2.7.2.6 HANS CONZELMANN

The law does not come to an end as a moral demand but as a way of salvation.[258] Its requirements have been fulfilled by Christ; we are therefore ransomed from it and have died to it (Rom 7:6). He believes, however, that the concept of salvation history alone is insufficient to give a proper understanding since Paul's outline of salvation history is fragmentary. In Galatians 3 and 4 the history from Adam to Abraham is missing, whereas in Romans 5 there is a sweep from Adam to Moses with no reference to Abraham. Galatians 3 is concerned with the relationship between law and promise; Romans 5 is concerned with the relationship between law and sin. In both cases the law is an intermediate factor; Conzelmann, however, believes in the validity of the moral demand of the law because, in agreement with Bultmann,[259] he finds a distinction between the law as the will of God which has absolute validity for all the world, and the law as an ordinance of Moses which has validity only for an intermediate period in one part of the world.[260]

---

[255] Thus the only one who is *ho poiēsas anthrōpos* (Rom 10:5) is the one who walks *en Christō* (ibid., 67). See Ragnar Bring, "Paul and the Old Testament: A Study of Election, Faith and Law in Paul, with Special Reference to Romans 9.30-10:30," ST 25 (1971) 21-60, 49-50. For an effective critique of this point see Räisänen, *Law*, 55.

[256] Bring also believes that in 9:31 the phrase *eis dikaiosynē tou nomou* or *eis telos tou nomou* could be substituted for *eis nomon*; thereby *telos* would signify the deepest content and ultimate goal of the law.

[257] Bring, *Gesetz*, 47. For a similar exposition of the law see Bring, *Paul and the Old Testament*, 21-60.

[258] Conzelmann, *Outline*, 224-26. Others who hold that the law is not ended as a moral demand but as a way of salvation include: Maurer, *Gesetzeslehre* 53; Bultmann, *Theology* I, 268-9; E. Percy, *Die Probleme der Kolosser und Epheserbriefe* (Lund: C. W. K. Gleerup, 1946), 356-357; Wilckens, *Rechtfertigung*, 109; Schrage, *Einzelgebote*, 232.

[259] Bultmann, *Theology* I. 268-9.

[260] Rudolf Bultmann, "Christ the End of the Law," in his *Essays Philosophical and Theological* (London: SCM, 1955) 36-66 gives an approach which should perhaps be labeled as "existential." Christ is the end of the law in that he gives man the freedom to live on a future basis and to live for the future released from his past and from himself (ibid., 64). For him, Paul does not have the modern theory of evolution in mind whereby a stage in the development of the human mind has been surpassed as if a coherent knowledge of God has taken the place of an obscure or false one. Nor does Paul's rejection of the law follow from his belief in the worthlessness of OT ethics; the law is holy,

2.7.2.7 RICHARD LONGENECKER AND GEORGE ELDON LADD

For Richard N. Longenecker[261] and George Eldon Ladd[262] *eis dikaiosynēn* indicates that Christ terminates the law in its connection with righteousness; it is terminated, not as the standard and judgement of God, but in its contractual obligation as a means of obtaining righteousness.

2.7.2.8 HANS HÜBNER

Hans Hübner believes in the ongoing validity of the law but in a qualified sense. By the time that Paul wrote Romans he changed his mind. The law is valid for the believer in Romans but not in Galatians.

According to Romans the Mosaic law in its true intention is the "law of faith" (Rom 3:27), the law of the life-giving Spirit (Rom 8:2). Rom 3:31 establishes this law and accepts its pneumatic claim to justice.[263] Romans 13:8-10 indicates, and Rom 14 confirms, that it is only the so-called moral commands and not the Levitical regulations of the Law which are valid for the believer.[264] The validity of the law does not mean a *tertius usus legis*. The Mosaic law is spiritual (Rom 7:14; Rom 8:2); the justified man does not obey it as an external impulse but is driven by the spirit (Rom 8:14) and does of himself what the spiritual law "demands."[265]

The problem with the law has been that men have asserted themselves before God, have boasted and gloried in themselves, have fulfilled the law in order to make themselves righteous. By doing this they have perverted the Mosaic law into "the law of works" (Rom 3:27). They have, consequently, become enslaved to the law, they are "under the law," they are "under the dominion of the perverted law."[266] Christ is the end of the misuse of the Torah, the end of the law of the carnal man, the end of the law perverted by *hamartia* and *sarx* (Rom 10:4).[267]

2.7.3 PRELIMINARY EVALUATION

The preceding discussion on the validity of the law is sufficient to alert us to some of the issues and views on this topic. Arguments for my own view and

---

just, and good, and Christian morality is the fulfillment of the OT demands (Rom 13:8-10; Gal 5:14). The polemic of Rom 2:21-23 against the Jews presupposes the validity of the law (ibid., 40-41.); its fulfillment, however, is not the way to salvation (ibid., 41).

[261] Longenecker, *Paul*, 144-147.

[262] George Eldon Ladd, "Paul and the Law," *Soli Deo Gloria* (FS William Childs Robinson. (ed) J. McDowell Richards, Richmond: John Knox, 1968) 50-67, 57-58.

[263] Hübner, *Law*, 148.

[264] Hübner, *Law*, 84-5.

[265] Hübner, *Law*, 127, 145.

[266] Hübner, *Law*, 135.

[267] Hübner, *Law*, 138, 148.

against some of the views presented here will emerge in the following chapters but some preliminary comments are in order to offset my views from the preceding survey.

I believe that the "moral" law is valid for the believer; consequently, I will argue against the cosmological view of Schweitzer, the messianic age view of Schoeps, and the spirit and love views of Käsemann and Bruce. I believe further that at Rom 10:4 Christ is the end of the law and not the goal of the law. But Christ is not the end of the law as a means of salvation, nor the end of the law in its connection with righteousness, nor the end of a misused law. My position is that for the believer Christ is the end of the enslavement, condemnation, and death which the law brings.

2.8 CONCLUSION

In our discussion so far we have been exposed to some of the issues that arise from an attentive reading of the text, and to other issues which would perhaps escape an attentive reading but have become the subject of scholarly debate.

We have concluded that Paul does not distinguish between the arthrous and anarthrous use of *nomos*. *Nomos* is used in a variety of ways and, with few exceptions, refers to some aspect of the OT or Jewish law. The law originates with God. God ultimately gave the law to make transgressions increase. There is at least an implicit distinction between the ceremonial law and the moral law. Recent arguments that Paul's statements on the law are contradictory cannot withstand close scrutiny. Although Paul's understanding on the law may have deepened he does not show a fundamental development in his thinking from letter to letter. What he says about the law is explained better by the occasion of the letter.

In the next three chapters I shall provide arguments for preliminary positions which have been taken in this chapter. I will examine the question which I believe Paul is asking and answering. I shall argue that Paul does give a coherent total view of the law. Paul argues from solution to plight; the solution is the atoning death and resurrection of Jesus. If man could be saved by obeying the law it would mean that the death and resurrection of Christ was in vain. The plight for Paul is the fallenness of man. Man is enslaved not to the "ceremonial" law but to the "moral" law. Perfect obedience to the law brings life, but man is unable to obey the law since he has participated in Adam's sin, is fallen, is in the flesh. For the believer Christ ends the enslavement, condemnation, and death which the law brings. The man in Christ is not in the flesh but in the Spirit. Paul distinguishes between the law as it encounters those in the flesh and those in the Spirit, between the law as a means of salvation and as a norm of life. The moral law remains valid for the believer.

CHAPTER THREE

THE PROBLEM: SIN, DEATH, LAW, AND FLESH

W. Gutbrod claims that "Paul's radical understanding of the Law can be apprehended only in the light of his inner starting point, namely, the act of forgiveness and justification accomplished by the cross of Christ...."[1] J. A. Schoeps[2] notes that "Paul take[s] as his starting point the death of Jesus as a saving event and survey[s] retrospectively the meaning of the law." E. P. Sanders[3] has argued that for Paul in the matter of salvation the solution precedes the problem.

The death and resurrection of Jesus as the saving event, and man's participation in that death and resurrection is the solution to the dilemma of man, and at the same time Paul's fundamental starting point about the meaning of the law.

The law, sin, death, and flesh are the reasons for the dilemma of man. Man cannot save himself by means of the law. The law is aligned with sin and death, but at the root of sin is the problem of flesh. The elements in the dilemma are given at Romans 7:5: "While we were living in the flesh (*en tę̄ sarki*), our sinful passions (*ta pathēmata tōn hamartiōn*) aroused by the law (*ta dia tou nomou enērgeito*), were at work in our members to bear fruit for death (*tǭ thanatǭ*)."

In this chapter we shall consider the dilemma of man and the relation of the law to the dilemma. In the next chapter we shall consider the solution.

3.1 Sin And Death

Though the law be "holy" and the commandment "holy and just and good" (Rom 7:12), though "the oracles of God" (*ta logia tou theou*, Rom. 3:2), and "the giving of the law" (*hē nomothesia*, Rom 9:4) be in themselves blessings, the law in the concreteness of history has not met the dilemma of man and relieved it; it has sharpened and worsened it.

This is entirely due to the situation of man the sinner. He is in bondage to sin (Rom 6); and though he validates the bondage by his own evil acts (Rom 6:23; cf 5:12f), he is above all victim, "sold under sin" (*pepramenos hypo tēn hamartian*, Rom 7:14). Sin (*hamartia*) is conceived as a personified ruling power.[4] Although in a few passages the image is that of a king - i.e., sin reigns (*basileuei*), Rom

[1] Gutbrod "nomos," TDNT IV, 1075. against Beker, *Paul*, 236, 237, 242.

[2] Schoeps, *Paul*, 180.

[3] Sanders, *Palestinian Judaism*, 442-447.

[4] Cf BAGD, "hamartia," 43-44.

5:21; 6:12), has its arsenal of weapons (*hopla*, Rom 6:13), and pays its wages (*opsōnia*, Rom 6:23) of death - in most passages the image is that of a slave master. Men serve (*douleuein*, Rom 6:6) it, are its slaves (*douloi*, 6:17, 20), and are sold into its service (*pepramenos hypo tēn hamartian*, Rom 7:14) or are set free from it (*eleutherōthentes*, Rom 6:22) from it. Sin acts as Lord (*kyrieusei*, Rom 6:14), and has all men under (*pantas hyph' hamartian einai*, Rom 3:9) it, and all things consigned to it (*synekleisen ... ta panta hypo hamartian*, Gal 3:22; cf 3:23).[5]

For man the ultimate consequence of this rule of sin and enslavement to sin is death. Being a slave (*doulos*) of sin leads to death (Rom 6:16), and sinful passions (*ta pathēmata tōn hamartiōn*) bear fruit for death (*thanatos*) (Rom 7:5). The wages of sin (*ta ... opsōnia tēs hamartias*, Rom 6:23), and the end (*to ... telos*) of the one who sins (Rom 6:21; cf 6:16; 1:32), is death (*thanatos*). To "me" (= *egō* in Rom 7) it was sin (*hē hamartia*) that was working death (*egeneto thanatos*, Rom 7:13; cf 7:24); when sin revived (*anezēsen*) "I" (*egō*) died (*apethanon*, Rom 7:9).

The condition of man is ruinous. This ruinous state is traced back to Adam. Adam initiated a process of sin and bequeathed mankind a heritage of death. It was "through one man (*di' henos anthrōpou*)" that "sin came into the world ... and death through sin (*dia tēs hamartias ho thanatos*) and so death spread to all men because all men sinned" (*eis pantas anthrōpous ho thanatos dielthen eph' hō̧ pantes hēmarton*) (Rom 5:12). It was because of one man's trespass (*tō̧ tou henos paraptōmati*) that death reigned through that one man (*ho thanatos ebasileusen dia tou henos*, Rom 5:17). It was because of this sin that death reigned from Adam to Moses (*ebasileusen ho thanatos apo Adam mechri Mōüseōs*, Rom 5:14).[6]

But the rule of sin and death is finally broken! What has broken it? The act of God whose victory over sin was accomplished in the death and resurrection of Jesus (Rom 8:3). In Rom 6:7 the one who has died is freed from sin (*dedikaiōtai*[7] *apo tēs hamartias*). Sanday and Headlam[8] argue that here the sense of *dedikaiōtai* is forensic; the idea is that of a master claiming legal possession of a slave. When a slave has died the claims of the law are satisfied; the slave is no longer answerable and sin loses its case.[9] In Rom 6:10 the death Christ died he died to

---

[5] BAGD "hamartia," 43-44 also notes that it enters the world (Rom 5:12), revives (*anezēsen*), Rom 7:9), or is dead (*nekra*, Rom 7:8).

[6] It is in light of these verses in Rom 5 that the statements *"di' anthrōpou thanatos"* (1 Cor 15:21) and *en tō̧ Adam pantes apothnȩ̄skousin* (1 Cor 15:22) are to be read.

[7] *Dedikaiōtai* is the verb which elsewhere in Paul means "to justify."

[8] Sanday and Headlam, *Romans*, ad. loc. 159.

[9] *Dedikaiōtai* may be forensic here, at any rate the idea of sin as a slave master, as we have seen above, is clear. When a slave dies, his master has no further claim on him.

sin once for all (*tē̦ hamartia apethanen ephapax*). This verse, read in the light of 6:7, indicates that sin ceased to have any claim on Jesus.[10] Sin previously did have a claim on the one who knew no sin (*ton mē gnonta hamartian*), because he was made sin for us (*hyper hēmōn hamartian epoiēsen*) (2 Cor 5:21).

The believer has died with Christ (*apethanomen syn Christō̦*, Rom 6:8) and has been united with Christ in the likeness of his death (*symphytoi gegonamen tō̦ homoiōmati tou thanatou autou*, Rom 6:5).[11] He has been baptized (*ebaptisthēmen) eis Christon Iēsoun* and *eis ton thanaton autou* (Rom 6:3).[12] His old self (*ho palaios ... anthrōpos*) was crucified (*synestaurōthē*)[13] with Christ so that his sinful body might be destroyed (*hina katargēthē̦ to sōma tēs hamartias*, Rom 6:6). The believer, because of his identification with Christ, has died to sin (*apethanomen tē̦ hamartią*, Rom 6:2).[14] The result is that he has been set free from sin (*eleutherōthentes (de) apo tēs hamartias*, Rom 6:18, 22), is no longer enslaved to sin (*tou mēketi douleuein ... tē̦ hamartią*, Rom 6:6), and will not have sin acting as Lord over him (*hamartia gar hymōn ou kyrieusei*, Rom 6:14).[15]

---

[10] In Rom 6:9 it says explicitly that death no longer has dominion (*thanatos autou ouketi kyrieuei*) over Christ. It will be argued below that this is also the case for the believer.

[11] Here the idea of "form" rather than "copy" or "image" is to be preferred for *homoiōma*. Robert C. Tannehill, *Dying and Rising with Christ: A Study in Pauline Theology* (BZNW 32; Berlin: Töplemann, 1967), 35 notes that here it indicates the form of the reality itself rather than a second thing which is similar to the reality. The text, then, speaks of a direct union with Christ's death.

[12] This verse is to be understood in light of 1 Cor 10:2 and 12:13. In 12:13 all Christians, whether Jew or Greek, by one Spirit were baptized into one body (*en heni pneumati ... eis hen sōma ebaptisthēmen*). In 10:2 all Israelites were baptized into Moses (*eis ton Mōüsēn ebaptisanto*) in the cloud and in the sea. Bruce, *Romans*, 137 believes that just as baptism into Moses seals the Israelite's exodus from Egypt, so baptism in Rom 6:2 seals the believer's exodus from the bondage of sin.

James D. G. Dunn, *Baptism in The Holy Spirit* (SBT 2nd series 15; London: SCM, 1970), 139-143, notes that the subject of Rom 6 is not baptism but death to sin and the life which follows. In depicting this theme Paul uses the images of baptism, planting, and crucifixion to point to the spiritual transformation which takes place at conversion. Baptism at 6:3 is a metaphor and no more points to the water rite of Baptism than does 1 Cor 12:13.

[13] Cf *Christō̦ synestaurōmai* in Gal 2:20.

[14] The use of the perfects *gegonamen* (Rom 6:5), *dedikaiōtai* (Rom 6:7), and *synestaurōmai* (Gal 2:20) seem to indicate the enduring results of the believer's death to sin, whereas the aorists *ebaptisthēmen* (Rom 6:3), *apethanomen* (Rom 6:2), *synestaurōthē* (Rom 6:6), and *katargēthē̦* (Rom 6:6) indicate the once for all nature of the action. This is particularly the case since in Rom 6 the character of the believer's death is derived from Christ's death, and Christ died (*apethanomen = aorist*) to sin, once for all (*ephapax*) (6:10).

[15] It is on this basis that the Pauline imperatives make sense, i.e., the imperatives not to sin (Rom 6:15), not to let sin reign (*basileuō*) in one's mortal body (6:12), not to present one's members as weapons of wickedness to sin (*mēde paristanete ta melē hymōn hopla adikias tē̦ hamartią*, 6:13), and the imperative to consider oneself as dead to sin (*logizesthe heautous einai nekrous ... tē̦ hamartią*, 6:11). It is pointless to tell a slave not to act as one, because he has no choice in the matter; the case is otherwise, however, with a freed slave. In Paul when one becomes a Christian there is a change of Lordship. See Tannehill, *Dying and Rising*, 14-20; and Sanders, *Palestinian Judaism*, 466-68, 497-500, 507.

3.2. **The Law**

In the previous section we saw how mankind is enslaved to sin (Rom 3:9; 6:1-23; 7:14), and as a result is slated for death (Rom 1:32; 5:12-21; 6:16, 21, 23; 7:5, 10, 13, 24). In many of the texts previously quoted the problem is not merely with sin and death but with the law as involved in the process of sin and death (i.e. Rom 5:12-21; 6:14; 7:5, 9, 13, 14; 8:3; Gal 3:23). Two of the prominent passages are Romans 5:12-21 and Rom 7:1-25. In this section we shall look at these two passages, and then consider how the law is an instrument of sin, how it enslaves and condemns; and who it enslaves and condemns.

3.2.1 Romans 5:12-21

The situation of man the sinner is the result of the sins of men (Rom 6:23a; 3:23a) but there is also a prior cause in the sin of Adam (Rom 5:12-21, esp vv 12, 15-19). Immediately following the statement in 5:12, that it was through one man (Adam) that sin came into the world, we have the clause *eph' hǭ pantes hēmarton*. It bears on the question of the law.

3.2.1.1 Rom 5:12: Eph' Hǭ Pantes Hēmarton

This clause has given rise to an enormous literature, and to a wide variety of interpretations.[16] The various positions on *eph' hǭ* in Rom 5:12 can be summarized as follows: (a) *hǭ* is masculine; its antecedent is an implied *nomos* (Danker); (b) *hǭ* is masculine and *ho thanatos* is its antecedent (Stauffer); (c) *hǭ* is masculine and *henos anthrōpou* is its antecedent with *epi* equivalent to: (i) *en* (Augustine), or (ii) "because of"; and (d) *hǭ* is neuter and the phrase *eph' hǭ* is a conjunction meaning "because." Within this view *hēmarton* has been taken to refer: (i) to men sinning, not in their own persons, but by their participation in Adam's transgression (Bengal, Lagrange, Bruce); (ii) to men sinning in their own persons independently of, but after the example of, Adam (Pelagius); (iii) to refer to men sinning in their own persons but as a result of the corrupt nature inherited from Adam (Cranfield).[17]

Cranfield rejects (b) because it is difficult and forced, and the way *pantes* in 5:12d picks up *eis pantas anthrōpous* in 5:12c suggests that 5:12d is intended to

---

[16] For a selected bibliography on more recent literature see Cranfield, *Romans* I, 274-81 and F. W. Danker, "Romans V. 12. Sin under Law," NTS 14 (1968), 424-439, 435-6. For the ancient and modern history of its exegesis see Theodor Zahn, *Der Brief des Paulus an die Römer* (Leipzig: Deichert, 1910), 163ff.

[17] This summary is basically that of Cranfield, *Romans* I, 274-5. He lists various people who have taken each of these positions.

explain why death came to all men.[18] View (c) (i) is probably to be rejected because *en* would be more natural and *eph' hǭ* elsewhere in Paul (Rom 6:21; 2 Cor 5:4; Phil 3:12; 4:10) and the NT (Lk 5:25; Acts 7:33) does not have this meaning; finally *henos anthrōpou* is somewhat far removed from the context. View (c) (ii) takes account of the difference between *epi* and *en*, but it is open to the other objections of view (c) (i). View (d) (ii) is to be rejected because it does not do justice to the analogy between Christ and Adam, or to the solidarity of men with Adam in 5:12-21; furthermore it seems to contradict 1 Cor 15:22.

Cranfield's view (d, iii) has the difficulty that in the context of the Adam/Christ typology the effect on the many is not what they do in themselves but what happens to them because of their solidarity with either Adam or Christ. Also 5:19 says explicitly that the sin of the one man makes the many *sinners*. View (d) (i) that all men sin by their participation in Adam's sin is to be preferred.[19]

Danker, in propounding view (a) argues and cites examples to show that both in classical and in koine Greek (*eph' hǭ*) is used to express the formal contractual basis on which reciprocal obligations are met.[20] He also argues that, although the question is vexed if *eph hǭ* is read in this light, good sense can be made of the remaining Pauline passages in which it occurs (Rom 6:21; Phil 3:12; 2 Cor 5:4; Phil 4:10).[21] He also claims that *eph' hǭ*, so understood, makes good sense in Rom 5:12. If *eph' hǭ pantes hēmarton* means "on the basis of what (law) all sinned," it has the advantage of associating *eph' hǭ* with *nomos* in 5:13.[22]

Against Danker it has been claimed that there is nothing in the preceding context which would indicate the existence of an implied *nomos*.[23] *Nomos*, however, occurs in the following verse. A bigger problem is the use of *eph' hǭ* in the other passages in Paul. They, in spite of Danker's claim, in no way imply the existence of a *nomos*.

Even if Danker's exegesis of *eph' hǭ* is incorrect, however, Adam's sin is still to be seen in terms of law for at 5:14 Adam's sin is described as transgression (*parabasis*). Therefore all who participate in Adam's sin have sinned in terms of law. Elsewhere in Paul the punishment for disobedience to the law is condemnation (Rom 3:19; 8:1; cf 2:15; 2 Cor 3:9) and death (*thanatos*) (Rom 7:5,

---

[18] Cranfield, *Romans* I, 275-6.

[19] See Ridderbos, *Paul*, 96-99. A. J. M. Wedderburn, "The Theological Structure of Romans V. 12," NTS 19 (1973) 339-354, 351 observes that personal sinning is implied more in 5:12a ("sin came into the world through one man") than 5:12d.

[20] Danker, *Romans V. 12*, 429.

[21] Danker, *Romans V. 12*, 432-3.

[22] Danker, *Romans V. 12*, 428ff.

[23] S. Lewis Johnson Jr., "Romans 5:12 - An Exercise in Exegesis and Theology," in *New Dimensions in New Testament Study* (eds. Richard N. Longenecker and Merrill C. Tenney. Grand Rapids: Zondervan, 1974) 298-316, 304.

10, 13 [bis]; cf Rom 1:32; 2 Cor 3:7). This is precisely the punishment that comes to the many through their participation in Adam's transgression; it is Adam's trespass that brings condemnation (5:16, 18) and death (5:15, 17; cf 5:21).[24]

5:14 does not say that the sinning of the generations following Adam was not in terms of transgression, but merely that it was not in the likeness of the transgression of Adam (*epi tō̧ homoiōmati tēs parabaseōs Adam*). The reason given is not that Adam disobeyed a direct command and his descendants did not, but that Adam and only Adam is the type of Christ the one who was to come (*hos estin typos tou mellontos*). No subsequent transgression could have the consequences of Adam's transgression.

It will be argued below that both Gentiles and Jews outside of Christ are "*hypo nomon*."[25] At Rom 2:15 the Gentiles show "the work of the law" (*to ergon tou nomou*) written on their hearts. At Rom 11:32 God has consigned *all* to disobedience (*apeitheian*). At 1:32 Gentiles are worthy of *thanatos* because they know God's *dikaiōma* yet they willfully disobey.[26] Paul says to his Gentile readers of Galatia: "Before faith came we were confined under the law" (*hypo nomon ephrouroumetha*, 3:23).

3.2.1.2 Rom 5:13: Hamartia De Ouk Ellogeitai Mē Ontos Nomon

Some have argued that the statement "sin is not counted where there is no law" (Rom 5:13) makes no sense in the context.[27] The difficulty can be resolved in two different ways. They are punished for their participation in Adam's disobedience to the law and/or they are under law between Adam and Moses.

Nomos, I believe, should be understood in two different senses in 5:13. The text should be read in the following way: Sin was in the world before the giving of the Mosaic law but sin is not counted where there is no law; i.e., there is law before the giving of the Mosaic law, and sin is counted before the giving of the Mosaic law. The punishment for sin after the giving of the Mosaic law, namely death (Rom 5:21) is the same as before (5:14, 17). This indicates that there previously was law and that sin was previously counted.[28]

---

[24] Adam's sin is not merely "transgression" but also, "trespass" (*paraptōma*) (vv 15, 16, 17, 18, 20) and "disobedience" (*parakoē*) (5:19). "Trespass" and "disobedience" can also be seen in terms of law. Disobedience to God has to be disobedience to a direct command or law of God. At 5:20 it is the introduction of the Mosaic law which causes the already existing singular "trespass" (not "transgression") to abound. "Trespass" therefore exists in the context of law.

[25] See below 100-104.

[26] On *to dikaiōma tou theou* in 1:32 as a reference to God's Torah see Wilckens, *Römer* I, 115 and II, 128. On the universal dimension of law in the OT see Sidney Greidanus, "The Universal Dimension of Law in the Hebrew Scriptures," SR (1985) 39-51.

[27] see Bultmann, *Theology* I, 252; Alfred Loisy, *The Origins of The New Testament* (New Hyde Park, NY: University Books, 1962), 25; and Räisänen, *Law*, 145-7.

[28] *Ebasileusen ho thanatos* (5:14) anticipates *ho thanatos ebasileusen* (5:17), and *ebasileusen hē*

3.2.1.3 Rom 5:20: Nomos De Pareiselthen Hina Pleonasę To Paraptōma

Rom 5:20 does not contradict the above conclusions. The giving of the Mosaic law in salvation history does not bring eternal life or salvation to Israel. It causes the "trespass" (*paraptōma*) of Adam[29] to abound (5:20) and the sin and death which are the result of Adam's sin to reign (5:21). The introduction of the Mosaic law shows the depth of the plight of man as a consequence of Adam's sin and all the more reveals the need for the second Adam to reverse the effects of the sin of the first Adam. Ever since the fall, for the person outside of Christ, law (*nomos*) can only bring sin and death.

3.2.2 Romans 7

In Rom 6 we have seen that we were enslaved to sin and have died to sin. In Rom 7:1-6 we were enslaved to the law (cf vv 2, 6) and have died to the law (v 4). Our natural question is "Is the law sin?" This is the question that Paul asks at 7:7 and answers in 7:7-25.

In 7:1-6 the word *nomos* occurs at 7:1 (bis), 2 (bis), 3, 4, 5, 6, and in 7:7-25 it occurs at 7:7 (bis), 8, 9, 12, 14, 16, 21, 22, 23, 25. In 7:7-25 "I" (*egō*, 7:9, 10, 14, 17, 20, 24, 25) have a problem with the *nomos*. In 7:7-25 there is widespread disagreement over the meaning of *egō* and, consequently, over the meaning of *nomos* and the dilemma that *nomos* presents to *egō* in 7:7-12.

3.2.2.1 The Identity of Egō In Romans 7:7-13

Our understanding of the law as involved in the process of sin and death is enhanced by a consideration of *egō* in Rom 7:7-25.[30] A major question debated throughout the history of the Christian Church is whether the past tenses in 7:7-13 refer to *egō*'s pre-Christian existence, and the present tenses in 7:14-25 refer to his Christian existence.

The view that Rom 7:7-13 refers to Paul's experience under the law would interpret several phrases more or less as follows: *egō de ezōn* (v 9) would be a vivid figurative expression; *ouk egnōn* (v 7) and *chōris ... nomou* (v 9) would refer to childhood innocence; *hē entolē* (v 10) would be that part of the Torah which

---

hamartia en tǫ thanatǫ (5:21). The punishment is death for all of Adam's descendents (5:17); it is the same whether it is before (= 5:14) or after (= 5:21) the giving of the Mosaic law. Cf Roy, A. Harrisville, *Romans* (Minneapolis: Augsburg, 1980), 84-85; and Eberhard Jüngel, "Das Gesetz zwischen Adam und Christus," ZTK 60 (1963) 42-74, 50-70, on the question of law between Adam and Moses.

[29] *Paraptōma* in 5:20 recalls the *paraptōma* of Adam in 5:15, 16, 17, 18. Cf Luz, *Geschichtsverständnis*, 202-03.

[30] I have given a discussion on the identity of *egō* in an earlier form in Brice L. Martin, "Some Reflections on the Identity of *egō* in Rom 7:14-25," SJT 34 (1981) 39-47.

first brought Paul consciousness of sin (or would refer to his becoming a *bar mitzvah*); and *egō de apethanon* (v 10) would refer to the ensuing guilt.

This interpretation, however, has difficulties. It hardly does justice to the phrases *egō de ezōn* (v 9) and *egō de apethanon* (v 10). In Gal 1:14 Paul says that he was zealous for the traditions of his fathers, and in Phil 3:4-6 he points out that he had confidence in the flesh, as to righteousness under the law he was blameless. Nor is it likely that there ever was a time in Paul's childhood that he was *chōris nomou* (v 9).[31]

It is sometimes held that Rom 7:7-13 refers to God's giving the law to Israel at Sinai.[32] A recent proponent of this view is Douglas Moo.[33]

He observes that neither *epithymeō* nor its cognates occur in Genesis 1-3 but they do occur with reference to the wilderness generation in Ps 100 (106):14. Also *ouk epithymēseis* (Rom 7:7; 13:9) reproduces the decalogue exactly.[34] This is Moo's strongest argument; it indicates some relation to the Mosaic law.

To maintain this view, however, Moo has to argue (1) that there is no law between Adam and Moses and, consequently, that Gentiles do not possess the law;[35] and (2) that *ezōn* (Rom 7:9) does not refer to eschatological life,[36] and therefore the time before the Mosaic law was a period of life for Israel. Considerations against Moo's claim that there is no law between Adam and Moses have been given above,[37] and considerations against his claim, that *ezōn* does not have any theological force, and that Gentiles are not *hypo nomon* will be given below.[38]

Moo gives reasons for his view that could equally well support the Adamite view. (a) The focus of the immediate context of vv 8b-10 is on the law as a stimulant of sin and instrument of death.[39] (b) The passage appears to depict an historical sequence, with the consistent use of the past tense (contrast 7:14-25).[40] (c) In vv 14-25 where the subsequent struggle of Israel under the law is depicted, Paul writes with more subjectivity because the struggle is one that he has personally experienced.[41]

---

[31] See Werner Georg Kümmel, *Römer 7 und die Bekehrung des Paulus* (Leipzig: J. C. Hinrichs, 1929), 84-94; and Longenecker, *Paul*, 91-2.

[32] Chrysostom; Ethelbert Stauffer, "Egō," TDNT II 343-362, 358-62; van Dülmen, *Gesetz*, 101-2; 109-110. Jan Lambrecht, "Man before and without Christ: Romans 7 and Pauline Anthropology," *Louvain Studies* 5 (1974) 18-33; Gottlob Schrenk, "Entolē," TDNT II 545-556, 550-552.

[33] Douglas J. Moo, "Israel and Paul in Romans 7. 7-12," NTS 32 (1986) 122-135.

[34] Moo, *Romans 7. 7-12*, 123, 130-1.

[35] Moo, *Romans 7. 7-12*, 123, 127-129.

[36] Moo, *Romans 7. 7-12*, 128, 132 n 29.

[37] See above 72-74.

[38] See below 100-104, 118-120.

[39] Moo, *Romans 7. 7-12*, 126.

[40] Moo, *Romans 7. 7-12*, 126.

[41] Moo, *Romans 7. 7-12*, 129.

Moo, furthermore, has to make a number of important concessions to the Adamite view: (1) Men living between Adam and Moses did not sin in the likeness of Adam's 'transgression' implies a parallel between Adam and those who were subject to the Mosaic law.[42] (2) Rom 7:7-13 can to some extent be applied to Adam or Israel and Paul sees a basic similarity in the situations of Adam confronted by the Paradise command and Israel confronted by the Law.[43] And (3) in Rom 5:14 Adam is in some sense a "prototype" of man under the law. But he attempts to mitigate this point by claiming that the similarity consists in the situation of the confrontation with the divine command, not with possession of the same body of demands.[44] I would reply that there is no need to have the same body of demands. The point is merely that a similar relationship exists between law, sin, and death whether it is the Mosaic law or part thereof, or the law given to Adam.

He believes that the law given to Israel is primary and the allusions to Adam are secondary. I would argue the reverse. Israel's coming under the Mosaic law is a visible dramatic and decisive instance in which sin makes law its base of operations. But there are features of Rom 7:7-12 which do not fit the Mosaic law. Before the giving of the Mosaic law, death reigns (Rom 5:14); this is a decisive argument against the Israelite view. In Rom 7:7-12 the law confronts man in a situation in which he is alive. It is a different situation from 7:5. There man is "in the flesh"; i.e. he is fallen. According to Rom 5:20 the trespass is there before the giving of the Mosaic law. The Mosaic law merely enters in to increase the trespass that is already there, it makes evident the sinfulness of man.

Rom 7:7-13 should, then, be understood in the light of its parallels to the story of the fall of Adam in Genesis 3.[45] *Ouk epithymēseis* (v 7) is reminiscent of the tree which was to be desired (Gen 2:17);[46] *hē hamartia ... exēpatēsen*[47] is

[42] Moo, *Romans 7. 7-12*, 132 n 21.

[43] Moo, *Romans 7. 7-12*, 128.

[44] Moo, *Romans 7. 7-12*, 124.

[45] That this passage was to be so understood was held by the Church fathers Methodius, Theodore of Mopsuestia, Theodoret (See Kümmel, *Römer 7*, 85; Hübner, *Law*, 72). A Few recent exponents of this position are Longenecker, *Paul* 90-6; Stanislas Lyonnet, "Questiones ad Rom. 7,7-13," VD 40 (1962), 163-183; Stanislas, Lyonnet, "L'Histoire du salut selon le chapitre vii de l'Epître aux Romains," Bib 43 (1962) 117-151; Stanislas, Lyonnet, "'Tu ne convoitera pas' (Rom.7)'," in *Neutestamentica et Patristica: Eine Freundesgabe, Herrn Professor Dr. Oscar Cullmann zu seinem 60. Geburtstag überreicht* (NovT Sup 6; Leiden Brill, 1962) 157-165; Hübner *Law*, 70-76, 98; Käsemann, *Romans*, 196; and Otfried Hofius, "Das Gesetz des Mose und das Gesetz Christi," ZTK (1983) 262-283, 269-71. Against Räisänen, *Law*, 230-1; Gundry, *Frustration*, 229-33. Kümmel, *Römer 7* 86-87. Moo, *Romans 7:7:12*, 122-135, esp 123-128, 133; et. al.

[46] Lyonnet, *Tu Ne*, notes that "desire" without the object is found in Tg Neof Exod 10:17, and that Tg Neof uses *hmd*, a word whose Hebrew equivalent is translated with *epithymeō* in Gen 3:6. Also b Sabb 145b-146a says that "desire" was injected in Eve by the Serpent.

[47] Paul uses this verb in connection with the fall (2 Cor 11:3; cf 1 Tim 2:14); see Barrett, *Romans*, ad.

similar to "the serpent beguiled me" (Gen 3:13); *apekteinen* is to be understood in light of Gen 2:17; 3:3, 4; *hē entolē he eis zōēn* (v 10) is comprehensible in view of the tree of life in Gen 2:9; 3:24. This view gives full weight to life without the law (v 9) and to death (v 10). There was a time when in Adam "I" did live without law, and there was a time when in Adam "I" died.[48] The switch to the present tense in vv 14-25 indicates that the Genesis story is no longer in view. This position also correlates with the view in Judaism that Adam was made responsible for the Torah in the garden.[49] Sometimes in Jewish literature the commandment not to eat of the tree of the knowledge of good and evil was viewed as receiving the Torah *in nuce*; Adam and Eve's disobedience was seen as a breach of the tenth commandment which is quoted in 7:7; and coveting and lusting was seen as being at the root of all disobedience to the law.[50]

3.2.2.2 THE IDENTITY OF EGŌ IN ROMANS 7:14-25

The Greek fathers generally believed that 7:14-25 refers to the nonChristian; but the western Church up to and including the Reformation followed Augustine in his belief that it refers to the Christian. German Pietism marked a return to the pre-Christian view. The modern book that has basically sealed the argument for the pre-Christian view in German scholarship is Werner Georg Kümmel's *Römer 7 und die Bekehrung des Paulus*, published in 1929.[51] Anders Nygren[52] and many English speaking scholars have disagreed. Notable examples from this group are: C. E. B. Cranfield,[53] John Murray,[54] F. F. Bruce,[55] C. K. Barrett,[56] J. I. Packer,[57] James D. G. Dunn,[58] and David H. Campbell.[59]

---

loc., 144.

[48] See Longenecker, *Paul* 93-94. Moo, *Rom 7. 7-12*, 127 would have *ezōn* refer to Israel before the giving of the Mosaic law. The problem is that before the giving of the Mosaic law "death reigned" (Rom 5:14)

[49] Lyonnet, *Tu ne*, 159-163; Longenecker, *Paul*, 94-5; Moore, *Judaism* I, 274; and Hofius, *Gesetz*, 269-70.

[50] see Hofius, *Gesetz* 269-70; and A. J. M. Wedderburn, "Adam in Paul's Letter to the Romans," in *Studia Biblica III: Papers on Paul and Other New Testament Authors* (ed. E. A. Livingstone. JSNT Supplement Series 3; Sheffield: JSOT, 1980) 413-430, 420, 421, 428, and the texts and literature they cite in support.

[51] Leipzig: J. C. Hinrichs, 1929. For brief histories of the interpretation of this question see Sanday and Headlam, *Romans*, 184-5; Michel, *Römer*, 181-87; and Otto Kuss, *Der Römerbrief* (3 Vols; Regensburg: Pustet, 1957, 1963, 1978) II, 462-465.

[52] Nygren, *Romans*, 284-303.

[53] Cranfield, *Romans* I, 344-47, 355-70.

[54] Murray, *Romans* I, 256-273.

[55] Bruce, *Romans*, 150-156.

[56] Barrett, *Romans*, 146-153.

[57] James I. Packer, "The 'Wretched Man' of Romans 7," SE II, 1964, 621-627.

[58] James D. G. Dunn, "Rom. 7, 14-25 in the Theology of Paul," TZ 31 (1975) 257-273; James D. G.

The main arguments that Rom 7:14-25 in some way refers to the Christian may be summed up as follows:[60] (a) 7:7-25 is not a parenthesis but is in the context of the account of the meaning of the Christian life in Rom 5-8;[61] (b) *egō* in vv 7-25 is most naturally autobiographical and, so, (c) the past tenses refer to Paul's pre-Christian experience; (d) a pre-Christian view of vv 14-25 contradicts Paul's "...as to righteousness under the law blameless..." (Phil 3:6; cf Gal 1:13-14);[62] (e) the positive claims made for *egō*[63] contradict Paul's view of the natural man in Rom 1:18-3:20; 8:5-8; (f) vv 14-25, like Gal 5:17, describe the one who is living in two aeons simultaneously;[64] (g) the plight of a non-Christian in v 25b coming after the announced victory through Jesus Christ in v 25a is a *non sequitur* and "anticlimactic."[65] In addition Dunn[66] has claimed (h) that the pluperfect *ęǳein* (v 7) has an imperfect sense, and therefore the covetousness he once experienced is still a part of his Christian present.

The pre-conversion view, against which the above arguments are directed, can be differentiated into at least four positions: (1) Paul's pre-conversion experience; (2) a Jew's pre-conversion experience; (3) the experience of everyman (*egō* = an indefinite *tis*); and (4) Paul's pre-Christian past viewed from a now Christian perspective. Against each of these differentiated positions a few of the above points would especially apply: against (1), (c) and (d); against (2), (b), (c), and (d); against (3), (b) and (e); and against (4), (a).

There have been, however, at least five important points made against the "Christian" position:[67] (i) the absence of references to the Spirit in 7:7-25 in

---

Dunn, *Jesus and The Spirit* (London: SCM, 1975), 312-316. This position has also been taken recently by the Chinese scholar Ronald Y. K. Fung, "The Impotence of the Law," in *Scripture, Tradition, and Interpretation: Essays Presented to Everett F. Harrison by His Students and Colleagues in Honor of His Seventy-fifth Birthday* (eds. W. Ward Gasque and William Sanford La Sor. Grand Rapids: Eerdmans, 1978), 34-48. For a list of others see Dunn, *Rom. 7, 14-25*, 258 n 8.

[59] David H. Campbell, "The Identity of *egō* in Romans 7:7-25," in *Studia Biblica III: Papers on Paul and Other New Testament Authors* (ed. E. A. Livingstone. JSNT Supplement Series 3; Sheffield: JSOT, 1980), 57-64.

[60] Convenient summaries of these arguments are found in Nygren, ad. loc., 284-303; Dunn, *Rom 7, 14-25*, 260-264; Longenecker, *Paul*, 110.

[61] Dunn, *Rom 7, 14-25*, 260 and Nygren ad. loc., 287 are examples of those who are against seeing vv 7-25 as a digression; otherwise Barrett, *Romans*, ad. loc., 140.

[62] e.g., Cranfield, *Romans* I, ad. loc., 344.

[63] In particular *synēdomai gar tǭ nomǭ tou theou kata ton esō anthrōpon* (v 22) and *autos egō to men noi douleuō nomǭ theou* (v 25).

[64] See Nygren, *Romans*, ad. loc., 34, 293; Bruce, *Romans*, ad. loc., 151, 156; and Dunn, *Rom 7, 14-25* 264-69.

[65] Packer, *Wretched Man*, 625; cf Cranfield, *Romans* I, ad. loc., 345.

[66] Dunn, *Rom. 7, 14-25*, 261.

[67] For brief summaries of these points see Kümmel, *Römer 7*, 97-98; Longenecker, *Paul* 110; Murray ad. loc. 256-57; and Fung, *Impotence*, 37-38.

contrast to 7:6 and ch 8; (ii) the emphatic (*nyn* in 8:1; (iii) the cry of despair in v 24; (iv) *egō* is *sarkinos* in v 14 whereas the Christian is *en pneumati* in 7:5-6. and 8:5-9; and (v) a Christian *pepramenos hypo tēn hamartian* (v 14) contradicts Rom 6.

An attempt will now be made to respond to the major points raised by the "Christian position," to strengthen arguments made by their opponents, and to add new arguments of my own. Point (c) has been discussed and refuted above.[68] Point (b), which is debatable and point (d), which can be accommodated to my view, will be discussed below. Points (f), (g), and (h) can be disposed of briefly. A difficulty with (f) is that *egō* is absolutely impotent,[69] while in Gal 5:16-26 those that are *en pneumati* are able to triumph over the flesh (*sarx*).[70] A difficulty with (h) is that even if "I" still know what sin is it does not necessarily mean that it is a ruling power over "me." Regarding (g), v 25a can be understood as an interjection.[71]

Arguments (a) and (e) will require more discussion. First argument (a): Rom 7:7-25 is not a parenthesis *per se* but it is aimed at dispelling a reader's possibly false notion about the law. Paul has said that to man sin has brought enslavement (3:9; 6:6, 17, 20; cf 5:21; 6:12, 14; Gal 3:22) and death (6:16, 21, 23; 7:5). But the believer, by participating in Christ's death, has died to sin, has been freed from sin (Rom 6:1ff. especially vv 2, 6, 7, 11, 13-14, 17-18, 20, 22). He says the same thing about the law. To man the law has brought enslavement (7:6; cf 6:14; Gal 4:21-31; 3:23) and death (7:5; cf 5:12-21; 2 Cor 3:6f). But the believer by participating in the death of Christ has died to the law, has been freed from the law (7:4, 6; cf Gal 2:19f). A reader's natural question is "Is the law sin?" - precisely the question that Paul asks (7:7) and answers (7:7ff). The answer is that the law is not sin, yet it brings sin and death.

Rom 8:1-4 continues the themes of 7:4-6: that is, the believer in possession of the Spirit and set free from the law by the death of Christ. 7:5 is a cryptic summary of 7:7-25, while 7:6 summarizes Rom 8.[72]

Rom 5-8 is less about the meaning of the Christian life than is sometimes supposed. Rom 1-4 is summarized by 1:17 (= Hab 2:4: *ho de dikaios ek pisteōs*

---

[68] See above 76-78.

[69] See Ridderbos, *Paul* 127; Robert H. Gundry, "Moral Frustration of Paul Before His Conversion: Sexual Lust in Romans 7:7-25" in *Pauline Studies: Essays Presented to F. F. Bruce on His 70th Birthday* (ed Donald A. Hagner and Murray J. Harris. Grand Rapids: Eerdmans, 1980) 228-245, 238-239; and Räisänen, *Law*, 115.

[70] Although Fung takes the 'Christian' position on Rom 7:14-25 he gives an illuminating discussion on Gal 5:17 and admits that the Christian there is able to overcome the flesh (*Impotence*, 36-37).

[71] See Longenecker, *Paul*, 113.

[72] See Osten-Sacken, *Römer 8* 194; Wilckens, *Romans* II, 63, 118; Conzelmann, *Theology*, 229; Jewett, *Terms*, 145; cf Franz J. Leenhardt, *The Epistle to the Romans: A Commentary* (London: Lutterworth, 1961), 179.

zēsetai); it is designed to show *that* it is the one who is just (= justified) *ek pisteōs* rather than *ex ergōn* who will live. Rom 5-8 describes the blessings both present and future which result from justification by faith. 5:1-11 and 8:5-40 have many common themes. In 5:12-8:4, freedom from death (5:12-21), freedom from sin (6:1-23), and freedom from law (7:1-8:4) are proclaimed, and new aspects of the *dilemma* of man are examined.[73] For example sin is a personified power that rules and enslaves man (6:6f, 12-14, 17, 20; 7:14, 17, 20; 7:14, 17, 20); it is because of Adam that sin and death have come to all men (5:12-21; 7:7-13); and no matter how hard "I" try "I" am powerless to obey the law (7:14-25). Exhortation to live the Christian life occurs only at 6:1f, 11-19, and 8:12f and only in a general way. The specifics of this exhortation are given at 12:1-15:13.[74]

Finally argument (e): *egō* in vv 14-25 is indeed unlike man in 1:18-3:20, but also man in Rom 1 is unlike man in Rom 2. There are three different types of man each with a different view of himself and God but with one thing in common - each disobeys God, each does evil.[75] The man of Rom 1 knows, yet scorns, both God (v 21) and his *dikaiōma* (v 32). The man of Rom 2, on the other hand, endorses God's law, believes he obeys it, would instruct others in it (vv 17-20), and condemns those who disobey (vv 1, 3). The man of Rom 7:14-25 in his innermost being (*autos egō*, v 25; *ton esō anthrōpon*, v 22) delights in God's law yet realizes that even when he tries as hard as he can he is powerless to obey (vv 15, 16, 18-19, 21, 23, 25). The end of each type of man is *thanatos* (1:32; 7:24; cf 5:12, 14, 17, 21; 6:16, 21, 23; 7:5, 10, 13; 8:6) or its corollaries *krima* (2:3), *orgē kai thymos* (2:8), and *thlypsis kai stenochōria* (2:9).

The obstacles raised against the "pre-Christian" view are, then, largely counteracted. The positive arguments for it, moreover, are compelling. First, *rhysetai* (v 24) is the future tense of a verb meaning "rescue," an apt description of a cry for salvation.

Second, "I" am unable to do the good, unable to obey the law. In Romans 2 one needs to do the good to have eternal life (2:7-10), and to obey the law to be justified (2:13).[76]

Third, the "members" (*ta melē*) of the person in 7:23 (bis) are the similar to the "members" of the non-Christian in 7:5 and opposed to the "members" of the Christians in 6:13 (bis), 19 (bis). The person who has died to sin does not need to yield his members to sin but can present his members to God as instruments of righteousness (6:13; cf 6:19), in 7:23, however, a warfare is going on over which

---

[73] See above 13-14.

[74] *parastēsai* (12:1) seems to recall *paristanete* (6:13, 16), *parestēsate* (6:19), and *parastēsata* (6:13).

[75] See esp 1:32; 2:1, 3, 21-24; 7:15, 16, 18, 19, 21, 23, 25.

[76] The problem is not merely to do the good, but to do the good in order to be saved. Josef Blank, "Der Gespaltene Mensch: Zur Exegese vom Rom. 7, 7-25," BibLeb 9 (1968) 10-20, 14-20. notes that the problem of gaining salvation and the problem of doing the good go together.

he has no control and takes him captive to the law of sin. This is similar to 7:5 where the person living in the flesh has his sinful passions aroused by the law at work in his members to bear fruit for death.

Fourth, "I" am *pepramenos hypo tēn hamartian* (v 14) and sin (vv 17, 20; cf vv 23, 25, 7-9, 11, 13) is a ruling power over "me." This is the same plight as those outside of Christ both in Gal 3:22 (*hypo hamartian*) and in the punch-line statement of 3:9 (*hyph' hamartian*).

Fifth, *pepramenos hypo tēn hamartian* contradicts Rom 6. There Paul affirms in the strongest possible way that the Christian has been freed from sin (personified as a slave master). The believer has died with Christ (*apethanomen syn Christǭ*, v 8), and has been united with Christ in the likeness of his death (v 5). He has been baptized *(ebaptisthēmen) eis Christon Iēsoun* and *eis thanaton autou* (v 3). His old self (*ho palaios anthrōpos*) was crucified (*synestaurōthē*) with Christ so that the sinful body might be destroyed (*hina katargēthę̄ to sōma tēs hamartias*, v 6). Thus the believer, because of his identification with Christ, has died to sin (*apethanomen tę̄ hamartia*, v 2), is set free from sin (*eleutherōthentes ... apo tēs hamartias*, vv 18, 22; *ho gar apothanōn dedikaiōtai apo tēs hamartias*, v 7), is no longer enslaved to sin (*tou mēketi douleuein ... tę̄ hamartią*, v 6), and sin will not act as lord over him (*hamartia gar hymōn ou kyrieusei*, v 14).[77]

Sixth, *egō*'s problem is not only one of sin but also one of law. "I" agree that the law is spiritual (*pneumatikos*, v 14), good (*kalos*, v 16; cf v 12-13), and of God (*theou*, vv 23, 25). The problem is that "I" am *sarkinos* (v 14) and unable to do the good (*kalos*, vv 18, 21; *agathos*, vv 18, 19). The Christian, on the other, hand has died to the law (7:4; cf Gal 2:19). He is set free from the law (7:4, 6), belongs to Christ (7:4), lives to God (Gal 2:19), and bears fruit for God (7:4) rather than for death (7:5). He is set free from the law of sin and death, walks *kata pneuma* rather than *kata sarka* and is able to fulfill the *dikaiōma tou nomou* (8:2, 4). Thus the law is no longer a problem for him.

Seventh, *egō*'s problem is one of flesh (*sarkinos*, v 14; *sarx*, vv 18, 25). This is the same plight that the non-Christian has (7:5; 8:3). The Christian, on the other hand, is no longer *en sarki* but *en pneumati* (7:5, 6; 8:8, 9), no longer walks *kata sarka* but *kata pneuma* (8:4, 5), no longer has the *phronēma tēs sarkos* but the *phronēma tou pneumatos* (8:6). He is, then, no longer *sarkinos* but *pneumatikos*, and a *pneumatikos* law is no longer a problem for him (cf 7:14).

Lastly, *egō*'s dilemma is one of death (*thanatos*, v 24; cf vv 10, 11, 13). This is the plight of the non-Christian, the plight of the man who is *en sarki* (7:5), who lives *kata sarka* (8:13), who has the *phronēma tēs sarkos* (8:6); it is the plight of

---

[77] On the enduring character of the believer's death to sin see above 71 n. 14.

the one who participates in Adam's sin (5:12, 14, 17, 21), who is controlled by sin (6:16, 21, 23), who sins highhandedly (1:32).

Egō's plight, like the non-Christian in 7:5, is thus one of *hamartia*, *nomos*, *sarx*, and *thanatos*. But for the Christian the power of all of these is broken (even though the final victory is future). In the present he lives in a mortal (*nekros*) body (8:11), awaits adoption (8:23), glory (8:18-30), and eternal life (8:11, 13 etc.), yet he has hope (5:2-5; 8:20-24), is not a debtor (*opheiletēs*) to the flesh to live according to the flesh (*tę̄ sarki tou kata sarka zēn*, 8:12), possesses a spirit of sonship (*huiothesias*) rather than slavery (*douleias*, 8:15), is alive to God (6:11), and is in the Spirit (5:5; 7:6; 8:1ff). By the Spirit he can put to death the deeds of the body (8:13); walking *kata pneuma* he is able to fulfill the *dikaiōma tou nomou* (8:4). Only because he is a freed slave does it make any sense for him to be exhorted not to act as a slave (6:13, 14, 16, 19).

To "me," on the other hand, Pauline exhortations not to act as a slave would be pointless because "I" have no choice in the matter. This makes Fung's view untenable; Following C. L. Mitton he holds that *egō* in Rom 7:14-25 refers to the believer who has "slipped ... back to a legalistic attitude to God and to righteousness."[78] Similarly, according to Fung, Gal 5:18 leaves open the possibility of Christians who are *hypo nomon* and are not led by the Spirit (*pneumati agesthe*).[79] But then Rom 8:14, which indicates that those who are not led by the Spirit (*pneumati theou agontai*) are not *huioi theou* becomes problematical. Furthermore the legalistic Galatians wish to be *hypo nomon* (4:21), yet no longer are *douloi* (4:7), *hypo paidagōgon* (3:25), or *hypo nomon* (3:23). Only because they are freed slaves does Paul urge them to "stand fast" and to "not submit again to a yoke of slavery" (5:1).

None of this is true of "me." *Egō* in Rom 7:14-25, therefore, refers to someone outside of Christ. But to whom? The opponents of a pre-Christian position are no doubt right in excluding both a Jew's pre-Christian experience (= Rom 2) and Paul's (= Phil 3:6); there is no evidence that Paul or other Jews, as opposed to Luther, had an introspective conscience.[80] But their arguments against *egō* as either an indefinite *tis* or Paul's pre-Christian past from a now Christian perspective are not constraining.

Kümmel claims that *egō* in Rom 7 is to be understood as a *Stilform* or an indefinite *tis*. As evidence he adduces one passage from Philo (*de Somnis* I: 176), three from the Rabbis (*Mishna: Ber*. I:3; *Gemara: Ber*. 3a; *Pirke Aboth* 6:96), and three from Greek literature Demosthenes: *kata Philippou* g 9:17;

[78] Fung, *Impotence*, 40; C. L. Mitton, "Romans vii Reconsidered," ExpT 65 (1954) 132-135, 133.

[79] Fung, *Impotence*, 41-42.

[80] See Krister Stendahl, "The Apostle Paul and the Introspective Conscience of the West," HTR 56 (1963) 199-215, 202-03.

Pseudo-Xenophon: *De republica Atheniensium* 1:11; 2:11).[81] Karl Georg Kuhn believes that this usage occurs in 1QS 11:9, 10 and that Rom 7 is to be understood in light of it.[82] Ethelbert Stauffer also sees a gnomic or general usage of *egō* in Rom 3:7; 1 Cor 6:12; 10:29-30; 14:11-19; and Gal 2:18-21.[83] Luz strikes a somewhat different note and suggests that the closest parallel to "I" in Romans is the use of the first person singular in such passages as Jer 10:19-22, Mic 7:7-10, Lam 1:9-22, and Pss Sol 1:1-2:6 as a reference to Jerusalem or Israel. In these passages the writer by using "I" shows a close personal identification with the horrors that have befallen city and people.[84]

Egō could refer to an indefinite *tis* but only to someone who loves God's law yet knows he cannot obey the law. Good sense results from the passage, however, if Paul is strongly but not exclusively identifying himself with "I." In 7:7-13 he could be thinking of his own history in Adam, and in 7:14-25 of his past from a present perspective. Paul as a Jew did have a zeal for God but only as a Christian does he realize that it is *ou kat' epignōsin* (10:2; cf Phil 3:4ff); only now does he realize that salvation can only come through the death of Christ.[85]

I conclude, then, that in 7:7-25 *egō* has an autobiographical element but is not necessarily exclusively autobiographical. The past tenses (7:7-13) with reference to "I" (*egō*) refer to Paul's and our involvement in Adam's disobedience to the law at the fall, and the present tenses (7:14-25) refer to Paul's past and our past from a now Christian perspective.

3.2.3 The Law Cannot Be Obeyed

We have seen in Rom 7:14-25 that even the one who tries his utmost is powerless to obey the law. But to obtain righteousness and life through the law it must be obeyed. In Rom 2:13 it is not the hearers (*akroatai*) of the law but the doers (*poiētai*) of the law who will be justified. Rom 2:13 is in the context of everyone being condemned (1:18-3:20). It is also a general statement similar to 2:6 ("He will render to every man according to his works."). 2:6 is amplified in 2:7-10; those who do good get life and its corollaries (2:7, 10), and those who do evil get death and its corollaries (2:8, 9). The point is that no one is righteous (3:10), no one does good, no one obeys the law (3:10-19).

---

[81] Kümmel, *Römer 7*, 126-32.

[82] Karl Georg Kuhn, "*Peirasmos - hamartia - sarx* im Neuen Testament und die damit zusammenhangenden Vorstellungen," ZTK 49 (1952) 200-222, 210.

[83] Stauffer, "Egō," TDNT II, 357. On Gal 2:18-21 see Karl Kertelge, "Exegetische überlegungen zum Verständnis der paulinischen Anthropologie nach Römer 7," ZNW 62 (1971) 105-114, 107.

[84] Luz, *Geschichtsverständnis*, 59 n 87; also Moo, *Rom 7. 7-12*, 129.

[85] Rom 7 seems to be the product of Paul's mature Christian thinking rather than his "conversion experience." Cf Ridderbos, *Paul*, 142.

In Rom 10:5[86] (= Lev 18:5; cf Gal 3:12; Lk 10:28) it is the one who practices (*poiēsas*) the *dikaiosynēn tēn ek tou nomou* who will live (*zēsetai*)[87] by it (*en autois*).[88] But the point is that no one is able to obey the law. And this OT text, which on the surface holds out the promise of life, is in reality a pronouncement of judgment.[89] In Gal 3:10 (= Deut 27:26) those who rely on the works of the law are under a curse because they do not "abide (*emmenei*) by all things (*pasin*) written in the book of the law and do (*poiēsai*) them."[90] In Gal 6:13 those who receive circumcision do not themselves keep the law. The man of Rom 2 endorses God's law, believes he obeys it, and would instruct others in it (vv 17-20); yet he does not obey the law (vv 1, 3, 21-24). The man of Rom 7:14-25 delights in God's law yet knows that even when he tries his utmost he is powerless to obey it (vv 15, 16, 18, 19, 21, 23, 25). For the one in the flesh the law is impotent (Rom 8:3); through the law comes only the knowledge of sin (Rom 3:20).[91] Because one cannot observe the law, the commandment which promises life brings death (*hē entolē hē eis zōēn hautē eis thanaton*, Rom 7:10).

This interpretation coheres with Paul's view that the law cannot bring life (Gal 3:21). Since all have already sinned (Rom 5:12; 3:23) it is no longer even a theoretical possibility to obtain salvation by perfect obedience to the Torah, if by perfect obedience is meant sinlessness during one's whole lifetime (past, present, and future).[92] At Rom 2:13 and Gal 3:10-12 the contexts indicate that Paul's

---

[86] Adopting the reading of Kurt Aland, et. al., eds. *The Greek New Testament* (3rd ed. New York/London/Edinburgh/Amsterdam/Stuttgart: United Bible Societies, 1975), 557; and Eberhard and Erwin Nestle, Kurt Aland et. al. (eds.), *Novum Testamentum Graece* (26th ed; Stuttgart: Deutsche Bibelstiftung, 1979), 427. On the textual and grammatical difficulties of this verse see Bruce M. Metzger, *A Textual Commentary on The New Testament* (London: United Bible Societies, 1971) ad. loc., 524-25; Käsemann, *Romans* ad. loc. 285; and Andreas, Lindemann. "Die Gerechtigkeit aus dem Gesetz: Ewägungen zur Auslegung und zur Textgeschichte von Römer 10 5," ZNW 73 (1982) 231-250.

[87] *Zēsetai* in vv 11 and 12 must refer to the same thing. In v 11, Paul is undoubtedly making reference to the life of the age to come. In v 12, therefore, *zēsetai* cannot mean that the one righteous through the law shall live, in the sense of receive strength and be preserved in life, through his obedience to the law. Against Bring, *Galatians*, 136. Regarding Rom 10:5 and Gal 3:12, Hofius, *Gesetz*, 265 n 11, observes that not only the future *zēsetai* but also the comments of Tg. Onq. and Tg. Ps. -J. on Lev 18:5 indicate that Paul is speaking of eternal life.

[88] *En* by analogy with the Hebrew in Lev 18:5 should be understood instrumentally. cf Lindemann, *Gerechtigkeit*, 241; Hofius, *Gesetz*, 265.

[89] See Hofius, *Gesetz*, 272.

[90] See for example Hofius, *Gesetz*, 265, and Käsemann, *Romans*, 285. Against Bruce who believes that even if one did obey the law he still would not receive righteousness and life (Bruce, *Galatians*, ad. loc. 159-160).

[91] Knowledge of sin includes not merely an understanding that we are sinners, but also a real experience of the power of sin. See Hofius, *Gesetz*, 269.

[92] In Phil 3:6, where Paul says that as to righteousness under the law (*kata dikaiosynēn tēn en nomǭ*) his former life was blameless, he seems to be speaking from his former Jewish, rather than his present Christian point of view. Cf pp 1, 96.

purpose, far from exhorting one to live a better life, is to show that those who would gain salvation through obedience to the Torah are condemned.[93]

Not everyone would agree with the preceding exposition. I shall now deal with recent views on three texts which would blunt the force of the preceding points. The texts are Gal 3:10; Gal 5:3; and Rom 2:14-15, 25-27.

3.2.3.1 GALATIANS 3:10

Gal 3:10 reads: "For all who rely on works of the law are under a curse; for it is written 'Cursed be every one who does not abide by all things written in the book of the law, and do them'" (Deut 27:26). The traditional view has been that the law cannot be obeyed perfectly.[94]

But recently some have taken a different view:[95] Daniel P. Fuller, for example, argues that the curse is on those who are conforming to the law's commands and that nothing is said about failure to observe the entire law. The phrase "works of law" refers not to the law's commands but to Jewish misrepresentation of the law. Fuller then has to argue that Deut 27:26 does not condemn those who are not observing the law but those who are legalistically devoted to the law.[96] But Thomas Schreiner observes that in Deut 27 the curses are exacted because one does not observe some part of the law. Deut 27:26 is a generalizing summary which censures those who fail to observe any part of the law. Paul uses the phrase "works of law" to show that even those who are most devoted to the law cannot keep the law perfectly.[97]

Some have held that at Gal 3:10 Paul does not say that the law cannot be fulfilled, the fault is rather that it drives men to do things.[98] Räisänen notes that this interpretation is possible for v 10 but not for vv 11 & 12. Had Paul wished to

---

[93] It is paradoxical that not only because of its transgression of the law (Rom 2) but also because of its zeal for the law (Rom 9:31-33), Israel has been unable to obtain righteousness and life before God. The reason Paul can make both points is that all have sinned and are therefore slated for condemnation and death, and that righteousness and life can only come through Christ.

[94] See for example John Calvin, *The Epistles of Paul the Apostle to the Galatians, Ephesians, Philippians and Colossians* (ed. D. W. Torrance and T. F. Torrance; Grand Rapids: Eerdmans, 1965), 53; Lightfoot, *Galatians*, 137-8; Burton, *Galatians*, 164; Oepke, *Galater*, 72; Schoeps, *Paul*, 175-177; and Hübner, *Law*, 18-19, 43-44.

[95] For a recent argument for the traditional view and a consideration of some of those who oppose it see Thomas R. Schreiner, "Is Perfect Obedience To The Law Possible? A Re-examination of Galatians 3:10," JETS 27 (1984) 151-160. Schreiner considers the views of Daniel P. Fuller, Hans Dieter Betz, F. F. Bruce, George Howard, and Heinrich Schlier.

[96] Daniel P. Fuller, "Paul and 'the Works of the Law'," WTJ 38 (1975) 28-42, 32-33.

[97] Schreiner, *Obedience*, 155-6.

[98] e.g., Schlier, *Galater*, 132-4; Maurer, *Gesetzeslehre*, 22; Karl Kertelge, *Rechtfertigung bei Paulus. Studien zur Struktur und zum Bedeutungsgehalt des paulinischen Rechtfertigungsbegriffs* (Münster: Aschendorff, 1967), 209.

emphasize that "doing" is bad he would best have omitted v 10 or at least removed "*ouk*" from it![99]

From a somewhat different perspective E. P. Sanders argues against those who in Gal 3:10-12 hold that the law could not be satisfactorily fulfilled, that one cannot do all the law. Paul cites Gen 15:6 (v 6) and Hab 2:4 (v 11), the only two passages in the LXX in which the *dik-* root is connected with *pistis*. The quotation, *Eneulogēthēsontai en soi panta ta ethnē* in v 8 is based on Gen 18:18, not 12:3, since Paul's major intention is to include the Gentiles and the term *ethnē* does not appear in 12:3. Gen 15:6 is, therefore, the first passage in the Abraham story which mentions the blessing of the Gentiles. Abraham is the link between Gen 15:6 and 18:18. From Gen 18:18 he "proves" that *Gentiles* are blessed in Abraham, and in Gen 15:6 that Abraham was *righteous* by *faith*.[100] Deut 27:26, *Epikataratos pas hos ouk emmenei pasin tois gegrammenois en tǭ bibliǭ tou nomou tou poiēsai auta*, quoted in v 10 is the only LXX passage in which *nomos* is connected with "curse." The thrust of Gal 3:10 is borne by *nomos* and "cursed," not by "all" which happens to appear.[101] The same argument applies to Schlier's emphasis on *poiein*.[102]

According to Sanders in Gal 3:8-14 the main proposition is that God *righteouses* the Gentiles by *faith* (3:8). 3:10 (= Deut 27:26) announces the negative proof that those who are under the law are under a curse. 3:11 (= Hab 2:4) proves that no one can be righteoused by the law. In v 12 faith excludes the law for Lev 18:18 specifies that one must do the commandments. In vv 11-12 righteousness is by faith and the law is not by faith. In v 13 God has provided for the removal of the curse of the law. 3:14 is a chiastic summary; the first *hina* clause reiterates v 8 (the blessing of Abraham for the Gentiles), and the second *hina* clause reiterates vv 1-5 (The Spirit is received through faith). These two assertions serve the larger negative argument against the requirement to keep the law (= 2:16). Thus 3:10-13 is subsidiary to 3:8.[103]

Sanders mistakenly assumes that to be cursed by the law you first have to accept the law. In Galatians all outside of Christ are under the law and are cursed by the law, whether they accept it or not and whether they realize it or not (Gal 3:13; Gal 3:23).[104] Although he is correct on the main thrust of Gal 3:8-14, Paul

---

[99] Räisänen, *Law*, 94.

[100] Sanders, *Jewish People*, 21.

[101] Sanders, *Jewish People*, 21.

[102] Sanders, *Jewish People*, 54 n 26.

[103] Sanders, *Jewish People*, 22.

[104] Käsemann, *Romans*, 51, 62 observes that unlike Judaism (cf Moore, *Judaism* I, 227-31) Paul does not have to presuppose that the Gentiles know the Torah or reject the Torah to establish man's guilt. For further critique of Sanders see Räisänen, *Law*, 95.

still quotes a text which states that you are cursed if you do not "do" (*poiēsai*) "all" (*pasin*) the law. The usual view is that the law cannot be fulfilled.[105]

Sanders has tried to argue that it is Paul's own words not the words he quotes from the OT which tells us what Paul means. This is a doubtful principle. If, however, it is granted for the sake of argument, Gundry notes that Paul's introductory statement "... all who rely on the *works* of the law" (3:10) indicates performance of the law and not mere acceptance of the law. Gundry further observes that at Deut 27:26 the Hebrew *yāqîm* means "confirm," that is a basic intention to keep the law whereas the LXX has *emmenei* ("abides by"), a term that requires legal perfection. He notes also that at v 12 Paul says that the one who does the things written in the law will receive eternal life (*zēsetai*).[106] Sanders claims that Paul is pitting Lev 18:5 (Gal 3:12) against Hab 2:4 (Gal 3:11), but Gundry observes it is more likely that Paul quotes Hab 2:4 to show that faith underlines righteousness or eternal life, and Lev 18:5 to show that eternal life might have come through complete obedience to the law.[107] 3:13 is then followed by the theme of the curse which comes because of disobedience.[108 & 109]

3.2.3.2 Galatians 5:3

Gal 5:3 is a text which is in some respects similar to Gal 3:10. It reads: "I testify again to every man who receives circumcision that he is bound to keep the whole law (*hoti opheiletēs estin holon ton nomon poiēsai*)." According to Betz, Paul is here referring to a rigorist Jewish view, which had come to be generally accepted, that circumcision was not sufficient to ensure salvation; the whole Torah also had to be rigidly obeyed in all its 613 commandments.[110] Hübner takes the view that Paul had been a Shammaite who thought that all of the law must be obeyed without exception, that proselytes too must successfully do all the law.[111]

But Sanders replies that Paul does not say that the law should not be accepted because all of it cannot be kept. This position assumes (1) that one must keep all of the law, (2) that one cannot keep all of the law, (3) that there is no forgiveness of transgression, and (4) that accepting the law necessarily leads to being cursed.[112] According to Sanders all Jewish groups believed that the law must be

---

[105] So for example van Dülmen *Gesetz* 32; Hübner, *Law* 18-19; Luz, *Geschichtsverständnis*, 149; Schoeps, *Paul* 176-77; Wilckens, *Rechtfertigung* 92.

[106] Robert H. Gundry, "Grace, Works, and Staying Saved in Paul," Bib 66 (1985) 1-38, 23-24.

[107] Gundry, *Grace*, 25; cf Hübner, *Law*, 38-41.

[108] See also Gundry's (*Grace*, 25-6) comments on Gal 5:3 and 6:13 where performance is indicated in Paul's own words.

[109] Sanders' view on this passage has been largely a reaction to Hübner, *Law*, 18-20; Hübner, *Law*, 151-153 has now given a response to Sanders in favor of the traditional view.

[110] Betz, *Galatians*, 259-60.

[111] Hans Hübner, "Gal 3,10 und die Herkunft des Paulus," KD 19 (1973) 215-231; Hübner, *Law*, 23.

[112] Sanders, *Jewish People*, 27.

accepted, all believed that the law could be kept, but none believed that obedience must be perfect, all believed in repentance and other means of atonement for transgression.[113] Even in the Dead Sea Scrolls where perfection is urged provision is made for atonement.[114] Sanders surmises that behind Paul's warning in 5:3 is the view that the law appeared burdensome and inconvenient for Gentiles, that Paul is warning them that they would have to obey such things as the food laws.[115]

In response to Sanders, Jas 2:10 states "whoever keeps the whole law but fails in one point has become guilty of all of it"; the position that all the law must be kept perfectly is therefore known. But Paul I believe is not arguing on the basis of Jewish presuppositions. He is not arguing on the basis of what Jews *think* is true but what is *really* true from his Christian standpoint. He is not saying that Judaism holds that the law cannot be kept but that the law cannot really be kept (cf Romans 7). God, not Judaism, makes you a debtor to do the whole law. Judaism might believe in various means of atonement but there is really no atonement for sin outside of the death and resurrection of Jesus. Christ is our passover lamb (1 Cor 5:7; cf Rom 3:25; 1 Cor 11:25; cf Heb 10:1-4).

The Galatians do not understand the real implications of what they are doing. Being circumcised implies an obligation to obey the law perfectly in order to be saved. It implies a denial of the necessity for the atoning death and resurrection of Jesus, it implies that Christ died in vain (Gal 2:21).[116]

In the context "receiving circumcision" (5:2) is equivalent to submitting again to a yoke of slavery (5:1), to attempting to "be justified by the law" (5:3); it implies falling from grace (5:3), and Christ being of no advantage to them (5:2). Asserting that justification comes through the law indicates that Christ died to no purpose (2:21). Christ is the one whom God "raised ... from the dead" (1:1), whom God sent forth "to redeem those who were under the law" (4:5). Christ is the one "who gave himself for our sins" (Gal 1:4), who "redeemed us from the curse of the law," who became "a curse for us" (3:13). Through faith in Christ (2:15-21; 3:2, 5, 11, 14, 22-25) we are set free (5:1), are justified (2:16-17; cf 3:21), are sons of God (3:26; 4:5-7). Through faith in Christ we belong to him (3:27-29), we receive the Spirit (3:2, 5; cf 5:16-25), we have hope (5:5).

---

[113] Sanders, *Jewish People*, 28.

[114] Sanders, *Palestinian Judaism*, 284-287; 298; 298-305. Sanders, *Jewish People*, 56. n 54.

[115] Sanders, *Jewish People*, 29.

[116] George E. Howard, *Paul: Crisis in Galatia. A Study in Early Christian Theology* (SNTSMS 35; Cambridge: Cambridge University Press, 1979), 16, argues that the emphasis in Gal 5:3 falls on the word *opheiletēs*; the threat is that the one who accepts circumcision comes under bondage to the law and thus to sin.

3.2.3.3 ROM 2:14-15 AND 2:26-27

Rom 2:14-15 and 2:26-27 appear to contradict the rest of Rom 2 for here it seems that Gentiles fulfill the law. At Rom 2:14-15 "Gentiles who do not have the law do what the law requires" and at 2:26-27 an uncircumcised man who keeps the precepts of the law will have his uncircumcision regarded as circumcision and will condemn those who have the written code and circumcision yet break the law.

To reconcile these statements with the rest of Rom 1:18-30, where no one obeys the law, a variety of viewpoints have been proposed: (a) Some precepts of the law are sometimes fulfilled by some Gentiles.[117] (b) The reference is to Gentile Christians.[118] (c) The reference is to pre-Christians, whether Jew or Gentile.[119] And (d) the reference is hypothetical.[120] Against (a) Räisänen correctly notes that *ton nomon telousa* (v 27) and *ta tou nomou* (v 14) refer to the law as a whole, and Gentiles fulfilling a few requirements of the law would hardly condemn the Jew (v 27).[121] Against (b) Räisänen correctly argues that here Gentiles fulfill the law by nature whereas Gentile Christians fulfill it by the fruit of the Spirit (Rom 8:4; Gal 5:22-24).[122]

Klyne Snodgrass[123] has recently argued that these passages in Rom 2 are neither contradictory, nor a reference to Gentile Christians, nor hypothetical. They are to be taken at face value; salvation belongs to the doers and judgment is according to works. The reference is to pre-Christians, whether Jew or Gentile, who rely on God and respond in obedience to the light that God has given and the grace that God has shown.[124] It is the opposite of justification by works or works righteousness. Works righteousness means presenting yourself to God as righteous in order to be accepted by God.[125]

The expressions *poiētai nomou* (2:13) and *dikaiōmata tou nomou phylassȩ̄* (2:26) are positive for Paul while *erga nomou* is negative. *Erga nomou* must have meant something like "works done in the flesh," that is, works done from a merely human context.[126] God's justifying the ungodly (Rom 4:5) means that

[117] Nygren, *Romans*, ad. loc. 122-25, 133-34 Maurer, *Gesetzeslehre*, 38-39.

[118] Zahn, *Römer*, ad loc; Markus Barth, "Die Stelle des Paulus zu Gesetz und Ordnung," EvT 33 (1976) 466-526, 521 n 62; Cranfield, *Romans* I, 155-6; et. al.

[119] Klyne R. Snodgrass, "Justification by Grace - To The Doers: An Analysis of Romans 2 in the Theology of Paul," NTS 32 (1986) 72-93.

[120] Grafe, *Gesetz*, 25-26; Van Dülmen, *Gesetz*, 77, 82. For a summary and bibliography of other viewpoints on this text see Snodgrass, *Doers*, 72-74.

[121] Räisänen, *Law*, 103.

[122] Räisänen, *Law*, 104.

[123] Snodgrass, *Doers*, 72-93.

[124] Snodgrass, *Doers*, 79, 80, 81, 82, 84.

[125] Snodgrass, *Doers*, 83; cf 78.

[126] Snodgrass, *Doers*, 84.

people may come to God in Christ, but it does not mean that they may remain ungodly.[127] Faith must be seen in the context of obedience.[128] Other texts in Paul have a similar theme,[129] and judgment according to works is, moreover, strongly rooted in the Biblical tradition.[130]

I agree with Snodgrass that for Paul faith and obedience go together, and that for one who is in the Spirit and a new creation in Christ Jesus (2 Cor 5:17), the natural response to God's grace is obedience. But I would deny that there is any evidence that the person of Rom 2 has experienced God's saving grace either as a Christian or as a pre-Christian. There is no evidence that the person of Rom 2 has faith, or that God has in anyway empowered him to be obedient. "The work of the law written on their hearts" (Rom 2:15) does not speak of "empowering" them but of either "accusing" or "excusing" them on judgment day (Rom 2:15); it must therefore mean something like the requirement of the law written on their hearts.[131]

Snodgrass' distinction between obedience to the law (which is good) and doing works of law (which is bad) is artificial.[132] The statements which claim that doing the good (2:7-10) and doing the law (2:13) bring justification and eternal life, are, moreover, similar to righteousness by means of the law in Rom 10:5 - i.e., *ho poiēsas auta anthrōpos zēsetai en autois* - and to the need to obey the law perfectly (Gal 3:10, 12). This is the opposite of righteousness by faith (Rom 10:6; Gal 3:11).[133]

Snodgrass also posits an arbitrary distinction between the singular *ergon* which is positive and the plural *erga* which is negative.[134] The reason *erga* or *erga nomou* is negative is that they occur in contexts where there is an attempt to be saved by them. Ephesians, regardless of whether it is Pauline, illustrates the point; in Eph 2:8 where *erga* are a means of being saved they are negative, but at 2:10 where *erga* are the result of God's work they are positive. He also eliminates the plural *erga* in Rom 2:6 from the negative category merely on the ground that it is an OT quotation.

---

[127] Snodgrass, *Doers*, 86.

[128] Snodgrass, *Doers*, 85; In support Snodgrass lists texts such as Rom 3:31; 8:4; 13:8, 10; Gal 5:14; 6:2.

[129] i.e. Rom 14:10-12; 1 Cor 3:13-15; 2 Cor 5:10; 9:6; 11:15; Gal 6:7; Col 3:25; Eph 6:8; 1 Tim 5:24-25; 2 Tim 4:14; Snodgrass, *Doers*, 74.

[130] Snodgrass, *Doers*, 90 n 44 gives a list of passages.

[131] See Ridderbos, *Paul*, 288.

[132] Snodgrass, *Doers*, 84.

[133] See Lindemann, *Gerechtigkeit*, 231-250, esp 244-46; 249-50.

[134] Snodgrass, *Doers*, 84.

Snodgrass insists that Rom 2 nowhere requires perfect obedience,[135] but he overlooks the fact that in Romans only those "in Christ" are *en pneumati*; and only those *en pneumati* are able to fulfill the law at all. Those not *en pneumati* are *en sarki* and unable to obey the law (Rom 7:4-6; 7:14-25; 8:4-9). For them the law can only bring sin and death (Rom 7:4-8:4; esp 7:5, 7-12, 14, 23, 25; 8:2, 3). Through the law comes only knowledge of sin (Rom 3:20). Before God has shown his mercy he has consigned all to disobedience (Rom 11:32).

Rom 2:14-16 and 2:26-27 are to be understood in light of the context of Rom 1:18-3:20. Rom 1:18-3:20 is to be seen in terms of an inductive argument with the delayed assertion and climax coming in 3:9-20; no one obeys the law and everyone is guilty before God. Jews are not any better off than Gentiles for all men both Jews and Greeks are under the power of sin (3:9). Paul backs up this statement with a catena of Scriptural texts (3:10-18) "No one is righteous ... no one seeks God ... no one does good" (3:10-12). Before God every mouth is stopped and the whole world is held accountable to God. No one is justified in God's sight by works of law for through the law comes only knowledge of sin (3:20).[136]

Rom 1 aims at the Gentile who knows of God's decree (*dikaiōma*) yet highhandedly disobeys. Rom 2 is aimed at the Jew who endorses God's law, who believes he obeys it, who would instruct others in it (vv 17-20), and who condemns those who disobey (vv 1-3); yet he also disobeys. The Jewish reader of Rom 1 would have cheered on Paul in his condemnation of the Gentile. But Paul has been setting him up. Rom 2 begins with Jewish premises and makes three general statements with which his Jewish opponent would agree: "He will render to every man according to his deeds" (2:6); "God shows no partiality" (2:11); and "it is not the hearers of the law who are righteous before God but the doers of the law will be justified" (2:13).[137]

The argument in Rom 2 is progressive. 2:7-10 sums up 2:6. The one who does good whether Jew or Greek (2:10) receives God's blessings ("eternal life"; "glory," "honour," "peace") (vv 7, 10). The one who does evil whether Jew or Greek (2:10) receives God's judgment ("wrath," "fury," "tribulation," "distress") (2:8, 9). 2:11 is a bridge between 2:7-10 and 2:12-13; God is impartial, he does not favor either Jew or Greek, God treats people on the basis of what they do.

2:12 is the negative application of 2:6-11. Those who sin will be judged whether they have the law or not (2:12). 2:13 is the positive application of 2:6-11

---

[135] Snodgrass, *Doers*, 75, 79, 83.

[136] Against Räisänen who argues on the basis of Rom 2:14-16 that Paul at heart does not subscribe to the assumption of universal guilt which can only be removed through the death of Christ (Räisänen, *Law*, 187).

[137] This correlates with my view in Rom 1-8 that Paul is speaking with an imaginary Jewish interlocutor in the style of the diatribe in order to bring him to faith (cf above 12-13 n 21).

"the doers of the law ... will be justified." 2:14-16 applies 2:13 to the Gentiles. Gentiles, although they do not have the law, have the work of the law written on their hearts and so depending on whether they have obeyed the law will be either "accused" or "excused" (2:15). 2:17-24 applies 2:12b-13 to the Jews; the Jews are not justified and are judged by the law because they have disobeyed the law. 2:25 adds further that circumcision is only of value if one obeys the law. One's circumcision becomes uncircumcision if one breaks the law (2:25) and one's uncircumcision becomes circumcision if one keeps the law (2:26).

If Paul states in Rom 2 that Gentiles actually obeyed the law it would of course contradict what he says about Gentiles in Rom 1 and 3 and would defeat the entire purpose of his argument. If on the other hand Paul is making a general statement in a vivid manner about the consequences of Gentiles obeying the law without stating that they really do obey the law, it makes good sense in the argument of Rom 2. Rom 2 does not state that Gentiles keep the law but states vividly that if they did they would be justified rather than Jews.[138]

Rom 2 is not designed to show that Gentiles keep the law but that Jews are equally guilty with Gentiles in breaking the law. The Gentiles in Rom 2 are the foil to show that the Jew is guilty before God.

3.2.4 Boasting In The Law Is Excluded

Rudolf Bultmann contended that Paul was against the law because keeping it leads to boasting and self-righteousness; his key texts were Rom 3:27; Ch 4; 7:7-25; 10:2-3; Phil 3:4-9.[139]

Hans Hübner holds that Bultmann's view is correct only for Romans; but viewed in isolation even Romans 1-3 merely criticizes improper behavior, not boasting in one's own fulfillment of the law. In the light of Romans 4, however, the phrase "works of law" in 3:27 means the perverted use of the law or works-righteousness. Abraham did not fulfill the work which would produce righteousness (cf 3:9-20) yet he wanted to be righteoused by works; but because of his faith, God forgave him for both (4:7).[140]

---

[138] Against Cranfield, *Romans* I, 155-56; Räisänen, *Law*, 104; Sanders, *Jewish People*, 126; Snodgrass, *Doers*, 73; 84. Prominent among those who argue that the text is hypothetical are Hans Lietzmann, *An Die Römer* (HNT; 4th ed. Tübingen: Mohr [Siebeck], 1933), ad. loc., 40-42; Günther Bornkamm, "Gesetz und Natur (Rom. 2, 14-16)," in *Studien zu Antike und Urchristentum. Gessamelte Aufsätze* (BEvT 28. Munich: Chr. Kaiser, 1963) II, 93-118, 110; Harrisville, *Romans*, 43-50; John Knox, *The Epistle To The Romans* (IB; New York Abingdon, 1954), 409, 418; and Kuss, *Römerbrief*, I, 64-68, 90.

[139] Bultmann, *Theology*, I, 264-267; see Sanders, *Jewish People*, 30, 44; and Räisänen, *Legalism*, 68.

[140] Hübner, *Law*, 101-124.

E. P. Sanders has recently challenged the view that Paul is against boasting and meritorious achievement. According to Sanders, Paul's argument against "boasting" in Rom 3:27 (as in 2:17, 23) is against the special status of the Jews. In 3:29 God is the God of Gentiles as well as Jews, he "righteouses" (Sanders' term) the uncircumcised and the circumcised on the same basis, i.e., on the basis of faith (3:30).[141]

Sanders argues against Hübner and claims there is no hint that Abraham *tried* to be righteoused before God by works. Paul's argument, based on Gen 15:6, is scriptural-factual. Abraham was righteoused, it was not by works, and he could not boast. Abraham is a paradigmatic type which shows how God righteouses: it is by faith, it has always been by faith. Paul's argument shows that Abraham was not in fact righteoused by works, and in any case works would not count towards righteousness, since God counts only faith. God deals with both circumcised and uncircumcised on the same ground (4:9-13). The promise to Abraham and his offspring (4:14) is an argument directed against privileged status not against boasting in meritorious achievement.[142]

Phil 3:9 and Rom 9:30-10:13 distinguish two righteousnesses - one by law, the other by faith. The distinction of Phil 3:9 is clearer than Rom 10:4-6 because at 3:9 the obvious meaning is that Paul himself had righteousness by the law, while Rom 10:3 says the Jews sought that righteousness, without explicitly stating that they found it.[143]

"My own righteousness" (Phil 3:9) is the same as "their own righteousness" in Rom 10:3. It is not, however, "self-righteousness." It is the righteousness which comes by law; it is the result of being an observant Jew, and is in and of itself a good thing (cf "zeal," Rom 10:2; "gain," Phil 3:7), but is shown to be "wrong" (cf "loss," Phil 3:7-9.) by the revelation of "God's righteousness," which comes by faith in Christ.[144]

In Philippians the only thing wrong with the old righteousness seems to be that it is not the new one. Paul has confidence in the old righteousness but his "fault" as a zealous Pharisee was not his attitude, but boasting in a "gain" which he later saw as "loss." The same attitude occurs in Rom 9:30-10:3. Jews will not be saved because they seek the righteousness based on the law, zealously to be sure, but blindly, because real righteousness is based on faith in Christ.[145]

Sanders is correct to argue against Hübner, that Abraham wanted to be righteoused by works, and against Bultmann, that what is really wrong with the

---

[141] Sanders, *Jewish People*, 32-33.

[142] Sanders, *Jewish People*, 33, 34, 60; cf Howard, *Crisis*, 56; Räisänen, *Legalism*, 70 n 43; Räisänen, *Law*, 187.

[143] Sanders, *Jewish People*, 43.

[144] Sanders, *Jewish People*, 44-45.

[145] Sanders, *Jewish People*, 140.

law is that fulfilling it leads to boasting.[146] But he is incorrect to claim that regarding the attainment of salvation Paul is not against boasting. "God chose what is low and despised in the world ... so that no human being might boast in the presence of God." (1 Cor 1:29) God is the source of our life in Christ Jesus, therefore we are to boast in the Lord (1 Cor 1:30, 31).[147] Those who are truly circumcised boast in Christ Jesus and put no confidence in the flesh (Phil 3:3). It is unthinkable to boast in anything but the cross of the Lord Jesus Christ (Gal 6:14). The reason that Paul is against boasting and meritorious achievement as such seems to be that it takes away from the glory due to God alone. In Romans the gospel is pre-eminently the "gospel of God" (1:1). In a situation of universal sinfulness God is faithful (Rom 3:3), reveals his righteousness (3:21.22), sets forth Christ as a *hilastērion* (3:25), justifies us freely (3:24), and reconciles us to himself (5:11). At the climax of Romans God has consigned all to disobedience that he might have mercy on all (11:32). This fact evokes a doxology (11:33-36). With reference to salvation, God alone must receive the glory, for all things are "from him and through him and to him" (11:36).

Sanders is also incorrect when he claims that the only thing wrong with the old righteousness is that it is not the new one. He does not clearly see that righteousness and salvation are similar terms. Fulfilling the law in order to be righteous makes the death of Christ as a saving event unnecessary (Gal 2:21). He is wrong to argue that there is a real righteousness by law; Gal 3:21 asserts that righteousness does not and could not come by law. Because of his fallenness man is unable to be saved by the law (Rom 8:3); through the law comes only knowledge of sin, not power over sin (Rom 3:20).

Contra Sanders Paul does indeed argue against individual works righteousness; works righteousness puts God in your debt. A key text is Rom 4:4: "To one who works his wages are not reckoned as a gift but as his due." The words "one" and "his" indicate individual performance. The words "wages" and "due" indicate indebtedness. The opposition of "gift" and "due" indicates that works and grace are mutually exclusive. Also at 11:6 - where Paul says "But if it is by grace, it is no longer on the basis of works; otherwise grace would no longer be grace" - "works" and "grace" are mutually exclusive; Sanders is therefore hard pressed to distinguish between "self-righteousness" and "my own righteousness" or "their own righteousness."

Robert Gundry notes other passages where Paul in essence criticizes Jewish self-reliance and self-righteousness: At Rom 10:3 they do not submit to God's righteousness but seek *to establish* their own righteousness. At 10:5 it is the one who *does* (*poiēsas*) the righteousness which is from the law who will live by it.

---

146 For a similar critique of Bultmann see Räisänen, *Law*, 165-174, esp 168-171.

147 At Eph 2:9 we are saved by God's grace not because of works "*lest* any man should boast."

He concludes that Paul is criticizing Jewish unbelief not *instead of* their attempt to perform the law but *as caused by* their attempt to perform the law.[148] Gundry further observes that - in view of Sanders discussion of Palestinian Judaism in his book *Paul and Palestinian Judaism* - while it may be true that the Jew does not view himself as earning salvation by works of law it is at least correct to say that good works are necessary to activate God's grace for the forgiveness of sins.[149]

Gundry[150] correctly points to a list of items in Phil 3:2-11 which point to Paul's pre-Christian attitudinal sin of self-righteousness: he boasted; he had confidence in the flesh. He viewed his practice of Judaism as gain, as superior to his opponents who boast in the flesh. Now (vv 12-16) he does not consider himself to have arrived, then he did.

Phil 3 should be regarded as Paul's pre-Christian view of things. What is wrong with the righteousness that Paul thought he had as a good observant Jew is not that it is the old righteousness but that it is not real righteousness. Real righteousness does not come through the law but only on the basis of what God has done in Christ (Rom 8:3; Gal 2:21; 3:21).[151] The fundamental value that Paul maintains is not that he is against privileged status but that the death and resurrection of Jesus as an atonement for sin was necessary.

If Paul is really concerned with special status rather than the works of the law why cannot Gentiles adopt the Jewish law and then have the same status as Jews? Why could the Gentiles not then boast as well?[152] Why on this basis is faith in Christ necessary? What would be the matter with uncircumcised (and still Gentile) Abraham boasting (Rom 4:2)?

Paul is not entirely against privileged status nor boasting in privileged status. Although Paul does not call it boasting that is precisely what he does when he glories in the special status of the Jew in Rom 3:1-2; 9:4-5. To the Jew has been committed the oracles of God (Rom 3:1-2). The Gospel is to the Jew first and also to the Greek (Rom 1:16; cf Rom 2:9, 10). Israel is a natural olive branch but the Gentiles are a wild olive branch (Romans 11). It is true, though, that both Jew and Gentile are saved by faith (Rom 3:30) and that there is no distinction between Jew and Greek in the matter of salvation (Rom 10:12).

Paul does indeed allow boasting but not in anything that one does, only in what God has done, or what God has done in Christ (Gal 6:14).[153] Boasting in Israel's election (Rom 3:1; Rom 9:4-5) is boasting in something that God has

---

[148] Gundry, *Grace*, 18-19; See also his comments on Rom 9:31 and 10:8 (ibid, 18-19).

[149] Gundry, *Grace*, 19-20.

[150] Gundry, *Grace*, 14.

[151] For a similar distinction in Paul cf Sanders, *Jewish People*, 140; Sanders, *Palestinian Judaism*, 494, 499, 505, 506.

[152] Cf Gundry, *Grace*, 21-2.

[153] Cf Betz, *Galatians*, 318.

done. Boasting in the cross of Christ (Gal 6:14; cf Rom 5:2; 11) is boasting in something that God has done in Christ.

3.2.5 The Law Is An Instrument Of Sin

The law, far from restraining sin, makes it increase. Apart from the law, sin lies dead (*chōris gar nomou hamartia nekra*, Rom 7:8). The law both produces transgressions (*hou de ouk estin nomos oude parabasis*, Rom 4:15) and increases the trespass (*nomos de pareisēlthen hina pleonasę̄ to paraptōma*, Rom 5:20). The law gives sin its power (*hē de dynamis tēs hamartias ho nomos*, 1 Cor 15:56); it is an instrument of deception (*hē gar hamartia aphormēn labousa dia tēs entolēs exēpatēsen me*, Rom 7:11), and arouses sinful passions which bear fruit for death (*ta pathēmata tōn hamartiōn ta dia tou nomou enērgeito en tois melesin hēmōn eis to karpophorēsai tǭ thanatǭ*, Rom 7:5). It is through the law that there is a curse (*tēs kataras tou nomou*, Gal 3:13), wrath (*ho gar nomos orgēn katergazetai*, Rom 4:15), and the charging of sin against one's account (*hamartia de ouk ellogeitai mē ontos nomou*, Rom 5:13).

Texts like Rom 7:7-11, 4:15; 5:20; 1 Cor 15:56 indicate more than man realizing his sinfulness by means of the law,[154] or that the law makes sin a conscious and wilful activity and thereby makes man guilty;[155] the law is the catalyst that helps to bring about sinning.[156] It is, however, incorrect to say that the law causes men to sin;[157] in 7:7-11 sin uses the law to cause men to sin. But the ultimate purpose of the law is not to make "sin reign in death," it is rather that "grace might reign" and result in eternal life (Rom 5:21).[158]

3.2.6 The Law Is Aligned With Death

Not only is the law an instrument of sin; it is also aligned with death (*hē gar hamartia aphormēn labousa dia tēs entolēs exēpatēsen me kai di' autēs apekteinen*, Rom 7:11). It is the very commandment which promises life that brings death (*hē entolē he eis zōēn hautē eis thanaton*, Rom 7:10). "I" was once

---

[154] Cf Duncan, *Galatians*, 3:19 ad. loc.; Ladd, *Law*, 64; Cranfield, *Law*, 45; Cranfield, *Romans* II, 846-47; Wilckens, *Römer* I, 177; Wilckens, *Entwicklung*, 171.

[155] Oepke, *Galater*, ad. loc. Gal 3:19; D. E. H. Whiteley, *The Theology of St. Paul* (Philadelphia: Fortress, 1964), 80-1; Cranfield, *Law*, 46; Cranfield, *Romans* II, 847; Sanday and Headlam, *Romans*, ad. loc. Rom 5:20; Luz, *Geschichtsverständnis*, 187.

[156] Commenting on Rom 7:12 Harrisville, *Romans*, 112, states: "The law is not sin, though I had not known sin without it; though through its commandment sin worked covetousness in me; though apart from the law sin is dead; though without the law I was once alive; though sin revived with its entry; though intended for life it issued in death; though through its command sin deceived and slew me."

[157] Against Räisänen, *Law*, 142.

[158] See Beker, *Paul*, 244-245.

alive without law (*chōris nomou*, Rom 7:9); when the commandment came sin sprang to life and "I" died (*elthousēs de tēs entolēs hē hamartia anezēsen, egō de apethanon*, Rom 7:9). It is because of the sin (*hē hamartia*, Rom 5:12) and transgression of Adam (*henos anthrōpou*, Rom 5:12; *tou henos*, Rom 5:15) which is in terms of law (Rom 7:7-13; 5:12-21) that mankind dies. The whole period of the Mosaic economy is described as "the dispensation of death" (*hē diakonia tou thanatou*, 2 Cor 3:7). It is the law or "the written code" which kills (2 Cor 3:6).

3.2.7 The Law Condemns

Adam's trespass brought condemnation for all (Rom 5:16, 18). The Mosaic dispensation is a dispensation of condemnation (2 Cor 3:9). Because of man's disobedience to the law he is "accused" (Rom 2:15) and "condemned" (Rom 2:1); every mouth is stopped and the whole world is held accountable to God (Rom 3:19).[159] But for the one in Christ the condemnation is removed (Rom 8:1; 34).[160]

[159] One does not need to have the specifically Mosaic legislation to be condemned. One commandment which is disobeyed would be sufficient to do this.

[160] The question of judgment according to works is an admittedly difficult topic and can only be alluded to briefly here. For discussion and bibliography see Kuss, *Römerbrief* II, 396-432; Sanders, *Palestinian Judaism*, 515-518; Sanders, *Jewish People*, 105-113, 118-122. Snodgrass, *Doers*, 72-93; Ridderbos, *Paul*, 178-181. Gundry, *Grace*, 1-38; Karl P. Donfried, "Justification and Last Judgement in Paul," ZNW 67 (1976) 90-110. Donfried, *Judgement*, 90-110, argued that Paul expects final judgement for Christians on the last day and this can result in salvation or wrath. Snodgrass agrees. Sanders (*Palestinian Judaism*, 516-18; and *Jewish People*, 105-113) holds that good deeds are the condition not of getting saved but of staying saved. But Gundry (*Grace*, 1-38, esp 35.,) believes that faith is the necessary and sufficient condition of staying saved with good works being the sign of staying saved. In general I agree with Gundry, although we must assume that Paul meant his warnings to be taken seriously.

Within a Christian community it is likely that some have not really experienced the transforming power of the Spirit and are self consciously on the side of the flesh and are indulging in the things of the flesh. Hence the warnings of Gal 5:19-21; Rom 8:13; 6:16 1 Cor 6:9-10.

But it is questionable if someone, who is a new creation in Christ Jesus (2 Cor 5:17) and has been transformed by the Spirit, can really be on the side of the flesh and sow to the flesh (Rom 8:5-13; Gal 5:19-21; Gal 6:8). By definition he is on the side of the Spirit and sows to the Spirit, and wants to live his life in accordance with the Spirit. The natural result is that he produces the fruit of the Spirit (Gal 5:22-24). Paul does recognize, however, that Christians can be "tempted" and "overtaken" (Gal 6:1). Hence Paul's reminder of the power of the Spirit which is available to them, and the need to rely on it.

It is true that those who highhandedly practice gross sin will be excluded from salvation (see Rom 1:29-31; Gal 5:19-21; 1 Cor 6:9-10). But significantly, although the Corinthian church has much immorality in it, the Corinthian Christians as a group are no longer what they once were; they were washed, sanctified, and justified (1 Cor 6:11), and are excluded from the unrighteous of 1 Cor 6:9-10. There is hope that even the immoral person of 1 Cor 5:5 will ultimately be saved.

Paul has every confidence that he will be saved (see e.g., Phil 1:19-23) and likewise assures other Christians (see e.g., Rom 8:17-39). They are not to live in dread of condemnation and death. Outside of Christ one faces the wrath of God, condemnation, and eschatological death, but in Christ there is "no condemnation" (Rom 8:1; 34), and nothing can separate us from God's love in Christ Jesus our

3.2.8. THE LAW ENSLAVES

Finally the law brings enslavement. It is the law (*tou nomou*) which holds man captive (*en hō̧ kateichometha*, Rom 7:6). "I" am enslaved (*douleuō*, Rom 7:25) and made captive (*aichmalōtizonta*, Rom 7:23) to the law of sin (*tō̧ nomō̧ tēs hamartias* (Rom 7:23), *nomō̧ hamartias* (Rom 7:25).[161] Just as man is *hyph' hamartian* (Rom 3:9), he is also kept under restraint (*synkleiomenoi*) and confined (*ephrouroumetha) hypo nomon*, (Gal 3:23).

There are further indications that we were enslaved to the law. Before Christ came we were children, we were slaves (Gal 4:1, 3). But "Christ has set us free" (*tȩ̄ eleutheria̧ hēmas Christos ēleutherōsen*) (Gal 5:1), we must not "submit again to a yoke of slavery" (*stēkete ... oun kai mē palin zygō̧ douleias enechesthe*) (Gal 5:1). To be "under law" (*hypo nomon*) again (Gal 4:21) is to become a child of the slave woman and not of the free woman (Gal 4:21-31).

3.2.8.1 HYPO NOMON

That the law brings enslavement is indicated by the fact that the man outside of Christ is not *hypo nomou* but *hypo nomon*; he is under the dominion of the law.[162] Sometimes in the Pauline Corpus *hypo* plus the accusative means *under* or *below* and answers the question "whither?" or "where?" It answers the question "whither?" in the phrase "*hypo tous podas*" (1 Cor 15:25, 27; Eph 1:22; Rom 16:20). It answers the question "where?" in the phrases "*hypo ta cheilē*" (Rom 3:13), "*hypo tēn nephelēn*" (1 Cor 10:1), "*hypo ton ouranon*" (Col 1:23), and "*hypo zygon*" (1 Tim 6:1).[163] But other times *hypo* plus the accusative means under the power, rule, sovereignty, or command of something. It is used in this sense in the following phrases: *hypo charin* (Rom 6:14, 15); *hypo nomon* (Rom 6:14, 15; Gal 3:23; 4:4, 5, 21, 5:18; 1 Cor 9:20 [4 times]; *hyph' hamartian* (Rom

---

Lord (Rom 8:35-39). The warning in Rom 11:21 should probably be seen in terms of salvation history, in terms of the exclusion of Gentiles and the inclusion of Jews. That is, the present situation of the exclusion of Jews and the inclusion of Gentiles could be reversed (cf Rom 11:17-26).

The Christian, however, does have to face the judgment seat of God/Christ (Rom 14:10; 2 Cor 5:10; cf 1 Cor 4:4; 9:27) in order to give an account and to receive good or evil (2 Cor 5:10) reward or loss (1 Cor 3:14-15) depending upon what he has done. But these texts do not indicate that the Christian will thereby lose his salvation.

The case is different for those who have "believed in vain" (1 Cor 15:2; cf Gal 4:11) or experienced the Spirit and miracles "in vain" (Gal 3:3-4). The question here is whether this is "real" believing and "real" receiving of the Spirit. Those who are severed from Christ in Gal 5:4 are those who reject the gospel and would be justified by the law. The implication is that they have rejected Christ (see Gal 2:21).

[161] The law of sin is the same law as the OT law; the OT is aligned with sin. It agrees with what has been said previously concerning the law's connection with sin.

[162] See Mussner, *Galaterbrief*, 255; Hübner, *Law*, 48.

[163] See BAGD, "hypo," s.v. 843.

3:9); *hypo [tēn hamartian]* (Rom 7:14; Gal 3:22); *hypo kataran* (Gal 3:10); *hypo paidagōgon* (Gal 3:25); *hypo epitropous kai oikonomous* (Gal 4:2); and *hypo ta stoicheia tou kosmou* (Gal 4:3).[164] To be under a sovereignty, rule, power or command can be, but is not necessarily, enslaving. It is, for example, not enslaving to be "under grace" (*hypo charin*) (Rom 6:14-15). At 1 Cor 9:20-1 *hypo nomon* means simply to be Jewish, to accept the Jewish law as authoritative. But in some passages at least *hypo* plus the accusative implies that the non-Christian is a slave. We were "under the power of sin" (*hyph' hamartian*, Rom 3:9), "*sold* under sin" (*pepramenos hypo tēn hamartian*, Rom 7:14), and "*consigned* under sin" (*synekleisen ... hypo hamartian*) (Gal 3:22). "We were slaves to the elemental spirits of the universe" (*hypo ta stoicheia tou kosmou ēmetha dedoulōmenoi*) (Gal 4:3). We were "under a curse" (*hypo kataran*) (Gal 3:10), "under a taskmaster" (*hypo paidagōgon*) (Gal 3:23), and "under the law." To be "under the law" (*hypo nomon*) (Gal 4:21) is to be children of the slave woman (Hagar) rather than of the free woman (Sarah) (Gal 4:22-26, 29-31). "We were *confined* under the law, *kept under restraint*" (*hypo nomon ephrouroumetha synkleiomenoi*) (Gal 3:23). But Christ came to "*redeem* those who were under the law" (*hypo nomon exagorasę̄*) (Gal 4:5).[165]

3.2.8.2 The Gentiles Are Hypo Nomon

Not everyone agrees that the Gentiles are *hypo nomon* in either Romans or Galatians. With reference to Romans, Moo[166] argues that *nomos* is Israel's peculiar possession and is not a possession of the Gentiles at Rom 2:12, 14; 3:2, 9:4 (cf 1 Cor 9:21; Eph 2:14-15). He believes that only in Rom 2:14-15 - where the Gentiles become a law to themselves and show the work of the law written on the heart - is the limitation of the law to Israel contradicted. But in the same passage (2:12) Paul has explicitly denied that the Gentiles possess the law.

I would reply that even though the Gentiles do not self-consciously posses the fully revealed law that was given to Israel on Sinai, and are thus in one sense without law, they are confronted with the *nomos* enough to be enslaved and condemned. At Rom 2:14-16 the Gentiles who do not have the law (*ta mē nomon echonta*) show the work of the law (*to ergon tou nomou*) written in their hearts; unlike the Jews they do not have the written law, yet they know enough of it to be "accused" (*katēgorountōn*).[167] At Rom 1:18-32 there are Gentiles who know both God (*gnontes ton theon*, v 21) and his decree (*to dikaiōma tou theou*, v 32) yet highhandedly they disobey; consequently, they are worthy of death (*thanatos*, v 32). At 11:32 God has consigned all *to disobedience* (*eis apeitheian*) that he

[164] See BAGD, "hypo," s.v. 843.

[165] See Hübner, *Law*, 33-34.

[166] Moo, *Romans 7. 7-12*, 123-24.

[167] See Käsemann, *Romans*, 64.

may have mercy upon all. At Rom 3:19 - after a catena of quotations from the Psalms and Isaiah to show that all are sinners and all are without excuse (vv 10-18) - we are told that the law speaks to those who are *en tǭ nomǭ* "that every (*pan*) mouth may be stopped and the whole world (*pas ho kosmos*) may be held accountable to God."[168] At Rom 6:14 the reason sin will not now act as Lord over the Roman Christians is that they are not *hypo nomon* but *hypo charin*. The implication is that previously they were not *hypo charin* but *hypo nomon* and *hyph' hamartian* (cf Rom 3:9; and Rom 6). At Rom 7:4-6 before the Roman Christians could belong to Christ, bear fruit for God, or serve in the new life of the Spirit, they first had to be set free from the law and die to the law. Previously they were in the flesh and their sinful passions were aroused by the law and bore fruit for death (7:5).

With reference to Galatians many believe that both Jews and Gentiles are *hypo nomon*.[169] But not everyone agrees. Gaston[170] for example argues that in Galatians *hypo nomon* refers exclusively to Gentiles. A decisive argument against this view, however, is Christ's being born of a woman, born *hypo nomon* (Gal 4:4).[171] Others argue, though, that those *hypo nomon* are exclusively Jews.

Of crucial importance is the identity of *hēmeis* in Gal 3:13; "Christ redeemed us from the curse of the law, having become a curse for us...." Many claim that this refers to an inclusive group of Jewish and Gentile Christians.[172] But others believe that it refers exclusively to Jewish Christians.[173]

The most recent exponent of this view is T. L. Donaldson.[174] He argues that 3:13, 14; 3:23-29, and 4:3-7 are to be understood in light of the salvation history of Jews and Gentiles in Romans. Paul moves in a salvation history sense from Jews under the law (3:13; 4:23-25; 4:5) to the redemption of the Jews from under

---

[168] For further support see Hahn, *Gesetzesverständnis*, 32-35, 59; Räisänen, *Law*, 19-22; and Hübner, *Law*, 33-34, 150; against Sanders, *Palestinian Judaism*, 509, 474 n 2. Hahn, *Gesetzesverständnis*, 51-52, 55 is ambiguous about seeing the Gentiles under law in Galatians as opposed to Romans. For this he is rightly criticized by Hübner, *Law*, 150.

[169] e.g., Bruce, *Galatians*, 166-67; Howard *Crisis*, 58-60. Guthrie *Galatians*, 102-104; Schlier, *Galater*, 136-37; Pierre Bonnard, *L' Epître de Saint Paul aux Galates* (Neuchatel: Delachaux & Niestle S. A., 1953), 68-9; Mussner, *Galaterbrief*, 231-234; 268-270.

[170] Lloyd Gaston, "Paul and the Torah," In *Anti-Semitism and the Foundations of Christianity* (ed. A. T. Davies, 48-71. New York: Paulist, 1979), 62-64.

[171] See T. L. Donaldson, "The 'Curse of the Law' And the Inclusion of the Gentiles: Galatians 3:13-14," NTS 32 (1986) 94-112, 108 n 10, for critique.

[172] e.g., Sanders, *Jewish People*, 68-69, 72; Howard, *Crisis*, 58-60; Guthrie, *Galatians*, 102-104; Schlier, *Galater*, 136-37. Mussner, *Galaterbrief*, 231-234; 268-270.

[173] e.g., Betz, *Galatians*, 148; Burton, *Galatians*, 169; Duncan, *Galatians*, 99-102; Richard B. Hayes, *The Faith of Jesus Christ* (Chico, California: Scholars Press, 1983), 86-92; Lightfoot, *Galatians* 139-40; Zahn, *Galater*, 156-160.

[174] Donaldson, *Curse*, 95-99.

the law (3:13, 25; 4:5) to salvation for the Gentiles (3:14a) or salvation for all both Jews and Gentiles (3:14b, 26-29; 4:6-7).[175]

He concedes that all both Jews and Gentiles are consigned *hypo hamartian* (3:22) but only Jews are *hypo nomon*. He argues that the Gentile Galatians, if they succumb to Judaizing pressure would be returning not to the law but to the elemental spirits. *Hēmeis* in 3:13 should be understood exclusively for the following reasons: a) *Hēmas* and *ta ethnē* (v 14) are emphatically placed at the beginning of their respective clauses; this suggests a contrast. b) The context of 3:6-14 implies strongly that those subject to the curse (*hēmeis* v 13; *hosoi ex ergōn nomou* v 10) are to be seen as Torah observers; and c) at Gal 2:15 *hēmeis* refers to Jews.

Donaldson's points are not cogent. He believes that on the basis of 2:15, *hēmeis* at 3:13 must be restricted to Jews but he does not consistently hold to the identity of "we/us" or of "you" in his schema. On the one hand "us" (3:13) and "we" (3:25) refers exclusively to Jews, and on the other "we" (3:14b, 4:5, 7) refers to both Gentiles and Jews. On the one hand "us" (= Jews) (3:13) is contrasted with "Gentiles" (3:14), and on the other "we" (= Gentiles and Jews) (3:14b) is contrasted with Gentiles (3:14a). On the one hand "we" (= Jews) (3:23, 25) is contrasted with "you" (Gentiles and Jews) (3:26-29) and on the other "we" (Gentiles and Jews) (4:5b, 7) is contrasted with "you" (Gentiles) (4:6, 7)

For Donaldson to be consistent he should also have "we" in 3:14b and 4:5b as a reference to Jews, and "you" 3:26-29, and 4:6-7 as a reference to Gentiles. A good guess why he does not come to this conclusion is that it does not make sense in the context. The second *hina* clause at 3:14b obviously explains the first and the "we" of v 14b has to include the Gentiles of v 14a. At Gal 3:26, 28 the "you all" is obviously a reference to Jews and Gentiles, and seems to be equivalent to "we" in 3:23, 25. At 4:5b-7 Paul equates "we" are sons (4:5b) with "you" are sons (4:6, 7). If the "we" of 4:5b referred to Jews and the "you" of 4:6,7 referred to Gentiles then Paul would be making the odd statement that "since you (Gentiles) are sons, God has sent the Spirit of his Son into our (Jewish) hearts"! The burden of proof is therefore on Donaldson to show why "we" in Gal 3:13, 23 refers exclusively to Jews.

There is a contrast between *hēmeis* and *ethnē* in 3:13, 14, but it contains the same contrast as the two *hina* clauses of v 14. There is a contrast between *ta ethnē* (14a) and *labōmen* (14b). The contrast is not one of Gentiles (14a) versus Jews (13, 14b), but Gentiles (14a) versus Gentiles and Jews (13, 14b). The idea of v 14a is that in Christ Jesus even the Gentiles might receive the blessings of Abraham. The second *hina* clause explains that "the blessing of Abraham" is the "promise of the Spirit." It was taken for granted that Jews would receive both.

---

[175] Donaldson, *Curse*, 95-107, esp 95, 97.

What is new is that Jew and Gentile receive both on the same basis, not on the basis of law but of faith (3:14b; cf Gal 3:2).

Meaning depends on context. At Gal 2:15 Paul explicitly says "we Jews." This does not mean that "we" always refers to "Jews" in Galatians. Unless otherwise indicated it would be natural to see "we" as referring to Paul and his Galatian readers and "you" as referring to his Galatian readers who are mainly but not exclusively Gentile. This is the best way to understand "we" in 3:23-29 and 4:3-7. The alteration between "we" and "you" is merely a stylistic change; he could just have easily used "we" only or "you" only.

The *hyper* formula with reference to the death of Christ occurs at 3:13; it is universal in scope elsewhere in Galatians (Gal 1:4; cf 2:20)[176] and elsewhere in Paul (Rom 5:6, 8; 8:32; 1 Cor 15:3; 2 Cor 5:14, 15, 21; 1 Thess 5:10; cf Eph 5:25).[177]

At 3:22 "all" (*panta*) are *hypo hamartian* (3:22), a phrase parallel to *hypo nomon* (3:23). Moreover *synkleiomenoi* (3:23) recalls *synekleisen* (3:22); both are to be understood in light of God consigning (*synekleisen*) all (*tous pantas*) to disobedience (Rom 11:32). In Romans to be under the power of sin you need to be under the power of the law, for apart from the law sin lies dead (cf Rom 7:8). Unbelieving Gentiles are not *hypo nomon* in the sense that they are self-consciously Jews, but they are *hypo nomon* and under the curse of the law in the sense that they are under its enslaving, condemning and killing effects. At Rom 2:12, 13 the Gentiles are *anomōs* ("without law") and will perish without law; they will be justified only if they have obeyed the law. At the judgment they will be "excused" or "accused" on the basis of their obedience or disobedience to the law (2:15). At Rom 3:19 the whole world (= "all men both Jews and Greeks" (3:9)) is under the law (*en tǭ nomǭ*) and accountable to God. At 11:32 God has consigned all to disobedience. The danger Paul sees is not that the Gentiles would be *self-consciously* returning to the law but that they would be *really* returning to the law. They never were self-consciously under law in the first place; but they wish to be *hypo nomon* (Gal 4:21), they wish to be justified by means of the law (Gal 5:4). Gal 3:8-14 is therefore relevant to a group of Gentile Christians who wish to be under law. They would be cursed unless they obeyed the law perfectly (Gal 3:10; cf vv 10-13). They would also be denying the necessity and efficacy of Jesus' atoning death (Gal 2:21).

Gal 3:13; 23, 4:5 therefore indicate that outside of Christ Gentiles as well as Jews are *hypo nomon*. "We" (Gal 3:13, 23) and the universal context of the work

---

[176] Gal 1:4; cf *paradontos heauton hyper emou*, Gal 2:20.

[177] i.e., *hyper asebōn apethanen*, Rom 5:6; *hyper hēmōn apethanen*, Rom 5:8; *hyper hēmōn pantōn paredōken auton*, Rom 8:32; *apethanen hyper tōn hamartiōn hēmōn*, 1 Cor 15:3; *hyper pantōn apethanen*, 2 Cor 5:14, 15; *hyper hēmōn hamartian epoiēsen*, 2 Cor 5:21; *apothanontos hyper hēmōn*, 1 Thess 5:10. Cf *paredōken hyper autēs* (Eph 5:25).

of Christ (Gal 3:13; 4:5) indicate that even the Gentile is *hypo nomon* and therefore under the curse of the law. That "we" are no longer under the law as a *paidagōgos* (3:23-25) is coupled with the fact that "you all" (Gentiles and Jews) are in Christ Jesus and are sons and heirs (3:26-29). At Gal 4:4-5 God sent forth his Son to redeem those under the law so that "we" might be sons.

At Gal 4:3 Paul says that he and his readers were at one time enslaved to the *ta stoicheia tou kosmou* and at 4:9 he cannot understand why his readers turn to the *ta stoicheia* again. On the one side, among the *stoicheia tou kosmou* seems to be the Torah with its statues, and on the other side is the world of false gods whom the recipients of the letter once served (4:8f). For the Galatians to be under the law is to be in as hopeless a position as non-Christian pagans.[178]

3.3 FLESH

The fundamental problem with the man outside of Christ with his enslavement to the law is that he is "in the flesh" (*en sarki*) rather than "in the Spirit" (*en pneumati*) (Rom 7:5, 14). He is a debtor (*opheiletai*) to the flesh to live according to the flesh (cf 8:12). The law is powerless to bring us salvation since we are in the flesh (Rom 8:3).[179] The text reads: *to gar adynaton tou nomou, en hǭ ēsthenei dia tēs sarkos*. This is not merely a relative weakness but an absolute powerlessness. Cranfield notes that the phrase *en hǭ ēsthenei dia tēs sarkos* depends on *adynaton* and indicates that the fault was not with the law but with flesh.[180] The one who is *en sarki* cannot please God, cannot obey the law (Rom 8:7, 8). I am *sarkinos* sold as a slave under sin (7:14). In "me" (*en emoi*) that is in my flesh (*sarki*) nothing good dwells (7:18), and with my flesh I am enslaved to the law of sin (7:25).

The problem of "flesh" (*sarx*) and its relation to the problem of law, sin, and death is brought out at Rom 7:5: "While we were living in the flesh (*en tę̄ sarki*), our sinful passions (*ta pathēmata tōn hamartiōn*) aroused by the law (*dia tou nomou*) were at work in our members to bear fruit for death (*tǭ thanatǭ*)." The man in Christ, however, is not *en sarki* but *en pneumati* (Rom 7:5f; 8:5-9)[181] and the law is no longer a problem for him because it is *pneumatikos*. As a Christian,

---

[178] See, Hübner, *Law*, 33-34. Cf Gerhard Delling, "stoicheion," TDNT VII 670-87, 683-84. For various meanings of the word *stoicheia* outside of the NT, see Delling, ibid., 670-683, and Eduard Lohse, *Colossians and Philemon* (Hermeneia; Philadelphia: Fortress, 1971), 96-98.

[179] see Hofius, *Gesetz*, 267 n 17; Michel *Römer*, 189-90.

[180] Cranfield, *Romans* I, 379.

[181] Gal 4:23, 29; 5:24; 6:8 also imply that the non-Christian is *en sarki*, and Gal 3:2-5, 14; 4:6, 29; 5:5, 25; 6:8 imply that the Christian is *en pneumati*. Cf Hofius, *Gesetz*, 266.

therefore, he walks not *kata sarka* but *kata pneuma* and is able to fulfill (*plērōthē*) the *dikaiōma tou nomou* (Rom 8:4).[182]

As in the Greek[183] and Jewish[184] worlds, Paul's use of *sarx* is varied and reflects many of their meanings.[185] He uses *sarx* to refer to flesh (1 Cor 15:39), body (2 Cor 12:7; Gal 2:20), human descent or relationship (Rom 1:3; 9:5; 4:1; 9:8), man as a whole (Gal 2:16; Rom 3:20; 1 Cor 1:29), and weak human nature (Rom 6:19; 8:3). A prominent feature of *sarx* in Paul is the opposition between *sarx* and *pneuma*.[186] But even here *sarx* and *pneuma* are contrasted in a variety of ways.[187] The human Davidic descent of Jesus is contrasted with Jesus'

---

[182] Räisänen, *Law*, 114-115, critiques those who would water down the Christian's fulfillment of the law in Rom 8:4.

[183] In Classical and Hellenistic Greek *sarx* can be used in a literal sense to distinguish man's flesh from his bone's, or by metonymy to refer to his body as opposed to his *nous*. See Burton, *Galatians*, 492, BAGD 743; LSJ 1585; Eduard Schweizer, "Sarx," TDNT VII 98-105, 108-110, 119-151, pp. 99-103. Anthony C. Thisleton, "Flesh," NIDNTT I 671-682, 671. In either case *sarx* refers to that which is corruptible and perishable. With Epicurus it was interpreted in the figurative sense as the seat of the affections and lusts (see LSJ 1585; Schweizer, "sarx," TDNT VII 103-105; cf Gal 5:19-21). *Sarx* can also distinguish humanity from the gods for the gods have no flesh (Thisleton, NIDNTT I, 671).

[184] The main Hebrew word for flesh is *bāśār*. It can have meanings similar to *sarx*, such as flesh versus bones and the human body in its entirety (Thisleton, *Flesh*, NIDNTT I, 671-73). But there are also new and distinctive uses. In the OT *bāśār* can refer to the foreskin in the religious rite of circumcision (N. P. "Bratsiotis, Bāśār," TDOT II 313-332, 324). But in the OT flesh sometimes denotes man as a whole, man in his essence (i.e. Gen 37:27; Job 34:15; Isa 40: 6, 8; 66:23 etc.). In the Greek world on the other hand man has flesh but is *not* flesh (Thisleton, NIDNTT I, 672-73).

The relationship that all men have with each other, in that they are *bāśār*, is sometimes applied to a blood relationship (e.g., Gen 2:23) or a marriage relationship (e.g., Gen 2:24) (Bratsiotis, *bāśār*, TDOT II, 328). Sometimes *bāśār* is viewed as inclining toward sin (e.g., Eccl 2:3; 5:5 (6); 11:10; Gen 6:12 (Bratsiotis, *bāśār* TDOT II, 329). The OT frequently has *bāśār* represent man in his transitoriness and creatureliness as opposed to God the creator and sustainer of life (Bratsiotis, *bāśār* TDOT II, 328-32). God's dominion includes God's *ruach* dwelling in *bāśār* (e.g., Num 16:22; 27:16; Job 10:11; 12:10; Ezek 37:1-14) (Bratsiotis, *bāśār*, TDOT II, 330-1).

The LXX translates the Hebrew *bāśār* as *sarx* and, consequently, *sarx* takes over these meanings. See Burton, *Galatians*, 492. Schweizer, *sarx*, TDNT VII, 108-9; Alexander Sand, *Der Begriff "Fleisch" in den paulinischen Hauptbriefen* (Regensburg: Pustet, 1967), 233-237. An important point in the LXX is the distinction of the cosmos into two spheres, that of spirits and that of flesh (Num 16:22; 27:16; cf Esth 4:17) (Schweizer, "sarx," TDNT VII, 108-10)

Many of these meanings for "flesh" are also present in Judaism (see Rudolf Meyer, "Sarx," TDNT VII, 110-119; Schweizer, "sarx," TDNT VII 119-123, 123; Brandenburger, *Fleisch und Geist*, 59-113; Sand, *Fleisch*, 246-288; and Kuss, *Römerbrief* II, 530-36). In the Dead Sea Scrolls "flesh" is especially closely related to sin (Meyer, "sarx," TDNT VII, 111-114).

[185] see e.g., Burton, *Galatians*, 492-3; BAGD "sarx," pp, 743-44; Schweizer, "sarx," TDNT VII, 124-144; Kuss, *Römerbrief* II, 506-21.

[186] On the history of the discussion of the relationship between *sarx* and *pneuma* in Paul see Egon Brandenburger, *Fleisch und Geist: Paulus und die dualistische Weisheit* (WMANT; Neukirchen-Vluyn: Neukirchener Verlag, 1968), 7-25; Kuss, *Römerbrief* II, 521-529; and Robert Jewett, *Terms*, 48-95. Cf Sand, *Fleisch*, 1-122.

[187] See Burton, *Galatians*, 494-95.

resurrection by the power of the Holy Spirit (Rom 1:3). The outward *sarx* is offset by the inward *pneuma* (Rom 2:28, 29; 1 Cor 5:5) aspect of man.[188] The one who would be saved by the flesh (= circumcision and works of law) is opposed to the one who would be saved by the Spirit (Gal 3:3; cf Phil 3:3). Hagar the slave woman was born according to the flesh and represents the law, while Sarah the free woman was born according to the Spirit and represents the promise (Gal 4:23, 29). The latter two contrasts between *sarx* and *pneuma* do not portray *sarx* as evil, but man left to himself apart from God. But the main Pauline contrast between *sarx* and *pneuma* reveals two powers which are opposed to each other, the one being evil and the other being good. We are either in one or the other, and belong to one or the other, and live in accordance with one or the other. This opposition between *sarx* and *pneuma* is brought out in Rom 7:5-6; Rom 7:14-8:16; Gal 5:16-25; Gal 6:8. This contrast, as well as the ones in Gal 3:3 and Gal 4:21-31, relates to the question of the law.

Rom 7:14-25, as we have seen, refers to a non-Christian who is "of the flesh" (*sarkinos*). At 7:25 "flesh" (*sarx*) is contrasted with *nous*; at 7:18 "nothing good dwells within me, that is in my flesh (*sarx*)," is correlative with "sin dwelling in me" (7:17) and is contrasted with "'I' delight in the law of God *kata ton esō anthrōpon*." *Nous* and the "inner man" are on the side of good and are opposed to "flesh" which is on the side of evil. The problem is that "flesh" is powerful and the "inner man" or the *nous* are impotent.

That part of "me" (*egō*) which is "flesh" has sin dwelling in it (17, 18, 20) is enslaved to the law of sin (7:25) and does what is evil (7:15, 16, 17, 19 20). That part of "me" which is "inner man" or *nous* delights in the law of God (7:22), wants to obey the law of God (7:25), wants to do the good, and does not want to do what is evil (7:15, 16, 18); it, however, is powerless to obey the law, powerless to do the good (19). The inner "me" is the real "me." It is not the real "me" which does evil (17, 20) but sin which dwells within me (17, 20). The real "me" is rescued from flesh (7:5; 8:5-9; Gal 5:24). The real "me" has no choice but to be enslaved to the flesh, to be a debtor to the flesh (cf Rom 8:12), and to do evil. But "I" do have a choice to decide whether or not "I" am on the side of the flesh, whether or not "I" want to do good or evil, whether or not "I" want to obey the law of God. The real "me" of Rom 7:14-25 is an *unwilling* slave of sin and the flesh. "I" am different from the person of Rom 1:18-32 who is a *willing* slave and the person of Rom 2 who is an *unwitting* slave.

Rom 8:1ff brings another element into the equation. At 7:14-25 the Spirit is absent, whereas in 8:1ff he is present. At 8:4-9 there is a contrast between the Christian who is "in the Spirit" and the non-Christian who is "in the flesh." *Nous*, which at 7:22, 25 is self-consciously opposed to the flesh and unaware of the

[188] See Sanders, *Jewish People*, 127.

Spirit, is to be distinguished from *phronēma* at 8:6, 7. *Phronēma* can be translated as "way of thinking," "mind," "mind-set," "aim," "aspiration," "striving."[189] It is not my *phronēma* but the Spirit's (cf Rom 8:27) or the flesh's; the genitives *tēs sarkos* and *tou pneumatos* are subjective.[190] Those who walk according to the Spirit set their minds on the Spirit, and are intent to follow the aims and aspirations of the Spirit (8:5-6), whereas those who walk according to the flesh set their minds on the flesh, are intent to follow the flesh and have sold out to the aims and aspirations of the flesh (8:5-6). Those who live according to the flesh, then, are similar to those described in 1:18-32. They are like those who sow to the flesh rather than to the Spirit (cf Gal 6:8). At Rom 7:14-25, on the other hand, I had no choice but to be enslaved to the flesh; but this situation no longer applies, for once we are confronted with the good news of what God has done in Christ to defeat "sin in the flesh," we have a choice to be either "in the flesh" and on the side of the flesh, or "in the Spirit" and on the side of the Spirit.

Paul also believes that the Jew is "in the flesh" and on the side of the flesh. The Jew, however, is profoundly concerned with the good and with obeying the law of God and with being justified in the sight of God. He, however, he has not seen the real plight of man as portrayed in Rom 7:14-25 and in the present situation also rejects the solution to that plight; namely, God's act in Christ and God's gift of his Spirit. The Jew thus is entangled with the flesh and is on the side of the flesh but does not realize the true nature of flesh and his true plight. He would be justified in the flesh (Gal 3:3; Phil 3:3-6), that is he would be justified on the basis of the circumcision of his flesh and on the basis of his Jewish privileges and observance of the law (Phil 3:3-6); he would be justified apart from the Spirit.

The dualism in Rom 7-8 and Gal 5-6 between the flesh which is evil and the Spirit which is good should not be seen as a natural dualism, or metaphysical dualism but a redemptive historical dualism which embraces the ethical.[191] *Pneuma* is the Holy Spirit and is closely associated with the risen Christ (cf Rom 8:1-11; esp vv 1, 2, 9-11).[192] *Sarx* seems on the other hand to be closely associated with Adam and to be a reference to fallen humanity.[193] Bruce notes that flesh for

---

[189] BAGD sv 866.

[190] cf Cranfield, *Romans* I, 386; cf Jewett, *Terms*, 156 who says they are not genitives of quality but of origin.

[191] See Ridderbos, *Paul*, 104.

[192] See below 120 where those who are risen with Christ possess the Spirit.

[193] For a discussion of *sarx* and *pneuma* as two evil powers which oppose each other and their connection to the Adam-Christ typology see Brandenburger, *Fleisch und Geist*, 42-58. cf Sanders, *Jewish People*, 89 n 31; Sanders, *Palestinian Judaism*, 553-4. Bultmann *Theology* II, 232-246 in many ways gives a comprehensive and brilliant understanding of *sarx*. He, however, has not yet appropriated these insights. He does not get beyond flesh as the sphere of the merely earthly apart from God, flesh as the realm of man's earthly, natural, and transitory existence.

Paul is a much more negative concept than body.[194] The body will be redeemed, but Paul nowhere says that the flesh will be redeemed (cf Rom 8:23).[195] Those who belong to Adam are "in the flesh," and those who belong to Christ are "in the Spirit." The "old man" (Rom 6:6), or ourselves in union with Adam, is similar to "flesh" in Gal 5:24. In Rom 6:6 the old man was crucified with Christ that the body of sin might be destroyed that we might no longer be enslaved to sin; in Gal 5:24 those who belong to Christ have crucified the flesh with its passions and desires. Making no provision for the flesh versus putting on the Lord Jesus Christ (Rom 13:14; cf Gal 3:27) is similar to putting off the old man (Adam) and putting on the new man (Christ) (Col 3:8, 9; Eph 4:22, 24).[196]

Elsewhere in Paul the powers of the new age have invaded this age and the decisive victory has been won but mopping up operations remain. There is both the "already" and the "not yet." "Between the times" ethical exhortation is needed. The same is true with reference to the believer's encounter with the flesh and the Spirit. Being in Christ and having the Spirit means that we have crucified the flesh (Gal 5:24), and are no longer obligated to the flesh (Rom 8:12); yet in the present there is war within us between the Spirit and the flesh. Although we would fulfill the desires of the Spirit (Gal 5:17) and would produce the fruit of the Spirit (Gal 5:22, 23) we still have to contend with the desires of the flesh (Gal 5:17) and beware of producing the works of the flesh (Gal 5:19-21). We are in the Spirit and have the life of the Spirit, still we must walk in accordance with the Spirit (Gal 5:25). The believer is enabled to do this through the power of the Spirit (cf Rom 8:13).

Underlying mankind's solidarity with Adam in sin (Rom 5:12), then, is its solidarity with him in flesh (cf 1 Cor 15:42-50). Hence the reversal that is salvation must be not only freedom from death, and therefore from sin, and therefore from law, it must ultimately be a new principle to take the place of flesh. Paul's celebration of the victory of salvation (Rom 8) accordingly takes the form of a pneumatology (vv 2-27). Sin is condemned "in the flesh" (v 3); now men walk "according to the Spirit" (v 4), setting their minds on the things of the Spirit (v 5). Here is the final key to Paul's view of Christ and the law.

---

[194] Bruce, *Paul*, 206.

[195] Yet at 8:13 *sōma* is used where we would logically expect *sarx*. *Sarx* occurs in the Western Text (D F G pc lat). See Nestle-Aland, *Novum Testamentum Graece*, 422.

[196] Cf Bruce, *Paul*, 205-206.

CHAPTER FOUR

THE SOLUTION: THE DEATH AND RESURRECTION OF CHRIST

It is through the death and resurrection of Jesus that the life of man *en sarki*, the life of man *hypo nomon*, his bondage to sin, and his destiny of death are all broken and reversed.

4.1 PARTICIPATION IN THE DEATH OF CHRIST

So far in the argument we have seen that one is a slave to sin and the law, that the law is involved in the process of sin and death, and that the Christian has been set free from sin by Christ's death.[1] Our expectation might then be that if one is freed from sin by Christ's death, he is also freed from the law by that death. This expectation is confirmed by four passages - Rom 7:4-6; 8:1-3; Gal 2:19-21; 3:13.

In each of these passages the resulting change in status is indicated by the aorist tense - *ethanatōthēte* (Rom 7:4), *katērgēthēmen* (Rom 7:6), *apothanontes* (Rom 7:6), *ēleutherōsen* (Rom 8:2), *exēgorasen* (Gal 3:13), *genomenos* (Gal 3:13), and *apethanon* (Gal 2:19); they seem to indicate the once for all nature of the action, whereas the perfect *synestaurōmai* (Gal 2:20) seems to indicate its enduring results.

4.1.1 ROMANS 7:4-6

Previously in Romans we have seen that salvation is a free gift (*charisma*) (5:15, 16; 6:23) which God gives by his grace (*charis*) through the work of Christ (3:24; 5:2, 15, 17). By participation in Christ's death and resurrection we have died to sin (6:1-23) and grace now reigns where sin once reigned (5:20, 21, 6:14). We are no longer under the rule of sin but of grace. At 6:13 Paul says that sin will not act as Lord over us. The reason we would expect Paul to give is that we are not under the rule of *sin* but of grace. Instead he says that we are not under the rule of *law* (*hypo nomon*) but of grace (*hypo charin*) (6:14-15). This prepares us for what Paul says about the law and the relationship of sin and the law in chapter 7. For the believer the same thing has happened to the law in 7:1-6 as has happened to sin in 6:1-23.[2]

---

[1] See above 69-71.

[2] cf Harrisville, *Romans*, 99-101. Tannehill, *Dying and Rising* 43 notes that several other features of 7:1-6 remind us of Romans 6, namely: *katargeō* (7:2, 6; 6:6), *kyrieuō* (7:1; 6:9, 14), *douleuō* or *doulos* (7:6; 6:6; 6:15-23), bearing fruit (7:4-5; 6:21-22), and the dative to indicate the lord to whom one lives or dies (7:4; 6:2, 10-11).

Rom 7:1 begins with a general statement: "the law is binding on a person only during his life." 7:2-3 illustrates this statement with an analogy from marriage law.[3] A woman is bound by law to her husband while he lives and is discharged (*katērgētai*) from the law concerning her husband when he dies and is free to remarry. It does not say that the law as such has changed but her relationship to the law has changed.[4]

7:4-6 expands on the meaning of 7:1. Just as the Christian, by participating in the death of Christ is no longer enslaved to sin, likewise he has died to the law through the body of Christ so that he may belong to another (*hymeis ethanatōthēte tǭ nomǭ dia tou sōmatos tou Christou eis to genesthai hymas heterǭ*, Rom 7:4). In the past his sinful passions aroused by the law were at work in his members to bear fruit for death (Rom 7:5), but now he is *discharged* from the law, dead to that which held him captive (i.e., the law) so that he might not *serve* under the old written code (*nyni de katērgēthēmen apo tou nomou, apothanontes en hǭ kateichometha, hōste douleuein hēmas ... ou palaiotēti grammatos*).

At 7:4 *tǭ nomǭ* is a dative of advantage or disadvantage.[5] *Ethanatōthēte* is aorist passive; it recalls 6:3-4, the believer's baptism and burial with Christ in his death.[6] The aorist tense indicates the once for all nature of the death, and the passive voice indicates that God has caused the death.[7] *Dia tou sōmatos tou Christou* does not refer primarily to the church as the body of Christ[8] but to

---

[3] This illustration has been viewed as an allegory and as an analogy. Origin, Augustine, Sanday and Headlam, J. C. O' Neil, Bruce et. al. have in various ways attempted to explain vv 2-3 as an allegory (cf Little, *Analogy*, 86). It is, however, difficult to apply the allegorical roles consistently in the context of vv 1-4 not to mention that there is no indication the text should be applied allegorically in the first place. It seems much more natural to view vv 2-3 as an analogy; but the analogy seems confusing since the logic of the situation would appear to demand that the woman herself die, that is the person no longer bound would be the one who has died (see Dodd, *Romans* ad. loc., 119-20; Lietzmann, *Römer*, ad. loc., 71-73; H. M. Gale, *The Use of Analogy in the Letters of Paul* (Philadelphia: Westminster, 1964), 192ff; Räisänen, *Law*, 61-2).

Recently Joyce A. Little, "Paul's Use of Analogy: A Structural Analysis of Romans 7:1-6," CBQ 46 (1984) 82-90, 87-89, has attempted to resolve the problems of this analogy by showing that it has a similar relationship to other analogies in Paul, that there is a forward movement in vv 1-6, and that vv 2-3 have an intimate connection with the argument of vv 1-6. For our purposes, however, the essential point is that death ends the obligations that are valid in life; we have died and we are no longer obligated to the law (see Käsemann, *Romans* ad. loc., 187).

[4] See Wilckens, *Römer* II, 64.

[5] see Cranfield, *Romans* I, 336; cf Tannehill, *Dying and Rising*, 18, 43.

[6] Note *ebaptisthēmen* (6:3, bis) and *synetaphēmen* (6:4); see Wilckens, *Römer* II, pp 64-5.

[7] see Cranfield, *Romans* I, 335-6; Tannehill, *Dying and Rising*, 45.

[8] Against Schweitzer, *Mysticism*, 18; John A. T. Robinson, *The Body* (London: SCM, 1952), 47. For the early Fathers who held this view see Wilckens, *Römer* II, 65 n. 253.

Christ's death on the cross,[9] for the phrase occurs in the context of Christ's death and resurrection (cf *tō̧ ek nekrōn egerthenti*). At 7:6 *katērgēthēmen* recalls *katērgētai* (7:2) and *apothanontes* (7:6) recalls *ethanatōthēte* (7:4).[10]

4.1.2 ROMANS 8:1-3

In Rom 8:1-3 the Christian has been set free from the law of sin and death (*ēleutherōsen me apo tou nomou tēs hamartias kai tou thanatou*, Rom 8:2), that is from the law which is aligned with sin and death.[11] Since we are in Christ and set free from the law, the law can no longer condemn us (*ouden ara nyn katakrima tois en Christō̧ Iēsou*, Rom 8:1). This being set free from sin and from the law will also mean being set free from "flesh," that is from our fallen humanity. Being set free involves both the incarnation and death of Christ (cf Gal 4:4; 3:13). God both sent his son in the likeness of sinful flesh (*ho theos ton heautou huion pempsas en homoiōmati sarkos hamartias*[12] and as a sin offering (*kai peri hamartias*)[13] condemned sin in the flesh (*katekrinen tēn hamartian en*

---

[9] see Kuss, *Römerbrief* II, 437; Michel, *Römer*, 167; Cranfield *Romans* II, 335-6; van Dülmen, *Gesetz*, 104; Osten-Sacken, *Römer 8*, 188-194; and Robert H. Gundry, *Sōma in Biblical Theology with Emphasis on Pauline Anthropology* (SNTSMS 29; Cambridge: Cambridge University Press, 1976), 239-40.

[10] See Cranfield, *Romans* I, 338-9.

[11] See above 29-32.

[12] This phrase is carefully chosen; it is neither *en sarki* (which would emphasize that human flesh was the realm in which sin gained a foothold and had domain), nor *en homoiōmati sarkos* (because it is docetic), nor *en sarki hamartias* (which would imply that there was sin in Christ, whereas in 2 Cor 5:21 he knew no sin), but *en homoiōmati sarkos hamartias*. Cf. Bruce, *Romans*, ad. loc., 161. According to the traditional interpretation, *homoiōma* indicates that Christ did not assume a fallen human nature (Ambrosiaster, Aquinas, Bengal; see summaries of their views in Cranfield, *Romans*, 380 n. 80). Barth *Church Dogmatics* I/2 151-59, however, argued that Christ assumed fallen humanity. Cranfield, *Romans*, 379-82, and Barrett, *Romans* et. al. agree and also assume Christ was sinless. Without discussing this specific issue Käsemann, *Romans*, 217 observes correctly that God sent his Son as a Sin offering and sent him deeply into the sphere of sinful flesh, but the limit in which he came into the sphere of human flesh is designated by *homoiōma*; he was passively exposed to sin but did not actively open himself up to it. Bruce, *Paul*, 204 notes that Christ came in real flesh (Col 1:22), but because sin gained no foothold in his life he is said to have come "in the likeness of sinful flesh." Vincent P. Branick, "The Sinful Flesh of the Son of God (Rom 8:3): A Key Image of Pauline Theology," CBQ 47 (1985), 246-262, would have Jesus really participate in sinful flesh. He gets around 2 Cor 5:21 by having it refer to the pre-existent Son!

[13] *Peri hamartias* (and perhaps also *hamartian epoiēsen* in 2 Cor 5:21) indicates that the death of Christ was a sin offering. In the LXX at Isa 53:10 (cf Isa 53:6, 12) the background is that of the suffering servant and *peri hamartias* translates the Hebrew *'asam* (guilt offering). In the LXX, however, *peri hamartias* regularly translates the Hebrew *hata'h* or *hatt't* (sin offering). *Peri hamartias* or (*hamartiōn*) occurs elsewhere in the NT at Heb 5:3; 10:6, 26; 13:11; and 1 Pet 3:18. With the possible exception of 1 Peter 3:18 it expresses the idea of a sin offering. For a discussion of this phrase see Harald Riesenfeld, "Peri," TDNT VI 53-56, 55; and N. T. Wright, "The Meaning of *peri*

tę̄ sarki) (8:3). *Katekrinen* seems to mean that God's sentence of condemnation was passed and executed on sin, and thus the power of sin was broken.[14] *Tēn hamartian en tę̄ sarki* (8:3) seems to recall "sin dwelling in me" and "nothing good dwelling in me, that is in my flesh" (7:18). *En tę̄ sarki* (8:3) would then refer to the realm of flesh in which sin was defeated rather than to the human flesh of Christ.[15] The work of Christ here correlates with the Adam-Christ typology. Because of Adam we are *en sarki*, and are part of fallen humanity; sin, condemnation, and death hold sway over us (cf 8:1, 2; 7:5; 5:12-21), and the introduction of the law only makes us sin all the more (Rom 7:5; 1 Cor 15:56). But because of Christ their power is broken. Because of Christ we are not *en sarki* but *en pneumati* (8:4-9) and *en Christǭ Iēsou* (8:1, 2). For those in Christ the law means Spirit and life, rather than sin and death.[16] For those *en pneumati* the law is not powerless on account of the flesh (8:3); they rather are able to fulfill the just requirement of the law (8:4).

4.1.3 GALATIANS 3:13

In Gal 3:13 we are redeemed from the curse of the law because Christ has become a curse for us (*Christos hēmas exēgorasen ek tēs kataras tou nomou genomenos hyper hēmōn katara*).[17] The law is not a curse per se; it is, rather, a curse to those who do not obey it perfectly. The curse in 3:13 refers back to 3:10 (= Deut 27:26): "Cursed be everyone who does not abide by all things written in the book of the law, and do them."[18]

3:13 must also be read in light of what has been said about the believer's freedom from sin. Just as all men, both Jews and Greeks, are *hyph' hamartian*, so all are "consigned" (*synkleiō*) both *eis apeitheian* (Rom 11:32) and *hypo nomon*; they are *hypo nomon* (Gal 4:5) and under the curse of the law (*hē katara tou nomou*, cf Gal 3:10, 13). Christ's purpose is thus to redeem (*exagorazō*) those (i.e., all men both Jews and Greeks)[19] who are both under the law (*hypo*

---

hamartias in Romans 8:3," in *Studia Biblica III: Papers on Paul and Other New Testament Authors* (ed. E. A. Livingstone. JSNT Supplement Series 3; Sheffield: JSOT, 1980) 453-459; Wilckens, *Römer* II, 126-127.

[14] See Friedrich Büchsel, "katakrinō," TDNT III, 951-52; Cranfield, *Romans* I, 382-3.

[15] Against Cranfield, *Romans* I, 383.

[16] See above 39-41.

[17] For further comments on the "curse of the law" see Betz, *Galatians*, 144-146; 148-152; Bruce, *Galatians*, 163-167; F. F. Bruce, "The Curse of The Law," in *Paul and Paulinism: Essays in honour of C. K. Barrett* (eds. Morna D. Hooker and S. G. Wilson; London: SPCK, 1982) 27-36; Friedrich Büchsel, "Katara," TDNT I, 449-451; Mussner, *Galaterbrief*, 234; Schoeps, *Paul*, 175-182.

[18] For a discussion on the meaning of Gal 3:10 see above 115-118.

[19] Cf Oepke, *Galater*, ad. loc., 74.

nomon, Gal 4:5) and under the curse of the law (*tēs kataras tou nomou*, Gal 3:13). The redemption involves both our identification with him (Gal 3:13; cf above Rom 6) and his identification with us (Gal 4:4-5); it involves both his *genomenon ek gynaikos, genomenon hypo nomon* (Gal 4:4) and his *genomenos hyper hēmōn katara* (Gal 3:13). In Gal 4:4-5 the means of Jesus' redemption is his humanity and his submission to the law (cf Rom 5:19), whereas in Gal 3:13 the means of redemption is his *genomenos hyper hēmōn katara*.[20] We have here an allusion to the suffering servant passages in Isaiah.[21] Christ by becoming a curse on our behalf and also in our place, redeems us from the curse of the law.[22]

4.1.4 GALATIANS 2:19-21

The Christian through the law has died to the law (*egō gar dia nomou nomǭ apethanon*, Gal 2:19). The Christian has died to the law (*nomǭ apethanon*, Gal 2:19; *hymeis ethanatōthēte tǭ nomǭ*, Rom 7:4) just as he has died to sin (*apethanomen tę̄ hamartią*, Rom 6:2; cf v 10); and just as he is dead to sin (*nekrous ... tę̄ hamartią*, Rom 6:11) so by analogy he is dead to the law. He has died to the law because he has been crucified with Christ (*Christǭ synestaurōmai*, Gal 2:20). Just as being crucified with Christ (*synestaurōthē*, Rom 6:6) means that he is no longer enslaved to sin (*tou mēketi douleuein hēmas tę̄ hamartią*, Rom 6:6) so by analogy it means that he is no longer enslaved to the law; he has died to the law and belongs to Christ (*eis to genesthai hymas heterǭ*, Rom 7:4).

---

[20] Franz-Josef Ortkemper, *Das Kreuz in der Verkündigung des Apostles Paulus* (Stuttgart: Katholisches Bibelwerk, 1967), 17, notes that a comparison of these two verses reveals a close connection between the idea of representation or substitution (*Stellvertretung*) and the OT idea of corporate solidarity (*altbiblischen Solidaritätsgedanken*).

[21] See Joachim Jeremias, "Pais Theou," TDNT V 678-717, 706, 710.

[22] *Hyper hymōn* does not in itself imply substitution. R. E. Davies, "Christ in our Place - The Contribution of the Prepositions," TynBul 21 (1970) 81-90 (cf. BAGD "hyper," 838-39), however, lists a number of passages in classical Greek (Thucydides I:141; Plato Gorgias 515C and Republic 590a; Xenophon Anabasis 7.4.9-10; Euripides Alcestis 689-701) and the LXX (Deut 24:16; Isa 43:3-4; Judith 8:12) where the idea of substitution is implied. In the Papyri there is an abundant use of *hyper* in the situation where one man has written a statement for someone else who was illiterate (ibid., 83). In the NT the translation of *hyper* as "instead of" or "in place of" makes good sense in the following passages: Rom 9:3; 1 Cor 15:29; Phlm 13; John 11:50-51; 1 Pet 2:21; 3:18; Rom 5:6-8; 2 Cor 5:14, 21; Tit 2:14; 1 Tim 2:6. Note the *hyper hēmōn* in Gal 3:13; 2 Cor 5:14, 21.

This view of *hyper* in Gal 3:13, although emphatically denied by Burton, *Galatians*, ad. loc., 171-72, is held by the following authors: Bultmann, *Theology* I, 296-7; Bonnard, *Galates*, ad. loc., 69; Guthrie, *Galatians*, ad. loc., 193; Schlier, *Galater*, ad. loc. 139; and Oepke, ad loc., 74-5. Ortkemper (*Kreuz*, 16) puts it this way: "*Hyper hēmōn* gibt den Grund dieses Geschehens an: an unserer Stelle und damit uns zugute; oder umgekehrt: uns zugute, weil an unserer Stelle."

Dying to the law, furthermore, takes place (*dia nomou*). This phrase does not mean that, since it cannot be fulfilled, the law exposes man to his sinfulness and points to the grace of Christ.[23] Nor does it mean, by analogy with Rom 7:9-11, that the law leads to sin which in turn causes the death of man, and that through death man is absolved from the law.[24] Nor can law be understood in two different senses here;[25] under this view *nomō̧* would refer to the Mosaic law and *nomou* to the *nomos tou pneumatos* (Rom 8:2) and the *nomou pisteōs* (Rom 3:27). The believer's death to the law, rather, takes place *dia nomou* because Christ was born under law (*genomenon ek gynaikos, genomenon hypo nomon*) (Gal 4:4), lived a life of obedience to the law, and died under the curse of the law. By becoming a curse (*katara*) he redeemed those who were under the *tēs kataras tou nomou* (Gal 3:13).[26] Since this death to the law *dia nomou* involves the incarnation and death of Christ, he can also say that it takes place *dia tou sōmatos tou Christou* (Rom 7:4).[27 & 28]

4.1.5 EXCURSUS ON DIA (EK) PISTEŌS IĒSOU CHRISTOU

Traditionally the phrases *dia (ek) pisteōs (Iēsou) Christou* (Rom 3:22; Gal 2:16; 3:22; Phil 3:9), *dia pisteōs Christou Iēsou* (Gal 2:16), and *ek pisteōs Iēsou* (Rom 3:26) were regarded as objective genitives and understood as "faith in

---

[23] Lightfoot, *Galatians*, 118. Burton, *Galatians*, ad. loc, 132-35; and Zahn, *Galater*, ad. loc., 123.

[24] Against Schweitzer, *Mysticism*, 188 n. 2.

[25] Against M. J. Lagrange, *Saint Paul Épître aux Galates* (Paris: J. Gabalda, 1950), ad. loc., 51.

[26] This is the view of Ortkemper, *Kreuz* 20-22; van Dülmen, *Gesetz* 26; Schlier, *Galater*, 98-101; Osten-Sacken, *Römer 8*, 190-191; Tannehill, *Dying and Rising*, 58-59; Wilckens, *Entwicklung*, 169-71 et. al. For the above summary on *dia nomou* see van Dülmen, *Gesetz*, 25-26.

[27] Passages besides Rom 6:1-23; 7:4-6 and Gal 2:19-20 which contain the idea of dying and/or rising with Christ are Gal 5:24-25; 6:14-15; 2 Cor 5:14-17; Col 2-3. See Tannehill, *Dying and Rising*, 50-55, 61-69.

[28] In Col 2:14 the clause *exaleipsas to kath' hēmōn cheirographon tois dogmasin ho ēn hypenantion hēmin* is problematical - especially the force of the dative *tois dogmasin*. Percy, *Probleme*, 89-90 argues that it is to be taken with the following clause to avoid superfluous repetition of *kath' hēmōn*. A second view is that of Bengel, Theodoret, and Chrysostom (cf Gerhard Kittel, "Dogma," TDNT II 230-32, 231) who take the dative as instrumental and link it with *exaleipsas*, thus making the *dogmata* the new command or edict of God.

A third view, however, seems preferable. Robinson, *Body*, 43 n. 1 interprets '*to ... cheirographon tois dogmasin*' as "our superscription to the ordinances." Thus it would be an example of a noun with a dative attribute; cf Nigel Turner, *Syntax*. Vol III of James Hope Moulton, *A Grammar of New Testament Greek* (4 Vols. Edinburgh: T. & T. Clark, 1963), 219. The *cheirographon* is, then, "our written agreement to keep the law, our certificate of debt to it." Our failure to keep the law has turned this certificate into a bond held against us to prove our guilt. It is, therefore, the charge which the law brings rather than the law itself which is cancelled by Christ.

Jesus (Christ)."[29] In more recent times, however, they have been understood by some to be in various ways a subjective (or both a subjective and an objective) genitive.[30] Richard Longenecker has argued that the phrase should be understood as a subjective genitive, as "the faithfulness of Jesus Christ." He connects this phrase with the obedience of Christ in Rom 5:19 (Phil 2:5-11) and stresses thereby that Christ met the full obligation of the law.[31]

Several arguments can be made in support of the "subjective genitive" view. D. W. B. Robinson[32] notes that neither Moulton-Milligan nor the ninth edition of LSJ give an example of *pistis* with the objective genitive;[33] nor is there any such usage in the LXX. Robinson further agrees with George Howard that in the twenty-four references in Paul where *pistis* followed by the genitive occurs - apart from *pistis Christou* or its equivalents - the phrase refers to the faith of the person, and never faith in a person.[34] Of the twenty-eight passages outside the Pauline corpus where *pistis* is followed by the genitive of the person or a personal pronoun, in only seven passages (Mark 11:22; Jas 2:1; Rev 2:13; 14:12; Acts 3:16; Col 2:12; 2 Thess 2:13) is an objective genitive possible, and in none of these is it demanded.[35]

If, then, the phrase *pistis Christou* and its equivalents in Paul are to be considered as subjective genitives, they could refer on purely linguistic grounds either to the "faith of Christ" or to the "faithfulness of Christ." Several linguistic considerations leave open the possibility that *pistis* here means "faithfulness." Rudolf Bultmann observes that in Greek literature *pistis* should sometimes be

---

[29] Sanday & Headlam, *Romans*, 83, note that up to their time it had been almost universally understood as an objective genitive.

[30] For a summary of these views see especially Markus Barth, "The Faith of the Messiah" HeyJ 10(1969) 363-370, 364 n. 2; D. W. B. Robinson, "Faith of Jesus Christ - A New Testament Debate," *The Reformed Theological Review*, 29 (1970) 71-81; BAGD "pistis," s.v. 662-65; Longenecker, *Paul* 149-151; Richard N. Longenecker, "The Obedience of Christ in The Theology of the Early Church," in *Reconciliation and Hope: New Testament Essays on Atonement and Eschatology Presented to L. L. Morris on his 60th Birthday* (ed. Robert Banks. Grand Rapids: Eerdmans, 1974) 146-149; Sam K. Williams, "The Righteousness of God in Romans," JBL 99 (1980) 241-290, 272-290.; Luke Timothy Johnson, "Romans 3:21-26 and the Faith of Jesus," CBQ 44 (1982) 77-90, 85-86; and Hayes, *Faith*, 160-162. For a summary of the debate at the end of the nineteenth century and the beginning of the twentieth century see Hayes, *Faith*, 158-160. For further bibliography see Bruce, *Galatians*, 138-9.

[31] Longenecker, *Paul*, 149-151; cf *Obedience*, 146-149.

[32] Robinson, *Faith*, 78.

[33] J. H. Moulton, and G. Milligan, *The Vocabulary of the Greek New Testament* (London: Hodder and Stoughton, 1930), and LSJ. In earlier editions of LSJ, however, two examples with the objective genitive were given.

[34] Robinson, *Faith*, 78; George E. Howard, "On the 'Faith of Christ'," HTR 60 (1967), 459-465.

[35] Robinson, *Faith*, 78-79.

translated as "faithfulness" or "reliability."[36] Artur Weiser[37] indicates that behind the *pisteuein* word group in the LXX, the Hebrew stem *'mn* is the most important qualitative (although not the most important quantitative) word.

In the actual Pauline usage of *pistis*, the idea of firmness or faithfulness cannot - especially in 2 Thess 1:4, where the phrase *tēs hypomonēs hymōn kai pisteōs en pasin tois diōgmois hymōn* is linked with the single definite article *tēs* - be excluded from the *pistis* of the Thessalonian Christians (i.e., 1 Thess 1:3, 8; 3:2, 5, 6, 7, 10; 5:8; 2 Thess 1:3, 11; 2:13; 3:2).[38] At Rom 3:3, moreover, the phrase *tēn pistin tou theou* refers to the faithfulness of God. In Romans faith and obedience are closely linked. It begins and ends with the aim that all nations might respond to the gospel with the "obedience of faith" (*eis hypakoēn pisteōs*) (1:5; 16:26). In Romans it is important to respond to the Gospel not only with faith but also with obedience (6:16-19; 10:16; 15:18).[39]

The phrases *eis pantas tous pisteuontas* (Rom 3:22), *tois pisteuousin* (Gal 3:22), and *epi tę̄ pistei* (Phil 3:9) are redundant if *pisteōs Christou* or its equivalents mean "faith in Christ." Against this argument one might say that they are placed there for emphasis.[40]

In the context of each of the passages where *pisteōs Christou* or its equivalents occur, *nomos* is explicitly mentioned; the phrase stands in contrast to *nomou* (Rom 3:22), *ek nomou* (Phil 3:9; Gal 3:21), *ex ergōn nomou* (Gal 2:16, bis). It is possible to say that one is "justified" (*dikaioō*, Gal 2:16), receives righteousness (*dikaiosynē*, Gal 3:22) and the righteousness of God (*dikaiosynē de theou*, Rom 3:22; *tēn ek theou dikaiosynēn*, Phil 3:9), not by observance of the law, but by the faithfulness of Christ. But it makes even better sense to say that they come not by observance of the law but through "faith in Christ." This contrast agrees well with the contrast between "faith" and "works (of law)" elsewhere in Paul (Rom 3:20, 27, 28; 4:2, 6; 9:3:32; Gal 3:2, 5; cf Eph 2:8, 9).

Paradoxically, if the faith and law statements are applied to Christ as opposed to us there is a sense in which they are not antithetical. There is a sense in which Christ brings us salvation by his faithfulness. But he also opens up the way to salvation for us by means of the law. He was "born of woman, born under the law, so that we might receive adoption as sons." (4:4-5). He "has redeemed us from the curse of the law having become a curse for us" (3:13).

---

[36] see Rudolf Bultmann, "Pisteuō," TDNT VI, 174-82, 197-228, pp. 176-77, 182; and BAGD 660-62.

[37] Artur Weiser, "pisteuō," TDNT VI 182-196, 188-90, 196.

[38] cf. Robinson, *Faith* 176-77.

[39] See L.T. Johnson, *Romans 3:21-26*, 85-6; cf Hayes, *Faith*, 139-191.

[40] Murray, *Romans* I, 112 claims that in Rom 3:22 *dia pisteōs Iēsou* stresses that salvation is only by faith and *eis pantas tous pisteuontas* stresses that it is always operative where there is faith. This argument, though, cannot apply to Gal 3:22 and Phil 3:9, since in those texts *panta* does not occur.

Strong arguments against the "subjective genitive" view have been given by Arland J. Hultgren.[41] He observes that whenever the phrase *pistis Christou* or its equivalents occur the article is lacking before both nouns. In Gal 2:16 the parenthetical clause (*kai hēmeis eis Christon Iēsoun episteusamen*) interprets the preceding and following *dia (ek) pisteōs (Iēsou) Christou*. Whenever Paul uses the prepositions *dia*, *ek*, or *en* followed by *pistis* in the absolute, it is the believer's faith that is in mind. The genitive of quality (under the influence of Hebrew and Aramaic) is frequent in the New Testament; *ek (en, dia) pisteōs Christou* qualifies or defines the believer's faith as being in Christ.[42] Longenecker's view, therefore, should probably by rejected.

Richard Hayes would go much further than seeing the genitives as a reference to the faithfulness of Christ. He claims that only at Gal 2:16 (= *hēmeis eis Christon Iēsoun episteusamen*) do we explicitly have faith in Jesus Christ mentioned. We do not have it explicitly mentioned in Gal 3-4 or in Romans.[43]

He believes that *ex ergōn nomou* and *ex akoēs pisteōs* present a contrast between human and divine activity, not human and human activity; *ex akoēs pisteōs* (3:2) does not refer to a human response but to the message of faith.[44] On the basis of parallels from Hebrews and the LXX and on the basis Abraham's seed being Christ (3:16), *ho dikaios ek pisteōs zēsetai* in 3:11 should be understood messianically.[45] Thus the messiah is justified and gains life by his own faith and not by law.[46] The same principle must therefore attain to Christ's people.[47] Abraham is not the prototype of the justified believer for Abraham believes in God not in Christ (Gal 3:6).[48] Christ is not the object of Abraham's faith; Abraham's faith is a foreshadowing of Christ's faith.[49] *Hoi ek pisteōs* (3:7, 9) does not primarily mean "those who have faith" but "those who are given life because of Christ's faith"[50] or because of Abraham's faith.[51]

Hayes' arguments are not convincing. Paul does explicitly talk about believing in Christ both in Galatians and in Romans (Gal 2:16; Rom 9:33; 10:11). The gospel does not become effective in us unless there is the proper

---

[41] Arland J. Hultgren, "The *Pistis Christou* Formulation in Paul," NovT 22 (1980) 249-263.

[42] Hultgren, *Pistis Christou*, 253-258.

[43] Hayes, *Faith*, 142, 169.

[44] Hayes, *Faith*, 143-149.

[45] Hayes, *Faith*, 150-57.

[46] Hayes, *Faith*, 165, 207, 209.

[47] Hayes, *Faith*, 207.

[48] Hayes, *Faith*, 165, 196.

[49] Hayes, *Faith*, 202.

[50] Hayes, *Faith*, 201.

[51] Hayes, *Faith*, 202-205, esp 202, 205.

human response. It must be received (Rom 5:17). *Ex akoēs pisteōs* should be understood in light of the similar phrase *eis hypakoēn pisteōs* (Rom 1:5; 16:26). In both cases it refers to receiving as opposed to rejecting the gospel. To receive the Spirit *ex ergōn nomou* (Gal 3:2) would be to reject the gospel (cf 2:21).

Ho dikaios ek pisteōs zēsetai has its closest parallel not in Hebrews or the LXX but in Rom 1:17, and there it is not messianic. Christ's task in Galatians is not to secure justification or life for himself but to bring salvation to us (1:5; 2:21; 3:13; 4:4, 5; 5:1; 6:14).

While we must read Galatians on its own terms it should give us pause when we are confronted with conclusions that seem so radically different from Romans. Abraham of course believed God (3:6); but in this context he believes in the promise of God, the promise that "in you (*en soi*) shall all nations be blessed" (3:8 = Gen 12:3). Paul later clarifies that this promise is made not only to Abraham but to Christ his seed (3:16). All nations are blessed in Christ because of his atoning death (3:13, 14). They are blessed in Abraham because they are blessed in Christ, Abraham's seed. In this context Abraham has to believe in his seed (Christ). At Gal 3:19 the promised seed is Christ; the statement that the law "was added ... until the offspring (*to sperma*) should come to whom the promise had been made" (3:19) is another way of saying that the law was added until Christ, God's promise to Abraham, should come (see 3:24). That Abraham had faith in Christ is also indicated by the fact that the gospel was preached beforehand (*proeuēngelisato*) to Abraham (3:8; cf Rom 4:13). Similarly in Rom 1:3-4 the subject matter of the God's gospel is Jesus Christ; this gospel God "promised beforehand through his prophets in the holy scriptures" (Rom 1:2). In the context of Galatians the content of the Gospel which is preached to the Gentiles is Christ (Gal 1:6, 8; 2:20; see Rom 1:2-4) and the Holy Spirit (cf 3:2, 3, 5, 14; 4:6). The Holy Spirit is closely identified with Christ for it is "the Spirit of his [God's] Son" (4:6).

The *hoi ek pisteōs* (3:7, 9; cf 3:8) are sons of Abraham because they like Abraham have faith in Christ. These are opposed to those who are *hoi ek nomou* (see Rom 4:14) or *hoi ex ergōn nomou* (cf 3:2, 5).

4.2 PARTICIPATION IN THE RESURRECTION OF CHRIST

4.2.1 LIFE

The death and resurrection of Christ, then, puts an end to man's bondage to law, sin, and death. By baptism into Christ's death (Rom 6:3-4) "we have died with Christ" (*apethanomen syn Christǭ*, Rom 6:8) and according to this logic "we shall also live with him" (*syzēsomen autǭ*, 6:8). The believer not only participates in the death of Christ, he is also destined to participate in the resurrection of Christ and, in fact, is already "alive to God in Christ Jesus" (*zōntas de tǭ theǭ en Christǭ Iēsou*, 6:11). The believer's ultimate participation is future,[52] but there is also a present aspect.[53] Believers, then, "should yield" themselves "to God as men who have been brought from death to life" (*parastēsate heautous tǭ theǭ hōsei ek nekrōn zōntas*, 6:13). Just as Christ was raised from the dead by the glory of the Father, the believer, too, is to walk in newness of life (*hina hōsper ēgerthē Christos ek nekrōn dia tēs doxēs tou patros, houtōs kai hēmeis en kainotēti zōēs peripatēsōmen*, Rom 6:4). In Christ he has God's gift - the life of the age to come (*to de charisma tou theou zōē aiōnios en Christǭ Iēsou tǭ kyriǭ hēmōn*, Rom 6:23; cf 5:21, 6:22). In his body he bears the death of Jesus so that the life of Jesus may be manifested in it (*pantote tēn nekrōsin tou Iēsou en tǭ sōmati peripherontes hina kai hē zōē tou Iēsou en tǭ sōmati hēmōn phanerōthę̄*, 2 Cor 4:10). Since he has been crucified with Christ he no longer lives, but Christ lives in him (*Christǭ synestaurōmai zō de ouketi egō, zę̄ de en emoi Christos*, Gal 2:20). He has died to the law so that he might live to God (*hina theǭ zēsō*, Gal 2:19), and bear fruit for God (*hina karpophorēsōmen tǭ theǭ*, Rom 7:4). Since he is no longer captive to the law he no longer serves under the old written code but in the new life of the Spirit (*hōste douleuein hēmas en kainotēti pneumatos kai ou palaiotēti grammatos*, Rom 7:6). It is the written code which kills but the Spirit which gives life (*to gar gramma apoktennei, to de pneuma zǭopoiei*, 2 Cor 3:6).

In direct opposition to the Jewish view that eternal life comes through observance of the Torah[54] these texts indicate that it is the believer's

---

[52] This future aspect is stressed in such passages as Rom 6:6, 8, 10, 11; 1 Cor 15:20, 22; 6:14; 2 Cor 4:14.

[53] See Gundry, *Sōma*, 57. He argues that the exhortations in Rom 6:4, 11, 13 imply the historicalness of the believer's resurrection with Christ but the point of 6:8 is to stress that the expectation of future resurrection is not cancelled. The present aspect of the believer's participation is especially brought out in Col 2:12; 3:1, 3. On dying and rising with Christ in Ephesians and Colossians see Tannehill, *Dying and Rising*, 47-54.

[54] See Pirke Aboth 6:7; Pss Sol 14:2; Bar 3:9; Lev Rab 18:3; Exod Rab 32:1; t. Sabb 15:17. See Betz, *Galatians*, 174; Moo, *Rom 7:7-12*, 134 n. 47; Schoeps, *Paul*, 175.; E. E. Urbach, *Sages*, I, 424-5.

E. P. Sanders has argued for a "covenantal nomism" in early Judaism. The elect are saved already and continue in that state so long as they truly repent of transgressions as they arise. (E. P. Sanders, "Patterns of Religion in Paul and Rabbinic Judaism: A Holistic Method of Comparison," HTR 66 (1973), 458-76; E. P. Sanders, *Palestinian Judaism*, 75, 236, 422-28) He argues that for Judaism and for Paul one must do works of law to stay saved. (Sanders, *Jewish People*, 105-113) Sanders' view of covenantal nomism in Judaism has been criticized by Jacob Neusner, but convincingly answered by Alan Segal. See Alan F. Segal, "Covenant in Rabbinic Writings," SR 14 (1985) 53-62 and the Sanders-Neusner debate in W. S. Green (ed.), *Approaches to Ancient Judaism* Vol. 2 (Missoula, MT: Scholars Press, 1980), 43-80. I argued above 98-99 n. 160 (cf below 147-149) that in Paul good works, or works of law, are are the sign of being saved and are not the condition of staying saved. See also Gundry, *Grace*, 1-38. I noted also that in Judaism good works or works of law are at least needed to activate God's covenant (cf above 95).

For early Judaism there is no present salvation in a Pauline sense. The Messiah has not yet participation in the resurrection of Christ which imparts life to him. They also indicate that *zaō* and *zōē* in the context of the law refer to eschatological life, and are equivalent to (*zōē aiōnios*).[55]

4.2.2 SPIRIT

These texts (Rom 7:4-6; 2 Cor 3:6; 1 Cor 15:45), as well as others (e.g., Rom 8:2, 10-13; Gal 5:25; 6:8) indicate that for Paul if one has eternal life he also has the Spirit, and vice versa. That being a Christian is correlative with having the Spirit is also indicated in such passages as Rom 2:29; 5:5; 8:4, 5, 6, 9, 14-16, 23; 14:17; 1 Cor 6:11; 12:13; 2 Cor 5:5; Gal 3:2, 3, 5, 14; 4:6, 29; 5:5, 16, 25; 6:8.

4.2.3 RIGHTEOUSNESS

Paul links righteousness and life. One cannot have righteousness without having life nor life without having righteousness. This inseparable link is indicated in several passages. In the pre-Pauline faith formula cited in Rom 4:25 "who was put to death for our trespasses and raised for our justification" (*hos paredothē dia ta paraptōmata hēmōn kai ēgerthē dia tēn dikaiōsin hēmōn*), the vocabulary of "raise," "resurrect," and "right-" (*dik-*) are already conjoined. This correlation calls for us to exploit the Pauline themes of righteousness in order to grasp Paul's theology of the resurrection and the role of the resurrection in breaking man's bondage to sin, death, and the law.

In full accord with the thought of Rom 4:25, but going beyond it, Paul declares in Gal 3:21 that "If a law had been given which could *make alive* (*ho dynamenos zōopoiēsai*), then righteousness (*hē dikaiosynē*) would indeed be by the law." That is, if an *A* (nomos) had been given which could produce *B* (*zōopoiēsai*) then *B* (*dikaiosynē*) would have been by *A* (*nomos*). Thus in Paul *zōopoiēsai* and *dikaioō* are correlated.

Dikaiosynē can be a virtual equivalent for life or salvation since the phrase *eis dikaiosynēn* is contrasted with *eis thanaton* and compared with *eis sōtērian*. The Christian is an obedient slave of the one he obeys, either of sin *eis thanaton* or of obedience *eis dikaiosynēn* Rom 6:16);. A man believes with his heart *eis dikaiosynēn* and with his mouth confession is made *eis sōtērian* (Rom 10:10).[56]

---

come and the Spirit has not yet been given. The belief that salvation comes through the atoning death and resurrection of the Messiah is foreign to them. To attain future salvation they must remain in the covenant and do works of law.

[55] Against Moo, *Rom 7:7-12*, 125, 128, 132.

[56] At Rom 8:10, however, it is connected with *zōē* in the same way that *hamartia* is connected with *nekros*. The phrase *eis dikaiosynēn* also occurs at Rom 4:3, 5, 9, 22; Gal 3:6.

Although righteousness and life are linked it does not follow that they are identical. *Dikaiosynē* is not only contrasted with *thanatos* but also with the legal term *katakrisis* (2 Cor 3:9) - although it is true that the *katakrisis* ends in death - and with such ethical terms as *adikia* (Rom 6:13-14),[57] *anomia* (2 Cor 6:14; Rom 6:19) *akatharsia* (Rom 6:19) and *hamartia* (Rom 6:18, 20; 8:10).

4.2.3.1 RIGHTEOUSNESS AND ROM 5:12-21

To understand the connection between *zōē* and *dikaiosynē* it will be of benefit to have a clear understanding of Rom 5:12-21. Hans Wilhelm Schmidt[58] points out that *dia touto* (5:12) refers back to the *sōthēsometha en tę̄ zōē autou* (5:10). Paul's thought on the saving power of the resurrection of Christ (5:10) provides the occasion for giving an extended comparison between Adam who initiates a process that culminates in death, and Christ who initiates a process that culminates in life (Rom 5:12-21; cf 1 Cor 15:21-22). It is Adam's one *hamartia* (5:12) (which as we have seen is in terms of law)[59] and one *paraptōma* (5:15, 16, 17, 18) which brings condemnation (*eis katakrima*, 5:16; *eis pantas anthrōpous eis katakrima*, 5:18) and death (*eis pantas anthrōpous ho thanatos dielthen*, 5:12; *hoi polloi apethanon*, 5:15; *ho thanatos ebasileusen*, 5:17; *ho thanatos ebasileusen hē hamartia en tǭ thanatǭ*, 5:21) to all men. It is Adam's disobedience (*parakoē*) which makes the many *sinners* (*hamartōloi*); it is Christ's obedience (*hypakoē*) which makes the many *righteous* (*dikaioi*, Rom 5:19).[60] Instead of Adam's *paraptōma* (5:15, 17, 18) Christ brings the *to charisma* (v 15a), the *hē charis tou theou kai hē dōrea en chariti* (5:15b), the *tēn perisseian tēs charitos kai tēs dōreas tēs dikaiosynēs* (v 17), and the *dikaiōma* (18). Instead of condemnation (*katakrima*, 5:16, 18) Christ brings the *dikaiōma* (v 16) and the *dikaiōsin zōēs* (5:18); and instead of death Christ brings life (*en zōę̄ basileusousin*, 5:17; *hē charis basileusę̄ dia dikaiosynēs eis zōēn aiōnion*, 5:21).

In this process which culminates in life in Rom 5:12-21, the *dikaios* word-group, occurs six times (*dikaios*, once 5:19; *dikaiōsis*, once, 5:18;

[57] Cf. *hē adikia hēmōn* versus *theou dikaiosynēn* (Rom 3:5).

[58] Schmidt, *Römer*, ad. loc., 97. Käsemann, *Romans*, ad. loc., 146 notes that if one sees the *dia touto* merely as a transitional particle, as Zahn (ad. loc., 259-60.), Lagrange (ad. loc.), and C. K. Barrett (ad. loc., 110) do, he overlooks the thought break which leads to a new argument. Käsemann sees Schmidt's interpretation as a possibility, but does not overlook the possibility of the view of Michel, *Römer*, ad. loc., 137 that it refers back to Rom 5:1-11 in its totality.

[59] If the *hamartia* is to be understood in terms of law, then the other terms for sin - i.e., *paraptōma*, *parabasis*, *parakoē* (and its opposite *hypakoē*) - and the sentence (*katakrima*) imposed are to be understood in terms of law as well. See above 72-74.

[60] See above 115-118 on the possible connection between Christ's faithfulness and his obedience to the law.

dikaiōma, twice, 5:16, 18; and *dikaiosynē*, twice, 5:17, 21), and, like *dikaiosynē* in the previous cases, the meanings seem to overlap between the judicial, the ethical, and the vital.

In 5:19 the *dikaioi* are contrasted with the *hamartōloi* (an ethical term); the status of the latter, however, is one which issues in death, and is the result of Adam's disobedience in terms of law; by contrast the status of the former is one which (in context) issues in life,[61] and is the result of Christ's obedience in terms of law.

Dikaiōma in 5:18 is contrasted with *paraptōma* and used synonymously with *hypakoē* (5:19). It seems, therefore, to refer to a right act in favor of a legal requirement.[62] In 5:16, however, *dikaiōma* (along with the other words which end in *-ma* - *dōrēma, krima, katakrima, charisma*, and *paraptōma*) is used for rhetorical effect[63] and is contrasted with *katakrima*; it seems, then, to refer to the sentence of justification and to be a synonym of *dikaiōsis*.[64]

In 5:18 the expression which is contrasted with *katakrima* - and which is the result of Christ's just act (*dikaiōma*) - is not *dikaiōma* (as in 5:16) or merely *dikaiōsis* (sentence of justification),[65] but *dikaiōsin zōēs*.[66] Just as on the divine side (in contrast to the human) the sentence and its result (death) cannot be distinguished in the word *katakrima*,[67] it also seems to be true that Paul cannot

[61] Although the emphasis is on the phrase *ek pisteōs* in the clause *ho de dikaios ek pisteōs zēsetai* (Rom 1:17; Gal 3:11), it is still the just (*dikaios*) who will live (*zēsetai*).

[62] Gottlob Schrenk, "dikaiōma," TDNT II 219-22, 221 notes that *di' henos* (v 18), in agreement with its other occurrences in 5:12-19, is to be read as masculine rather than neuter. Thus Christ, placed under the law (Gal 4:4), fulfilled it negatively by having no knowledge of sin (2 Cor 5:21) and positively by obedience unto death (Phil 2:8).

[63] According to BDF, 259 constructs in *-ma* "belong to the dainties of Hell. artists of style." Cf. also BAGD, "dikaiōma," 198.

[64] Cf. Schrenk, "dikaiōma," TDNT II, 222. For a summary of the various views on the meaning of *dikaiōma* in 5:16, 18 see Käsemann, *Romans*, 154, 156.

[65] This is the substantive which corresponds to the verb *dikaioō*.

[66] *Dikaiōsis* occurs elsewhere in Paul only at Rom 4:25, and there it is linked with the resurrection. The clause *paredothē dia ta paraptōmata hēmōn* is parallel to *ēgerthē dia tēn dikaiōsin hēmōn*. Schrenk ("dikaiōsis," TDNT II, 224) notes that if the second *dia* is interpreted causally, the sense is against the example of Abraham whose justification is the result of faith in God who raises the dead. It is best, therefore, not to view both *dia*'s as causal, or the first as causal and the second as final (contra Käsemann, *Romans*, ad. loc., 129; Schmidt, *Römer*, ad. loc., 88; Gottlob Schrenk, "dikaiōsis," TDNT II, 223-24, 224). Rather, since the clauses are parallel, both *dia*'s are final. Christ was thus delivered up to atone for our transgressions and raised in order that we might be justified. *Dikaiōsis*, appears, then, to be a gift of the resurrected Christ. This seems to agree with Rom 5:10 where reconciliation (*katallagentes*) comes through the death of Christ, and salvation (*sōthēsometha*) comes through his resurrection life (*zōē*). Cf. Schmidt, *Römer*, 88.

For a summary of the discussion on the liturgical derivation of Rom 4:25, cf. Käsemann, *Romans*, ad. loc., 128.

[67] See Büchsel, "katakrinō," TDNT III, 951-52.

think of the sentence of justification without having in mind its result (*zōē*). The phrase, therefore, means either justification which is life[68] or justification which issues in life;[69] at any rate, *dikaiōsis* and *zōē* are correlative.

Dikaiosynē is another of the *dikaios* group of words in Rom 5:12-21. In this passage it too is related to life although it is unclear in precisely what sense it is related. The genitive *tēs dōreas tēs dikaiosynēs* (Rom 5:17) seems to be epexegetic;[70] it is those who receive the gift which is righteousness who will reign in life. In 5:21 the contrast perhaps centers around the prepositions *en ... eis*[71] rather than *en ... dia*;[72] the opposite of *en tō̧ thanatō̧*, then, is *eis zōēn aiōnion* rather than *dia dikaiosynēs eis zōēn aiōnion*.

In the preceding texts *dikaiosynē* can have a judicial, an ethical, and a vital aspect. It is contrasted with such terms as *thanatos*, *katakrisis*, *adikia*, *anomia*, *akatharsia*, and *hamartia*, and is compared with *zōē* and *sōtēria*.

4.2.3.2 RIGHTEOUSNESS AND SALVATION

The righteousness which the Christian receives is intimately bound up with the salvation that God has provided in Christ. We cannot have *dikaiosynē* by means of the law (Gal 2:21; 3:21; cf Phil 3:9); to attain it this way would mean that Christ had died in vain (Gal 2:21). To Those who receive it, it is a free gift that God bestows (*hoi ... tēs dōreas tēs dikaiosynēs lambanontes*) (Rom 5:17). The Jews in contrast to the Gentiles tried but failed to obtain it on the basis of works rather than faith in Christ (Rom 9:30-33). We receive it by faith in the work that God did in Christ (Rom 10:6-10). God reckons righteousness (*logizetai ... eis dikaiosynēn*) (Rom 4:5, 6; cf 4:12) to everyone on the same basis which he reckoned it *(elogisthē ... eis dikaiosynēn*) (Gal 3:6; Rom 4:3, 9, 22; cf 4:9-13, 23) to Abraham, that is on the basis of his faith in God apart from works. To have it reckoned to us (Rom 4:3, 5) is equivalent to being justified (*edikaiōthē*, Rom 4:2; *ton dikaiounta*, Rom 4:2, 5). We not only receive righteousness in the present, but through the Spirit by faith we have hope for it in the future (*elpida dikaiosynēs*) (Gal 5:5).

4.2.3.3 RIGHTEOUSNESS AND THE CHRISTIAN LIFE

In these texts the righteousness which we receive from God as a gift can refer to the right standing that God gives to us, and need not refer to an ethical quality of righteousness which he gives to us. But the ethical quality which God

[68] The view of Käsemann, *Romans*, 156; Schmidt, *Römer*, ad. loc., 102, et. al.

[69] The view of Black, *Romans*, ad. loc., 91; Bruce, *Romans*, ad. loc., 133; Murray, *Romans*, ad. loc., 202; Ridderbos, *Paul* 161; et. al.

[70] See Käsemann, *Romans* ad. loc., 155.

[71] See Schmidt, *Römer* ad. loc., 103.

[72] Lietzmann, *Römer*, ad. loc., 65.

gives to us seems to be present at Phil 1:11 where we are to be "filled with the fruits of righteousness which come through Jesus Christ."[73] The Christian is exhorted to live a life characterized by righteousness on the basis of a real change which has taken place within him. He is a new creation in Christ (2 Cor 5:17), he is not in the flesh but in the spirit (Rom 8:4-9). He has died to sin (Rom 6). Since he is dead to sin and alive to God (Rom 6:11) he is to live a life characterized by righteousness (Rom 6:13, 17-19).

4.2.3.4 THE RIGHTEOUSNESS OF GOD

"The righteousness (*dikaiosynē*) of God" is a term which is closely related to *dikaiosynē*.[74] Just as man's faithlessness cannot nullify the faithfulness of God (*tēn pistin tou theou*) so man's wickedness (*adikia*) cannot nullify the righteousness of God (*theou dikaiosynēn*) (Rom 3:3, 5). The gospel is the power of God unto salvation, and in it the righteousness of God is being revealed for those who have faith (*dikaiosynē ... theou en autǭ apokalyptetai ek pisteōs eis pistin* (Rom 1:16, 17). But for those who have rejected God, the wrath of God is being revealed (*apokalyptetai ... gar orgē theou*) (Rom 1:18).

In a situation where all are under the power of sin (Rom 3:9) and the law makes the whole world guilty before God (Rom 3:19), the righteousness of God has now been revealed apart from the law (*nyni de chōris nomou dikaiosynē theou pephanerōtai*) and comes *dia pisteōs Iēsou Christou, eis pantas tous pisteuontas* (Rom 3:21, 22). God justifies us freely by his grace through the redemption that is in Christ Jesus (3:24) and shows his righteousness (*endeixin tēs dikaiosynēs autou*) by passing over former sins and by setting forth Christ as a sacrifice of atonement (*hilastērion dia tēs pisteōs en tǭ autou haimati*) (Rom 3:25). He now (*en tǭ nyn kairǭ*) shows his righteousness (*endeixin dikaiosynēs autou*) so that he might be just and the justifier (*eis to einai dikaion kai dikaiounta ton ek pisteōs Iēsou Christou*) (Rom 3:26).

The problem with the Jew is that he is ignorant of the righteousness that comes from God (*tēn tou theou dikaiosynēn*); he seeks to establish his own righteousness, and does not submit to the righteousness of God (*tę̄ dikaiosynę̄ tou theou*) (Rom 10:3). But Paul has rejected his former Jewish view of things and now prays that he may gain Christ and be found in him (Phil 3:8, 9), that he may have a righteousness not of his own based on law (*mē echōn emēn dikaiosynēn tēn ek nomou*) but a righteousness *dia pisteōs Christou*, the

[73] See Eph 4:24 where we are to "put on the new nature created after the likeness of God in true righteousness and holiness."

[74] The term occurs in the following forms in Paul: *dikaiosynē theou*; (Rom 1:17; 3:21, 22; 2 Cor 5:21); *theou dikaiosynēn*; (Rom 3:5); *tēs dikaiosynēs autou* (Rom 3:25, 26); *tēn tou theou dikaiosynēn* (Rom 10:3); *tę̄ dikaiosynę̄ tou theou* (Rom 10:3); *tēn ek theou dikaiosynē* (Phil 3:9); *hē dikaiosynē autou* (2 Cor 9:9).

righteousness from God that depends on faith (*tēn ek theou dikaiosynēn epi tę pistei*) (Phil 3:9).

Frequently in Paul *sōtēria* can be substituted for *dikaiosynē* and tolerably good sense can be made of the passage.[75] In all of the passages where "the righteousness of God" occurs good sense results if we substitute "the salvation of God." Our faithlessness does not nullify the faithfulness of God and God shows forth his salvation in a situation in which we are wicked (Rom 3:5). In the gospel the salvation of God is revealed (Rom 1:17). Now the salvation of God has been manifested apart from the law for all who believe (Rom 3:21-22). Through Christ's sacrificial death God shows forth his salvation (Rom 3:25, 26). Israel being ignorant of the salvation that comes from God and seeking to establish her own has not submitted to God's salvation (Rom 10:3). Paul would like to have that salvation from God that depends on faith (Phil 3:9). God made Christ to be sin for us so that in him we might become the salvation of God (2 Cor 5:21). His salvation endures forever (2 Cor 9:9).[76]

From the preceding discussion it is evident that "the righteousness of God" cannot be limited to the fact that God judges righteously (the pre-Reformation view),[77] yet the idea can be present. When God shows forth his righteousness he is both just and the justifier (Rom 3:26). When God's righteousness is compared to his scattering abroad and giving to the poor (2 Cor 9:9) it refers to his righteous action but this undoubtedly has to stem from his righteous character.

"The righteousness of God" cannot be limited to the righteousness which is valid before God,[78] although the righteousness that one receives from God by faith based on the sacrificial death of Christ is certainly valid before God. God is actively involved in the process of giving righteousness to men.

Bultmann has stressed the gift character of the righteousness of God but exclusively in individualistic terms. He especially bases his view on Rom 10:3 and Phil 3:9. It is a forensic-eschatological term which denotes the new relationship that the individual has with God and not the ethical quality of the person. It means that God does not count man's sin against him (cf 2 Cor 5:19).[79]

---

[75] i.e. at Gal 2:21; 3:16, 21; 5:5; Phil 3:6, 9; Rom 4:3, 5, 6, 9, 11, 13, 22; 5:17 21; 9:30, 31; 10:3, 4, 5, 6, 10.

[76] Cf Wilckens, *Römer* I, 202-208, who interprets the righteousness of God under various aspects of God's act of salvation in Christ.

[77] See Manfred T. Brauch, "Perspectives on 'God's Righteousness' in Recent German Discussion," in E. P. Sanders, *Paul and Palestinian Judaism* (Philadelphia: Fortress, 1977) 523-42, 525.

[78] This is Luther's view; Similar views are held by J. C. O'Neil, *Paul's Letter to The Romans* (Baltimore: Penguin, 1975), 38, 70-72, 168; and Ridderbos, *Paul*, 163; See Brauch, *Righteousness*, 525; Williams, *Righteousness*, 242; J. A. Ziesler, *The Meaning of Righteousness in Paul* (SNTSMS 20; Cambridge: Cambridge University Press, 1972), 12.

[79] Bultmann, *Theology*, I, 270-287; Rudolf Bultmann, "Dikaiosynē Theou," JBL 83 (1964), 212-216. His view has been summarized by Brauch, *Righteousness* 526-7. To some extent Bultmann has been

I agree with him on Phil 3:9 and to some extent on Rom 10:3. At Phil 3:9, where he does not want to be found with a righteousness of his own based on law but with the *tēn [dikaiosynēn] dia pisteōs Christou, tēn ek theou dikaiosynēn epi tę̄ pistei*, good sense results if he is referring to the individual's right standing with God at the judgment. This individualistic sense comes out strongly in Romans 4 where Abraham and those like him have righteousness reckoned to them on the basis of their faith. At Rom 10:3, where Israel has not submitted to the righteousness of God, there is, however, a more corporate sense.

Käsemann stresses that the righteousness of God not only has a gift character but also a power character (cf esp Rom 1:16-17). The power character is not only oriented towards the individual but also extends even to the entire creation. It refers to God's saving activity rather than merely his coming into right relation with the individual.[80] I agree with Käsemann that the righteousness of God has a power quality and can be present independently of the response of men. This comes out above all at Rom 3:5, and to some extent at Rom 3:25-26. At Rom 3:5 in the phrase *theou dikaiosynēn* the main stress is on God; God's righteousness is opposed to man's wickedness (*adikia*) and is parallel to "God's faithfulness" (*tēn pistin tou theou*) (Rom 3:3) - i.e. God's faithfulness to his covenant - which is demonstrated in the midst of man's faithlessness (*apistia*).[81] At Rom 3:25 God demonstrates his righteousness in a situation where he has had to overlook former sins. He does so by putting forth Christ as a *hilastērion*. The righteousness of God is present apart from the response of man but it becomes effective in man when he has faith (see Rom 1:17; 3:22, 25, 26). On the basis of Rom 1:16-17 the righteousness of God has not only a gift character but also a

followed by Conzelmann, *Theology*, 215-16; and Hans Conzelmann, "Die Rechtfertigungslehre des Paulus: Theologie oder Anthropologie?," EvT 28 (1968) 389-404. For others who hold that it is a genitive of origin see Williams, *Righteousness*, 243; and Ziesler, *Righteousness*, 11-12.

[80] Ernst Käsemann, "The Righteousness of God in Paul," in his *New Testament Questions of Today* trans W. J. Montague. London: SCM: 1969, 168-182. Käsemann's students (Müller, Stuhlmacher, Kertelge) have picked up on his insights and have given a greater exegetical foundation for them by considering the meaning of "the righteousness of God" in the OT and apocalyptic Judaism. Christian Müller, *Gottes Gerechtigkeit und Gottes Volk* (FRLANT 86; Göttingen, Vandenhoeck & Ruprecht, 1964); Peter Stuhlmacher, *Gerechtigkeit Gottes bei Paulus* (Göttingen: Vandenhoeck & Ruprecht, 1966); and Kertelge, *Rechtfertigung*. For a summary and critique of their views see Brauch, *Righteousness*, 529-36; 540-240. In a somewhat similar vein to Käsemann see also Stanislas Lyonnet, "Pauline Soteriology," in *Introduction to the New Testament* (eds. A. Robert and A. Feuillet; New York: Tournai, 1965) 820-865. For others who hold *dikaiosynē theou* to be a subjective genitive see Williams, *Righteousness*, 242. In addition to the above summaries of "the righteousness of God" in the OT and Judaism see Wilckens, *Römer* I, 212-222.

[81] Williams, *Righteousness*, 241-290 accepts the thoroughly theocentric nature of the righteousness of God. According to him it means God's faithfulness to his covenant, and does not refer to the gift or power character of righteousness. He might have come to a different conclusion if he had examined 2 Cor 5:21 where we clearly receive the righteousness of God. A similar criticism applies to Snodgrass, *Doers*, 75-76 who sees the righteousness of God as the vindication of God.

power character. "The power of God for salvation to everyone who has faith" is similar to "the righteousness of God revealed through faith for faith." Since the righteousness of God is God's saving power, it must result in the *sōtēria* of man; but it does not necessarily follow from this text that a real change in man has occurred. It might mean God's saving power that objectively comes into effect through the atoning death of Jesus Christ and whereby man is brought into right relation with God. In none of the texts where man receives the righteousness of God as a gift is it absolutely demanded that there has been a real change in man. It is, however, most likely that the idea of a real change in man is present. The one who is brought into right relation with God already is a new creation in Christ (2 Cor 5:17), is dead to sin and alive to God (Rom 6:11), is not in the flesh but in the spirit (Rom 8:4-9), and is empowered to obey God (cf Rom 8:4-9). On this basis it is expected that his life will be characterized by righteousness (Rom 6:13-19).[82]

Dikaiosynē, dikaiosynē theou, then (and also as we have seen above, *dikaiōsis*, *dikaios*, and *zōē*), are mutually related. Just as sin and death come through Adam, so righteousness and life come through, and only through, Christ.

4.3 Conclusion

Salvation does not come from observance of the law. To live *en nomǭ* (Gal 3:11; 5:4), *ek (tou) nomou* (Rom 4:14, 16; 10:5; Gal 3:18, 21; Phil 3:9), *dia nomou* (Rom 3:20; 4:13; Gal 2:21), or *hypo nomon* (Rom 6:14, 15; Gal 4:21; 5:18) is to die.[83]

Both the death and resurrection of Jesus are essential for man's salvation. By dying with Christ the believer is set free from flesh, law, sin, condemnation, and death. His fallen humanity has been crucified (Gal 5:24; cf 6:14; 6:6). He has died to sin (Rom 6), and the law (7:1-6), and is no longer under the sentence of death (5:12-21; 8:1).

By rising with Christ he receives righteousness and life, the salvation which the law promises to those who obey the law.[84] Those who have died and risen

[82] For summaries on the various views of the righteousness of God see Manfred T. Brauch, *Righteousness*, 523-42. Hübner, *Law*, 125-137; Stuhlmacher, *Gerechtigkeit*, 1-73; Williams, *Righteousness*, 241-245; and Ziesler, *Righteousness*, 7-14. For a summary of the history of the discussion see Wilckens, *Römer* I, 223-233.

[83] The various aspects of salvation that Paul expressly mentions as not coming from observance of the law are: being justified (*dikaioō*, Rom 3:20, 21, 28: 4:2; Gal 2:16 (three times); 3:11; 5:4), *dikaiosynē* (Rom 4:6; 10:5; Gal 3:21; Phil 3:9), *dikaiosynē theou* (Rom 3:21, 22), *hē epangelia* (Rom 4:16), *charis* (Rom 11:6), receiving the Spirit (*to pneuma elabete*, Gal 3:2), being lead by the Spirit (*pneumati agesthe*, Gal 5:18), and being an heir (*klēronomos*, Rom 4:14; *hē klēronomia*, Gal 3:18). Boasting (*kauchēsis*, Rom 3:27; *kauchēma*, Rom 4:2) is thus excluded.

[84] For an understanding of dying and rising with Christ see further Ridderbos, *Paul*, 206-214;

with Christ are "in Christ" and have received the Spirit. By the Spirit they are enabled to fulfill the law's just requirement (Rom 8:4).[85]

This finally puts us in a position to confront Paul's epitome affirmation that "Christ is the *telos* of the law" (Rom 10:4).

Tannehill, *Dying and Rising*, 1-134. cf. E. Schweizer, "Dying and Rising with Christ," NTS 14 (1967) 1-14; Sanders, *Palestinian Judaism*, 463-468, 487, 498, 501-2. For an understanding of the Christian's participation in/with Christ see Sanders, *Palestinian Judaism*, 435, 440, 453-463.

[85] See Friedrich Lang, "Gesetz und Bund Bei Paulus," in *Rechtfertigung: Festschrift für Ernst Käsemann zum 70 Geburtstag* (eds. Johannes Friedrich, Wolfgang Pohlmann, and Peter Stuhlmacher. Tübingen: Mohr [Siebeck], and Göttingen: Vandenhoeck & Ruprecht, 1976) 305-320, 316-17, on the importance of the death and resurrection of Jesus as the turning point between the old and the new aeon.

CHAPTER FIVE

THE SYNTHESIS: CHRIST THE END OF THE LAW

In the preceding chapter we concluded that, according to Paul, dying with Christ means the end of enslavement to sin, and the end to the enslavement, condemnation, and death which the law has brought. Rising with Christ means righteousness, life, and Spirit. Righteousness and life could only come through the death and resurrection of Jesus; it could in no way come through the law.

In this chapter we will see how these conclusions correlate with Rom 10:4 *telos gar nomou Christos eis dikaiosynēn panti tō̧ pisteuonti*. This verse, and especially the precise sense of *telos* is usually seen to sum up Paul's understanding of Christ and the law.

5.1 **TELOS IN ROMANS 10:4**

Robert Badenas[1] gives a history of the interpretation of *telos nomou* in Romans 10:4. He notes that, with rare exceptions, in the early and medieval church the Greek *telos* and the Latin *finis* were interpreted (a) in a perfective/completive sense or (b) in a teleological sense, rather than (c) in a temporal/terminal sense. The Greek *nomos* and the Latin *lex* were generally understood as the law and the prophets of the OT rather than as an ethical code. The phrase *telos nomou Christos* or *finis legis Christos* was seen as the OT predictions which pointed to Christ or as the purpose of the law which was fulfilled in Christ; it was not seen as bringing a discontinuity between the law and Christ.[2]

During the Reformation *telos* in a completive, perfective, or teleological sense prevailed, but later a temporal, terminal, or antinomian sense gained some prominence.[3] Erasmus, Calvin, and Bucer took it in a perfective sense[4], while Luther, Melanchthon, and Beza took it in a teleological sense.[5]

Catholic interpretation after Trent did not differ essentially from medieval views. But Lutherans tended to apply the negative view of the law which Luther had stated in other contexts to 10:4. The Reformed began to explain 10:4 as cancellation because of Christ's substitutionary fulfillment of the law.[6] The

---

[1] Badenas, *End*, 6-38.

[2] Badenas, *End*, 6-18, esp 17-18.

[3] Badenas, *End*, 19-26, esp 26.

[4] Badenas, *End*, 19.

[5] Badenas, *End*, 19-20.

[6] Badenas, *End*, 22.

Anabaptists tended to see the NT as superseding the OT and to see 10:4 in terms of abrogation.[7]

The eighteenth century with its lower view of Scripture contributed to the growing tendency of interpreting Rom 10:4 in the sense of abolition.[8] With nineteenth century Liberalism this became the prevailing interpretation.[9]

In the present situation there are multiple interpretations of Romans 10:4. There are those such as Cranfield, Howard, Kaiser, Rhyne, and Badenas who hold that "telos" means "goal."[10] Others such as Bring, Bruce, Barrett, Drane, Hellbardt, and Schneider believe that *telos* means "termination and goal."[11] Still others claim that "*telos*" means "termination." Those who hold the latter position can be divided into at least five categories: (a) the messianic age view, the law ceases when the messianic age begins (Schoeps and Fitzmeyer);[12] (b) the cosmological view, the law belongs to the natural world and the rule of angels (Schweitzer);[13] (c) the salvation history view, the law is abolished with regard

---

[7] Badenas, *End*, 22.

[8] Badenas, *End*, 24.

[9] Badenas, *End*, 25-27.

[10] Cranfield, "Law," 42-68; and Cranfield, *Romans* II, 515-20; Howard, "End" 331-337. Walter C. Kaiser Jr., "Leviticus 18:5 and Paul: Do this And You Shall Live (Eternally?)," JETS 14 (1971) 19-28; Rhyne, *Law*, 95-116 esp 103-104; Badenas, *End*, 1-151, esp 81-151; cf also Bläser, *Gesetz*, 177; M. Barth, *Stellung*, 516-17; Wilckens, *Rechtfertigung*, 101; Wilckens, *Römer* II, 221-224; Felix Flückiger, "Christus des Gesetzes *telos*," TZ 11 (1955) 153-157; W. S. Campbell, "Christ the End of the Law: Rom 10:4," *Studia Biblica III. Papers on Paul and Other New Testament Authors* (ed. E. A. Livingstone. JSNT Supplement Series 3; Sheffield, JSOT, 1980) 73-81; Meyer, *End*, 59-78; Daniel P. Fuller, *Gospel and Law: Contrast or Continuum?* (Grand Rapids: Eerdmans, 1980), 84-5 Osten-Sacken, *Römer 8* 255-56. cf K. Barth, *Romans*, 375; and Karl Barth, *Church Dogmatics* II 2, 269.

[11] Bruce, *Romans* 56, 203; Bruce, *The Law of Moses*, 264; Barrett, *Romans*, ad. loc., 197-8; Drane John W. *Paul: Libertine or Legalist?*, 133; Hans Hellbardt, "Christus, das *telos* des Gesetzes," EvT 3 (1936) 331-346, 345-46 (cf Gerhard Delling, "telos," TDNT VIII 49-57, 56. n 51); E. E. Schneider, "Finis Legis Christus," TZ 20 (1964) 410-422, 420; Bring, *Gesetz*, 35-72. For Bring Christ is the end of the law in that he puts an end to law-righteousness and the condemnation that the law brings. He is the goal of the law in that all that the law aimed at is summed up in him. Cf also Furnish, *Theology* 161; Andrew John Bandstra, *The Law and The Elements of The World: An Exegetical Study in Aspects of Paul's Teaching* (Kampen: J. H. Kok, 1964), 101ff; A. Feuillet, "Loi ancienne et Morale chrétienne d'après l'épître aux Romains," NRT 92 (1970) 785-805, 794; Ladd, *Law*, 58; and Leenhardt, *Romans*, 265-66.

[12] Schoeps, *Paul*, 171-175; J. A. Fitzmeyer, "Saint Paul and the Law", *The Jurist*, 27 (1967) 18-36.

[13] Schweitzer, *Mysticism*, 177-204.

to the attainment of salvation (Conzelmann, Sanders, Hahn, Sand);[14] (d) the end of a misused law view (Hübner);[15] and (e) the existential view (Bultmann).[16]

On the basis of the NT's usage none of the above positions can be ruled out;[17] *telos* sometimes means "goal," and sometimes "end."[18]

Badenas argues strongly that in Rom 10:4 the burden of proof is on those who would have *telos* mean anything other than "goal." Yet in the course of his argument he has to make a number of concessions to the temporal/terminal view. In the prepositional phrases in the NT where *telos* occurs Badenas concedes that *mechri telous* (Heb 3:14) refers to the eschatological end, but he downplays a seemingly obvious temporal meaning at 1 Thess 2:16; Heb 6:11; Rev 2:26; 1 Cor 1:8; Matt 10:22; 24:13; Mark 13:3; John 13:1; Rev 21:6 and 22:13.[19] Regarding the nominal use of *telos* he concedes that *telos* is used in the sense of termination or cessation at Mark 3:26 and Heb 7:3 and that there is a temporal element at Matt 24:6; Mark 13:7; Matt 24:14; 1 Pet 4:7. But he attempts to blunt a seemingly obvious temporal reference at Matt 26:58; 1 Cor 10:11; 2 Cor 3:13; 1 Pet 4:17; 2 Cor 11:15; Heb 6:8; Phil 3:19; Luke 1:33; Rom 6:21, 22.

Of the thirteen occurrences in the Pauline corpus he concedes that three times (1 Cor 1:8; 10:11; 15:24) *telos* refers to the eschatological end and twice it means final destiny (2 Cor 11:15; Phil 3:19), but he argues that five times it seems to have a teleological meaning (i.e. at Rom 6:21, 22; 10:4; 2 Cor 3:13; 1 Tim 1:5).[20] What is striking is that the only reference of the five which has a strong case to be understood teleologically is 1 Tim 1:5! In light of this his claim seems strange that unless the context of Rom 10:4 clearly requires a non-teleological meaning it is more normal to assume a normal Greek teleological meaning.[21]

Lexically it is possible that *telos* means "goal" but normally in Romans (i.e., 6:21, 22; 13:7) it means "end." "Goal," moreover, adds something extraneous to the theme of salvation by faith versus works in Rom 1-8 and 9:30-10:21, and it does not relate the law to the believer's participation in the death and resurrection of Jesus. It does not take adequate account of the "then" versus

[14] Conzelmann, *Theology*, 223-228; Sanders, *Palestinian Judaism*, 496-97; Alexander Sand, "Gesetz und Freiheit. Vom Sinn des Pauluswortes: Christus, des Gesetzes Ende," TGl 61 (1971) 1-14, 12; Hahn, *Gesetzesverständnis* 50 says that Christ is the end of the law "sofern es um das Gesetz der Werke geht...."

[15] Hübner, *Law*, 135, 138, 148; Hübner, *Thema*, 266-267. Cf Lang, *Gesetz und Bund*, 316.

[16] Bultmann, *End*, 36-66.

[17] Many of these views were earlier examined in detail. See above 73-88.

[18] see BAGD, "telos," 811-12; and Gerhard Delling, "telos," TDNT VIII, 54-56.

[19] Badenas, *End*, 71-73.

[20] Badenas, *End*, 78-79.

[21] Badenas, *End*, 79.

"now" aspect of the law nor does it do justice to the negative points Paul makes on the law. The ministry of the law was a ministry of death (2 Cor 3). We have died to the law and are set free from the law which held us captive (Rom 7:4-6). We are no longer under the law but under grace (Rom 6:14). The law is in a very real sense over and done with.

It is odd that in interpreting Christ as the *telos* of the law neither Rhyne nor Badenas consider the explicit statements about the relationship of Christ and the law which are made elsewhere in Romans and Galatians (e.g., Rom 7:4-6; Rom 8:2-4; Gal 3:13; Gal 4:4-5; 3:24). These texts indicate that Christ's work has in some sense brought the law to an end in order that salvation may come. I shall argue that this is the case in Rom 10:4.

Regarding the messianic age view Herman Ridderbos and E. P. Sanders[22] rightly ask why Paul did not appeal to the view that the law would be altered in the messianic age if he believed it and if it were Jewish doctrine. Sanders argues that it is not likely that ancient Judaism expected the law to be abrogated in the messianic age.[23]

Neither the messianic age view nor the cosmological view does justice to the positive points Paul makes on the law.[24]

Hans Conzelmann has rightly emphasized that the law as a moral demand does not come to an end. It does not, however, seem true to say that Christ has put an end to the law as a means of salvation, for in Paul's view, salvation never did or could come by the law (Gal 2:21; 3:21).[25] In Romans 4 Abraham and all the righteous of the old dispensation were saved by faith - in Christ (cf Rom 9:30-33). It was to Abraham (Gal 3:8) and through the prophets (Rom 1:2, 3) that the Gospel was preached beforehand. The rock that Israel stumbled over was Christ (Rom 9:33 = Isa 28:16; cf 1 Cor 10:4). Rom 10:4, moreover, seems to state that Christ is the *telos* of the law only for those who believe. Christ is not the end of a misused law for God has consigned man *hypo nomon*, has consigned man to disobedience (Rom 11:32) in order that he might have mercy on all (Rom 11:32).[26]

---

[22] Ridderbos, *Paul*, 137; Sanders, *Palestinian Judaism*, 479-80.

[23] Sanders, *Palestinian Judaism*, 479 n 25. See further Räisänen, *Law*, 237-240. See also Luz, *Geschichtsverständnis*, 144-145; Urbach, *Sages* I, 297-314; Bammel, *Nomos*, 120-128; Robert Banks, "The Eschatological Role of Law in Pre- and Post-Christian Jewish Thought," in *Reconciliation and Hope* (ed. Robert Banks. Grand Rapids: Eerdmans, 1974) 173-185, 173-179; Jacob Jervell, "Die offenbarte und die verborgene Tora," ST 25 (1971) 90-108; and Howard M. Teeple, *The Mosaic Eschatological Prophet* (Philadelphia: SBL, 1957) 14-17.

[24] See below 142-143.

[25] see Badenas, *End*, 36, 116.

[26] See Hofius, *Gesetz*, 275.

Most of the points that Cranfield makes are, no doubt, correct. It is true that for Paul Christ is the only one who fully obeys the law, that the ceremonies contained in the law point to Christ, that the Mosaic economy came with *doxa*, and that Rom 6:14; 7:4-6 imply that man is no longer under the curse of the law. But that these premises demand a conclusion excluding *telos* in the sense of "end" is, as we shall see, a *non sequitur*.[27]

George E. Howard is right to say that *gar* ... *de* (10:5-6) can mean "for ... and." But his construing of the immediate issue in Rom 10:1-13 as the "inclusion of the Gentiles" is excluded by the structure of the argument. The context is established by Paul's question: If Israel has failed to come into messianic salvation, does it follow that the word of God has failed (9:6)? In ch 9 Paul answers that Israel's not entering into salvation did not lead to a failure of the word of God but to an incredible success, the salvation of the Gentiles. The follow-up in ch 10 is a variation of the same question. No, it is not the word of God that failed, but Israel, by its own fault, has failed. Howard's exegesis does not fit into the thematic sequence.[28]

Some of Ragnar Bring's points are well made. Christ does indeed end the condemnation of the law (cf Rom 8:1) and does not abolish the prescriptions of the law. Again it is true that salvation for Paul is a two-act drama. It does not follow, however, that any of these considerations demand that *telos* means "goal" in Rom 10:4.[29]

It is true that for Paul Christ in his own person embodies perfect righteousness as C. K. Barrett and F. F. Bruce affirm. But this as we shall see does not define the force of *eis dikaiosynēn* in Rom 10:4.[30]

The position of G. E. Ladd and R. N. Longenecker, that *eis dikaiosynēn* means Christ is the end of the law in its connection with righteousness is also ill-conceived. A positive proposal will be offered below.[31]

The view proposed here correlates with both the positive and negative statements Paul makes on the law, and with the Pauline view of justification by faith rather than works of law. It agrees with other Pauline statements which indicate that Christ has in some sense terminated the law in order that salvation may come to the believer. It coheres with the considerations of the previous chapter where the believer dies to the law through his participation in the death of Jesus and receives righteousness and life through his participation in the resurrection of Jesus.

---

[27] See below 140-146.

[28] See above 61-62.

[29] See above 65-66.

[30] See Bruce, *Romans*, 203; Barrett, *Romans*, 198.

[31] An exposition of the views of Cranfield, Howard, Bring, Bruce, Barrett, Ladd, and Longenecker have been given above 59-62, 65-67.

Several texts indicate that Christ has in some sense terminated the law in order that salvation may come to believers. We "have died to the law *through the body of Christ*" in order that we might belong to Christ and bear fruit for God rather than for death (Rom 7:4-5). We have been discharged from the law which held us captive, in order that we might serve in the new life of the Spirit (Rom 7:6). Because of the impotence of the law on account of our sinful flesh, God sent his own Son as a sin offering (Rom 8:3) in order that we might receive the Spirit (Rom 8:4-9). God sent his son to redeem those who were under the law so that we might receive our adoption as sons (Gal 4:4, 5). Christ has redeemed us from the curse of the law so that we might receive the promise of the Spirit through faith (Gal 3:13, 14). Until Christ came we were under a *paidagōgos* and no better than slaves (Gal 3:24; cf vv 23, 25) "The law was our *paidagōgos* until Christ came in order that we might be justified by faith" (Gal 3:23). We are not "under the law" but "under grace" (Rom 6:14, 15). Because of God's gracious act in Christ (Rom 3:24; 5:15, 17, 20, 21) we have died to the rule of sin and the law (cf Rom 6:1-23; Rom 7:4-6) and stand in a gracious relationship to God (Rom 5:2).

These considerations would make us *a priori* expect that at 10:4 Christ has brought the law to its termination for the believer. However, in line with other texts about the relationship of Christ and the law there could also be some telic force in 10:4. Christ does not merely bring the law to its end, he also brings it to its appointed end. He brings the negative functions of the law to their appointed end so that all who believe may attain righteousness. It was God who caused the law to slip in that the offense might abound (Rom 5:20), it was God who added the law because of transgressions (Gal 3:19); it was God who consigned man under law (Gal 3:23). But it was also God who sent Christ to redeem man from this situation.

This view also agrees with the context of Rom 9:30-10:10.

5.2 TELOS IN ROMANS 10:4 AND THE CONTEXT OF 9:30-10:21

In Rom 9:30-10:10 as in Rom 1-8[32] Paul is contrasting salvation by works and by faith; he is contrasting the Gentiles who have received righteousness on the basis of faith and the Jews who pursued it on the basis of works. What is new in this passage is that Paul is speaking to the post-Christian situation where the

[32] Rom 1-8 is an exposition of Rom 1:17 (= Hab 2:4, *ho de dikaios ek pisteōs zēsetai*). Rom 1-4 establishes *that* it is the one who is just by faith as opposed to works who will receive eternal life. Rom 5-8 states the consequences of this fact for the believer. Rom 9-11 applies 1-8 to Israel and its unbelief. 9:30-10:21 explains that Israel in refusing to accept the Gospel is following a pattern set repeatedly throughout her history. On the structure and argument of Romans see above 13-14.

Jews have refused to believe in Christ, whereas in 1:18-3:20 Paul is speaking to the pre-Christian situation.[33]

5.2.1 ROMANS 9:30-10:3

In 9:30-33 the goal of both Jews (*Israēl*) and Gentiles (*ethnē*) is *dikaiosynē* (in the sense of salvation).[34] Gentiles did not pursue *dikaiosynē* yet attained it. Gentiles received it "by faith" (*ek pisteōs*) but the Jews tried to attain it "by works" (*ex ergōn*) (v 31). They pursued the law which promises righteousness (*nomon dikaiosynēs*) but did not meet the requirement of the law (*eis nomon ouk ephthasen*) because they did not obey the law. They, in contrast to Gentiles, refused to believe in Christ the "stone of stumbling and rock of offense" (*proskommatos kai petran skandalou*, v 33).[35]

In the phrase *nomon dikaiosynēs* most exegetes understand *nomos* as referring to the OT law but there is wide disagreement over the meaning of the qualifying genitive *dikaiosynēs*. The phrase has been viewed as the law which results in righteousness.[36] But some such as Huby, Lagrange, Schlier, Zahn and Jülicher interpret it as the law which demands righteousness (cf 8:3-4),[37] others as the law falsely understood as a way of righteousness,[38] and still others as the law which promises righteousness.[39] But the law which promises righteousness can be viewed: a) as promising righteousness because it bears witness to

[33] See Wilckens, *Römer* II, 213.

[34] Against Badenas, *End*, 104.

[35] Opposing the universal view that the rock at 9:33 is Christ, Paul Meyer claims that it refers to the Torah. He notes that the stone passages Isa 8:14 and 28:16 were already linked in Judaism and that elsewhere when they refer to Christ they make use of Ps 118:22 (Meyer, *End*, 63-4). Against Meyer I would note that elsewhere in Romans and particularly in 9:30-10:21 (i.e., 10:4, 9, 10, 14, 16) *pisteuein* refers either to believing in Christ or in God for salvation. Also the quotation of Isa 28:16 in Rom 10:11 refers to Christ and is meant to recall 9:33. Furthermore a major point of Romans 9-11 is to answer the question why Israel has stumbled when it comes to believing in Christ. See also Badenas, *End*, 106-7, 134.

[36] E. Kühl, *Der Brief des Paulus an die Römer* (1913) ad. loc., as cited in Käsemann, *Romans*, 277.

[37] J. Huby, *Saint Paul, épître aux Romains*. ed. S. Lyonnet: Paris; Beuchesne, 1957, 360; Heinrich Schlier, *Der Römerbrief* (HTKNT; Freiburg: Herder, 1977), 307; Zahn, *Römer* ad. loc.; et. al.; Cf Käsemann, *Romans*, 277.

[38] So Barrett, *Romans* 193; Schmidt, *Römer*, 172; et. al.

[39] So Michel, *Römer*, ad. loc.; Bläser, *Gesetz*, 173-77; Stuhlmacher, *Gerechtigkeit*, 92; Kurt Stalder, *Das Werk des Geistes in der Heiligung bei Paulus* (Zurich: EVZ-Verlag, 1962), 350. For summaries see Käsemann, *Romans*, 277 and Rhyne, *Law*, 99.

righteousness as in 3:21,[40] or b) as promising righteousness to those who keep or fulfill it.[41]

Käsemann claims that in Pauline theology the qualitative genitive cannot denote the result; it may indicate the demand but in this context it is the promise. The law is thus viewed as a witness of righteousness, as in 3:21.[42]

C. Thomas Rhyne believes that the proper interpretation of *nomon dikaiosynēs* in 9:31 largely determines the meaning of 9:32-10:21. Like Käsemann, Rhyne holds that *nomon dikaiosynēs* is the law which promises righteousness in that it is a witness to righteousness. The phrase refers back to 3:21 (where the law bears witness to righteousness by faith) and 4:1-25 (where Gen 15:6 argues for righteousness by faith), and looks forward to 10:6-8 (where Deut 30:12-14 proclaims righteousness by faith).[43]

According to Rhyne the Jews are faulted not with the fact that, but with the way in which, they pursue "the law of righteousness;" they pursue it *hōs ex ergōn* rather than *ek pisteōs*.[44] Attaining the law corresponds to attaining righteousness by faith in the case of the Gentiles (9:30). Thus attaining to the law and receiving righteousness by faith are practically identical.[45]

As in 3:27 there are two perspectives from which the law may be approached, *diōkein nomon dikaiosynēs ... ek pisteōs* versus *diōkein nomon dikaiosynēs ... ex ergōn*; they correspond to the contrast between *nomos pisteōs* and *nomos tōn ergōn*.

The law is not disparaged, it, rather, stands on the side of righteousness by faith (cf 3:21b-22, 27e; 3:31-4:25).[46] The Jews were able to perform the works of the law, but their ability to do the works of the law hindered their attaining the law by faith. They failed to reach the law because they misunderstood it and transformed it into a tool of personal achievement (cf 10:2-3, 5; see also 2:17, 23; 3:27d; 4:2; Phil 3:6, 9).[47]

---

[40] So Käsemann, *Romans* 277; Rhyne, *Law*, 100; Badenas, 103-4, 117, 119 see also C. E. B. Cranfield, "Some Notes on Romans 9:30-33," in *Jesus und Paulus: Festschrift für Werner Georg Kümmel zum 70. Geburtstag* (eds E. Earle Ellis and Erich Grässer. Göttingen: Vandenhoeck & Ruprecht, 1975) 35-43, 37-38.

[41] So Lietzmann, *Römer*, 94. Michel, *Römer*, 219, n 4; Wilckens, *Römer*, II, 212 n 944. see also Osten-Sacken, *Römer 8*, 252 n 25; Cf Rhyne, *Law*, 167. n 34.

[42] Käsemann, *Romans*, 277.

[43] Rhyne, *Law*, 100, 103, 104, 110, 114; 169 n 68.

[44] Rhyne, *Law*, 100-101; Also Cranfield, *Romans 9:30-33*, 39; Osten-Sacken, *Römer 8*, 253.

[45] So Osten-Sacken, *Römer 8*, 253. He believes that Käsemann, *Romans*, 277 and Barrett, *Romans*, 193 wrongly substitute *dikaiosynē* for *nomos*. Cf Rhyne, *Law*, 100, 167 n 41.

[46] Rhyne, *Law* 101; Rhyne, *Nomos Dikaiosynēs*, 489-90.

[47] Rhyne, *Law*, 101; Rhyne, *Nomos Dikaiosynēs*, pp 490. Cf Käsemann, *Romans*, 277.

Rhyne, however, can be criticized at several points in his exposition of *nomos dikaiosynēs*. It is true that the law promises righteousness in the sense that the Scriptures bear witness to it and that Christ fulfills the promise but it is questionable if that is the meaning in 9:31 where the context indicates there are two ways of obtaining righteousness. He does not properly take into account the contrast between Jews and Gentiles in 9:30-33. There seems to be at least an implicit criticism of the Jews who "pursued" for at 9:30 Gentiles obtained righteousness yet did "not pursue."[48] What Gentiles receive is righteousness, therefore what the Jews are striving for must be righteousness and not the law.[49] The contrast in 9:30-32 seems to be carried over into 10:5-6; therefore *hē de ek pisteōs dikaiosynē* (10:6) is equivalent to *dikaiosynēn de tēn ek pisteōs* (9:30), and *tēn dikaiosynēn tēn ek [tou nomou]* (10:5) is equivalent to *diōkōn nomon dikaiosynēs* (9:31). At 9:32 *ek pisteōs* seems to refer to Gentiles who did not pursue righteousness yet received the righteousness of faith (9:30), and *ex ergōn* at 9:32 seems to refer to the Jews who pursued the law of righteousness.

Rhyne claims wrongly that the Jews either did or could perform the works of the law. Romans 2 asserts that the Jews think they obey the law but do not really obey it. At 3:1-20 no one obeys the law. The point of Romans is that God has consigned all to disobedience - see Gal 3:23 where God has consigned all under sin - that he might have mercy on all (11:32). At 7:14-25, 8:7 fallen humanity (i.e., those in the flesh) cannot obey the law, whereas redeemed humanity is in the spirit and is able to obey (8:4, 7). Rhyne is mistaken when he claims that the Jews were able to perform the works of the law but this hindered them from attaining the law by faith. If the Jews really did obey the law then they would have eternal life (*zēsetai*) (10:5), be justified (2:13), and saved (10:1).

It seems much more probable that 9:31 should be interpreted as the Jews pursue the law which holds out the promise of righteousness for those who obey the law (= 2:13; 10:5), but they did not obtain the law, they did not meet the requirement of the law for they did not obey the law. This is precisely what Paul has said earlier in Romans.

Alternatively by *hypallagē*, *nomon dikaiosynēs* might mean righteousness of the law (= Calvin's view) if this is taken in the sense of righteousness by means of the law.[50]

---

[48] Wilckens, *Römer* III, 212, correctly notes that the contrast between running and not running is the same contrast as "My people" and "not my people" in 9:25-26.

[49] This criticism also applies to Meyer, *End*, 62-64, 66; and Badenas, *End*, 104. cf Schlier, *Römerbrief*, 306.

[50] See Luz's (*Geschichtsverständnis* 157) apparent attempt to interpret *nomos dikaiosynēs* as "die Gerechtigkeit des Gesetzes"; cf Rhyne, *Law*, 1981, 167 n 32. Against C. E. B. Cranfield, *Romans 9:30-33*, 37 n 3; Kaiser, *Leviticus 18:5* 25; and Rhyne, *Law*, 167 n 32.

Regarding the phrase *eis nomon ouk ephthasen* (9:31) Käsemann rightly rejects the view of Muller-Duvernoy that the law is not to be fulfilled, and the view of Lagrange that what was inherited must be constantly won afresh; the point is that the will of God which calls for righteousness cannot be reached in the law. Käsemann rightly rejects the protest of Bonhöffer and Jülicher that God would not leave honest striving unrewarded, or the view of Dodd and Althaus that the Jews had not had the requisite moral zeal; the text does not speak of moral power or of righteousness as a virtue but as a gift of salvation.[51]

The Jews, then, pursued the law which promises righteousness (*nomon dikaiosynēs*) but did not arrive at the law (*eis nomon ouk ephthasen*) in the sense that they did not meet the requirement of the law; they did not obey the law (9:33).[52] They did not attain righteousness because they did not receive it by faith in Christ (*hoti ouk ek pisteōs*) but tried to attain it by works in the sense of works of law (*all' hōs ex ergōn*) (9:32a).[53] They stumbled at Christ the stumbling stone (9:32b, 33) They, in contrast to Gentiles, refused to believe in Christ the "stone of stumbling and rock of offense" (*proskommatos kai petran skandalou*, v 33).[54]

In 9:30-33 *dikaiosynēn de tēn ek pisteōs* (v 30) is thus contrasted with *dikaiosynēn (de tēn ex ergōn)* and with *nomon dikaiosynēs* (v 31). In 10:3 *tēn tou theou dikaiosynēn* is contrasted with *tēn idian (dikaiosynēn)*. This raises the presumption that in 10:5, 6 *tēn dikaiosynēn tēn ek tou nomou* is contrasted with *hē de ek pisteōs dikaiosynē*.

We have seen above that the righteousness of God is a term virtually equivalent to the salvation of God.[55] At 10:3, then, Israel is ignorant of the righteousness or salvation that comes from God, refuses to submit to it in the sense that it refuses to receive righteousness as a gift from God and seeks to acquire it by herself.[56] In 9:30-33 and 10:6-10 this is what Israel is doing. She tries to gain righteousness by means of the law (10:5) and does not receive it by faith (10:6), she does not admit that God's saving work has been accomplished in Christ and is received as a gift by faith (10:6-10). Since she refuses to do this our previous discussion would indicate that she is *hypo nomon*, enslaved to the law, condemned by it, and under the sentence of death.[57]

---

[51] Käsemann, *Romans*, 277; cf Dodd, *Romans* ad. loc.

[52] cf Schlier, *Römerbrief*, 307.

[53] *ergōn* here recalls the statements earlier in Romans that righteousness is not received by works (Rom 4:2, 6), and a man is not justified by works of law (Rom 3:20, 28; cf Gal 2:16; 3:2, 5, 10) See Schlier, *Römerbrief*, 307; Wilckens, *Römer* II, 212.

[54] For a critique of Sanders' (*Jewish People* 34-42) views on Rom 9:30-33 see Gundry, *Grace*, 16-18.

[55] See above 124-127.

[56] Against Meyer *End*, 66, 68.

[57] See above 72-104.

5.2.2 ROMANS 10:5-6

Scholars who interpret *telos* as end in 10:4 usually see a sharp antithesis between 10:5 and 10:6. Käsemann, for example, notes that if Christ is the "end" as opposed to the "goal" of the law in 10:4, then in 10:5 and 10:6 the lawgiver Moses stands over against the personified righteousness of faith.[58] Of those who see *telos* as goal many do not,[59] but others do,[60] see a sharp contrast between 10:5 and 10:6-8.

Cranfield[61] is one who sees a contrast between 10:5 and 10:6. For him the *anthrōpos* is Christ. Christ fulfilled the law by perfectly obeying it and has, consequently, earned eternal life both for Himself and for those who believe in him; the contrast is between the righteousness of Christ and that of men. Räisänen, however, correctly points out that such an attempt is refuted by Gal 3:10-12; there the law and faith are opposed to each other and Lev 18:5 is cited in a similar manner.[62]

Käsemann notes that in 10:5 Paul quotes from Lev 18:5 (cf Gal 3:12; Rom 2:13) but the phrase *tēn dikaiosynēn tēn ek nomou* is put first and incorporated into the *hoti* clause. The phrase about the righteousness of the law is the object of *ho poiēsas* and sums up the first clause of Lev 18:5; for the sake of contrast and emphasis this phrase is moved forward. The legal righteousness represented by Moses demands achievement and promises temporal and eternal life only to the doer.[63] According to 2:17-3:19; Gal 3:10-12, Paul is convinced that no one can achieve salvation in this way. Receiving righteousness by obedience to the law is the opposite of the righteousness of faith and the righteousness of God.

5.2.3 ROMANS 10:6-10

It is fallacious to argue that since "righteousness by faith" in 10:6-8 is actually taken from the law itself (Deut) then Christ must be the fulfillment of the Torah in 10:4.[64] Räisänen points out that for the author of Hebrews the Old

---

[58] Käsemann, *Romans*, 284; Luz, *Geschichtsverständnis*, 92.

[59] e.g., Bandstra, *Law*, 104-5; Karl Barth, *Church Dogmatics* II, 2, 245; Bring, *Gesetz*, 54; Flückiger, *telos*, 155; Howard, "End" 336-37; Fuller, *Gospel* 70; Badenas, *End*, 119-125.

[60] Cranfield, *Romans* II, 520. Rhyne, *Law*, 105; Meyer, *End*, 69; Osten-Sacken, *Römer 8*, 255, and apparently Bläser, *Gesetz* 180. It should be noted that in a similar context *de* does introduce a contrast at 9:31.

[61] Cranfield, "Law" 49; Cranfield, *Romans* II, 521-2.

[62] Räisänen, *Law* 55.

[63] Käsemann, *Romans*, 285, 286, 288.

[64] Against Cranfield, *Romans* II, 519, and Osten-Sacken, *Römer 8*, 255.

Covenant is superseded yet he bases his argument on the OT.[65] Badenas has claimed that, since the arguments of 10:5 (= Lev 18:5) and 10:6-8 (= Deut 9:4; 30:12-14) are both based on the Torah, these texts cannot be contrasted for then Scripture would be pitted against Scripture.[66] This is fallacious; the quotation from Lev 18:5 is not designed to encourage one to obey the law in order to gain righteousness but to pronounce that anyone who attempts to gain righteousness this way is doomed (cf Gal 3:10-12).[67]

In Rom 10:6-8 Paul gives a pesher-like Christian interpretation to Deut 30:11-14,[68] an interpretation facilitated by the association of this passage with wisdom in ancient Judaism.[69] One who bases his righteousness on faith does not say in his heart "Who will ascend into heaven?" because that would mean that Christ had not yet come down and become incarnate (Rom 10:6); nor does he say "Who will descend into the abyss?" for that would mean that Christ had not been raised. He accepts the incarnation and resurrection of Christ and the fact that he has new life in Christ.[70] Therefore, in contrast to the man in Rom 10:5, he does not try to obey the law in order to gain life. He knows that the message of faith is in his "mouth" (*stoma*) and "heart" (*kardia*) (10:8), for it is with the *kardia* that one believes, and with the *stoma* that one confesses and thus receives *dikaiosynē* and *sōtēria* (10:10).

---

[65] Räisänen, *Law*, 55.

[66] Badenas, *End*, 119-120. Wilckens, *Römer* II, 226, correctly notes that it is an overinterpretation to distinguish between Moses who writes (*graphei*) (10:5) and the righteousness of faith which speaks (*legei*) (10:6). Against Schlier, *Römerbrief*, 311; Käsemann, *Romans*, 284; Michel, *Römer*, 256; et. al. Wilckens, ibid., 226 notes we cannot distinguish between the meaning of *legei* (10:11, 16, 19, 20, 21) and *gegraptai* (10:16).

[67] See Hofius, *Gesetz*, 272.

[68] See Bruce, *Romans*, 204; Käsemann, *Romans*, 285; Wilckens, *Römer*, II 224-25.

[69] See M. Jack Suggs, "The Word is Near You: Romans 10:6-10 within the Purpose of the Letter," in *Christian History and Interpretation: Studies Presented to John Knox* (eds. W. R. Farmer, C. F. D. Moule, and R. R. Neibuhr. Cambridge: Cambridge University Press, 1967) 289-319,

[70] Or alternately there might be a reference to the death and resurrection of Christ. Käsemann, *Romans*, 288-89, claims that Christ's ascension is linked here with the descent into Hades, thus with the descent into the realm of the dead (cf Sanday & Headlam, *Romans* ad. loc.; Michel, *Römer*, ad. loc.; Against Nygren, (*Romans* ad. loc.) and Barrett, (*Romans*, ad. loc.) he believes that the interpretation at the end of 10:7 excludes the incarnation. Cf Helmut Traub, "ouranos," TDNT V 497-502, 509-536, p. 526; E. Schweizer, "Zur Herkunft der Präexistenzvorstellung bei Paulus," EvT 19 (1959) 65-70, 67-68. For conclusions similar to those of Käsemann see James D. G. Dunn, *Christology in The Making; A New Testament Inquiry Into the Origins of the Doctrine of the Incarnation* (Philadelphia: Westminster, 1980), 184-187, 331-332.

5.2.4 EIS DIKAIOSYNĒN IN ROM 10:4

Eis dikaiosynēn panti tǭ pisteuonti means the same as similar phrases in its context. It is similar to *pisteuetai eis dikaiosynēn* (10:10), *he de ek pisteōs dikaiosynē* (10:6), and *dikaiosynēn de tēn ek pisteōs* (9:30). Attaining righteousness by faith in these passages is the same as submitting to the righteousness of God (10:3); it means receiving the righteousness which God gives. Receiving the righteousness which God gives (10:3) is the opposite of trying to establish one's own righteousness (10:3) and not submitting to the righteousness of God (10:3). Attaining to righteousness by faith (9:30; 10:4; 6, 10) is the opposite of attempting to attain righteousness by works (9:32) or by the law (10:5).

For righteousness to be attained in 10:4 two conditions must be met. Christ must bring the law to its *telos* and it must be received by faith. It is available for all (*panti*) whether Jews or Greeks who have faith (cf 10:12). The problem is that the Jews do not have faith. Faith in this context is understood to be faith in Jesus Christ the stumbling stone (cf esp 9:33; 10:11).[71]

Eis dikaiosynēn is contrasted with *eis thanaton* (Rom 6:16) and compared with *eis sōtērian* (Rom 10:10). This, coupled with the fact that *dikaiosynē* is a virtual synonym for life, indicates that *eis dikaiosynēn* (10:4) is a synonym of *eis sōtērian* (10:1). Also the closest verbal parallel in Paul is Rom 1:16 *to euangelion, dynamis gar theou estin eis sōtērian panti tǭ pisteuonti*. Thus in Rom 10:4 *eis dikaiosynēn* is not related to *telos* but to *panti to pisteuonti*. Grammatically *telos* is the equivalent of *dynamis ... theou* (Rom 1:16). *Christos* is not predicate, but subject.[72] Christ is not the goal of the law in that he realizes perfect righteousness[73] nor is he the end of the law in its connection with righteousness;[74] rather he is the end of the law so that righteousness or salvation might come to all who believe. And just as the Gospel is *not* the power of God *eis sōtērian* for those who do not believe (Rom 1:17), so Christ is *not* the end of the law *eis dikaiosynēn* for those who do not believe (Rom 10:4). Those outside of Christ are still *hypo nomon*, still enslaved to and condemned by the law.[75]

This interpretation of 10:4 is consistent with the fourfold explanatory use of *gar* in 10:2, 3, 4, 5.[76] The Jews have not entered into salvation *for* they have a misplaced zeal for God (10:2). They have a misplaced zeal for God *for* they are

---

[71] Against Badenas, *End*, 110.

[72] See Cranfield, *Romans* II, 515; against Meyer, *End*, 68, and Badenas, *End*, 111-112.

[73] Against Bruce, *Romans*, 203; and Barrett, *Romans*, 197-98.

[74] Against Longenecker, *Paul*, 144-147; Ladd, *Law*, 57-8.

[75] See Gutbrod, "Nomos," TDNT IV, 1075. Hofius, *Gesetz* 276-77 notes rightly that the law as such is not ended nor is it ended a way of salvation but its accusing and condemning function is ended.

[76] Against Badenas, *End*, 112, 122.

ignorant of God's righteousness and have not submitted to it (10:3). *For* God's righteousness means that Christ has brought the law to its appointed end so that righteousness may come for all who believe (10:4). *For* God's righteousness is the opposite of righteousness by means of the law (10:5) and is the same as righteousness by means of faith (10:6)

5.3 ADVANTAGES

This interpretation of *telos* in Rom 10:4 has the advantage that it adds nothing extraneous to what Paul has said about the law and justification by faith in either Romans or Galatians. If it is argued that *telos* as goal in Rom 10:4 agrees with Gal 3:24 where the law is a *paidagōgos ... eis Christon*, it must be said that in Gal 3:23 the law is a slave master, and in Gal 3:23, 25 there is a then-now contrast. In context as Oepke and Schlier, Betz and others have pointed out, *paidagōgos* seems to be more of a task master than an educator, and *eis* seems to have more of a temporal than an exclusively final sense.[77] *Eis Christon* can be final in the sense that God appointed the law as a pedagogue until Christ came.

This interpretation also has an advantage over the messianic age view of Schoeps and Fitzmeyer and the cosmological view of Schweitzer in that it does full justice to the positive points Paul makes on the law. These positive points are as follows: Of all the attributes there is none greater than love (*agapē*, 1 Cor 13), and all the law - including the commandments not to commit adultery, kill, steal, or covet (= the Decalogue; Exod 20:13-15, 17; Deut 5:17-19, 21) - is summed up in the one Pentateuchal commandment (Lev 19:18): "You shall love your neighbor as yourself" (Rom. 13:8-10; Gal 5:14). It is the one who loves his neighbor (*ho heteros*, Rom 13:8; *ho plēsion* Rom 13:10; Gal 5:14) who has fulfilled the law.

Paul also views the law positively when he states directly at Rom 7:22, 25; 8:7, and indirectly at several passages, that it is the law of God (*ho nomos tou theou*). The Corinthian Church is exhorted to keep the (*entolōn theou*) (1 Cor 7:19). It was a privilege for Israel that God gave them the law (*nomothesia*, Rom 9:4)[78] and entrusted them with his oracles (*episteuthēsan ta logia tou theou*, Rom 3:2).[79] For the Jew it is by understanding the law that God's will is known (Rom

---

[77] See Betz, *Galatians*, ad. loc., 177-8; Oepke, *Galater*, ad. loc., 86-88; Schlier, *Galater*, ad. loc., 124-126; Bruce, *Galatians*, 182-83; Sanders, *Jewish People*, 66.

[78] Here *nomothesia* is ranked with "the sonship, the glory, the covenants ... the worship, and the promises."

[79] After a careful examination of *logion* in the LXX, J. W. Doeve, "Some Notes With Reference To TA LOGIA TOU THEOU in Rom III 2," *Studia Paulina: In honorem Johannis de Zwaan septuagenarii* (eds. J. N. Sevenster and W. C. van Unnik. Haarlem; Erven F. Bohn, 1953) 111-123,

2:17-18.), and by breaking the law that his name is dishonored (Rom 2:23). In 1 Cor 9:8 Paul contrasts what the law says with his own human authority. In 1 Cor 9:9 (= Deut 2:54) and 1 Cor 14:21 (= Isa 28:11-12; Deut 28:49) OT quotations are introduced with "it is written (*gegraptai* = divine passive) in the law (*en gar tō̧ Mōüseōs nomō̧*," 1 Cor 9:9; *en tō̧ nomō̧* 1 Cor 14:21).[80] The law is holy, just, good, spiritual (Rom 7:12-14; cf 7:16), in accord with the promises of God (Gal 3:21), contains the *morphōsis* of *gnōsis* and *alētheia* (Rom 2:20), and (along with the prophets) bears witness to the righteousness of God (*dikaiosynē theou*, Rom 3:21).

Only in Christ is one able to walk *kata pneuma* rather than *kata sarka* and thus fulfill the *to dikaiōma tou nomou* (Rom 8:4); it is thus only for the one in Christ that the law has the character of spirit and life (*ho gar nomos tou pneumatos tēs zōēs en Christō̧ Iēsou*, Rom 8:2).[81] The law, if viewed from the standpoint of *pistis* (in contrast to *erga*), excludes the possibility of human boasting (*kauchēsis*, Rom 3:27).[82] Through faith the law is not destroyed (*katargoumen*) but established (*histanomen*, Rom 3:31).[83]

In Rom 7:4-6 Paul has stated that the Christian has died to the law and is discharged from the law. He then goes on to expound on its nature. He states emphatically that the law is not sin (*ho nomos hamartia; mē genoito*, Rom 7:7). Since Paul holds that the law is good he needs in the context of the argument to deny emphatically that it is sin. The natural supposition of the reader would have been that the law is sin since the Christian has died to both and has been set free from both.[84] It is not the law itself which is sin but it is sin which avails itself (*aphormēn ... labousa*, Rom 7:8, 11) of the law as its starting point. Georg Bertram notes that in passages in the Pauline corpus where *aphormē* occurs it is not the "starting point" or "occasion" itself which is bad, whether it be the apostolic right to support (2 Cor 11:12), widowhood (1 Tim 5:14), Christian

concludes that the *ta logia tou theou* in Rom 3:2 refer to God's revelation in Holy Scripture.

[80] Cf *ho nomos legei*, 1 Cor 14:34.

[81] See above 29-32.

[82] See above 26-27.

[83] For a discussion of various possibilities on the interpretation of Rom 3:31; cf Käsemann, *Romans* ad. loc., 104-105; *katargein/histanein* probably is equivalent to the rabbinic *bittēl* (Aramaic *battēl/qiyyēm* (Aramaic *qayyēm*) (See Hofius, *Gesetz*, 279 n 57) - For critique, however, see Hübner, *Law*, 141-144. *Nomos* seems to refer to the OT. Schmidt, *Römer*, ad. loc., 75 argues that *nomos* is part of the OT *Verheissungsgeschichte*. Paul's doctrine of justification by faith does not deny the OT history; on the contrary, only with the coming of Christ is its true meaning revealed. Only the law as *Werkgesetz* is set aside. Rom 3:31 looks backward and forward, and is similar in meaning to Rom 3:21. Rom 4:1-25 is a discussion of the *dikaiosynē theou* as *martyroumenē hypo tou nomou* (Rom 3:21).

[84] See above 69-71; 109-111; 113-114.

freedom (Gal 5:13), or the law (Rom 7:8, 11).[85] In Rom 7:13 it was not that which was good (i.e., the law) which brought death to "me" (egō); but it was sin working death in "me" through the law (*dia tou agathou*) so that sin might be completely exposed. Note the statements *hina phanę̄ hamartia*, and *hina genētai kath' hyperbolēn hamartōlos hē hamartia*. The law is *pneumatikos* but "I" am *sarkinos ... pepramenos hypo tēn hamartian*; "I" am thus unable to attain salvation.

With regard to the salvation history views of Conzelmann and Gutbrod et. al.[86] one ought not to say that the law is ended as a way of salvation if anything is implied by that which would designate the law as a genuine soteriological dispensation which now yields to what is one more, albeit superior, soteriological dispensation. Christ is the end of the law for every believer, every believer Jew or Greek.[87] The rock that the Jews stumbled (Rom 9:33) on can only be Christ (cf 1 Cor 10:4; *hē petra de ēn ho Christos*). In Rom 4 Abraham and all the righteous of the old dispensation are saved by faith (in Christ).

5.4 IMPLICATIONS

It would seem to follow that it is only the enslavement, condemnation, and death which the law brings that is ended in Rom 10:4. This is consistent with the view that the law is good, and equally, I believe, with the statements in Paul that tend to depreciate the law. By way of conclusion to this chapter, I would like to review some of the implications for this view of Christ as the *telos* of the law.

5.4.1 THE LAW AS AN EXPRESSION OF THE WILL OF GOD HAS NOT ENDED

How are the passages which indicate that the law is aligned with sin and death, that the Christian has died to the law,[88] that Christ is the end of the law[89] to be reconciled with the fact that for Paul the law is valid? The answer is that the law is terminated only in a special sense: Christ has ended the enslaving, condemning, and death-dealing effects of the law,[90] But the law as an expression

[85] Georg Bertram, "aphormē," TDNT V, 472-474.

[86] See above 58-59, 66.

[87] The law is ended for the Gentile as well as the Jew because outside of Christ, he is consigned *hypo nomon* (cf Gal 3:23; Rom 2:15). See above 100-104.

[88] See above 72-104.

[89] See above 19-20.

[90] Cranfield's criticisms against *telos* meaning "end" in Rom 10:4 can be accommodated to this view.

of the will of God is not ended,[91] nor is its obligation on the Christian ended, since love is the fulfilling of the law, and the Christian is commanded to love.[92]

5.4.2 THE CHRISTIAN CAN OBEY THE LAW

The law is no longer a problem for the man in Christ because he is no longer *sarkinos*, no longer *pepramenos hypo tēn hamartian* (Rom 7:14);[93] rather he is *en pneumati* and the law is *pneumatikos* (Rom 7:14).[94] He is no longer *en sarki* but *en pneumati*, no longer has the *phronēma tēs sarkos* but the *phronēma tou pneumatos* and is thus able to obey *hypotassetai* the *tǭ ... nomǭ tou theou* (Rom 8:5-9).[95] He no longer walks *kata sarka* but *kata pneuma* and is able to fulfill the *dikaiōma tou nomou* (Rom 8:4).[96]

5.4.3 THE CHRISTIAN'S RELATIONSHIP TO THE LAW HAS CHANGED

For Paul when one is saved the law has not changed but one's relationship to it has changed both from the point of view of God and man. From God's viewpoint man is no longer *hypo nomon* (Rom 6:14, 15; Gal 4:5; 5:18), no longer enslaved to sin or condemned to death. From the Christian's viewpoint

---

91 See also "it stands written" (*gegraptai* = perfect tense and Divine passive) in 1 Cor 9:9; 14:21 and *legei* (= present tense) in 1 Cor 14:34.

92 Cf Bultmann, *Theology* I, 262; and Victor Paul Furnish, *The Love Command in the New Testament* (London: SCM, 1972) 95-111.

93 On Rom 7:14 as a reference to the non-Christian see above 78-84.

94 See Gundry, *Grace*, 19; Keuck, *Gesetz*, 215-35 notes that this verse was widely held by the ancient Greek Fathers to refer to the Torah. They viewed the Torah as *pneumatikos* because the Holy Spirit is its author. He agrees (ibid., 234-235).

95 The law has not changed, what has changed is one's ability to obey the law. see Van Dülmen, *Gesetz* 67-8; Jürgen Roloff, *Das Neue Testament* (Neukirchener Arbeitsbücher; Neukirchen-Vluyn, 1977), 163.

96 Käsemann, *Romans*, 217-18, admits that the *dikaiōma tou nomou* means the legal claim as in 1:32 and that correspondingly *plēroun* means the keeping of a norm (cf Schrenk "dikaiōma" TDNT II 221-2). But to evade the implications of this he argues that Paul takes over an existing formula and applies it to the doing of God's will independently of the law. Wilckens, (*Römer* II, 129 n 526) and Räisänen, (*Law* 66) rightly criticize this procedure. Others have also evaded the implications that *dikaiōma* means the legal claim; Pierre Benoit, *Exégèse et théologie* II. *La théologie de Saint Paul* (Paris: Cerf, 1961), 30-31 argues that it is the verdict of the law and Leander Keck, "The Law and 'The Law of Sin and Death' (Rom. 8:1-4): Reflections on the Spirit and Ethics in Paul," in *The Divine Helmsman: Studies on God's Control of Human Events. Presented to Lou H. Silbermann* (eds. J. L. Crenshaw and S. Sandmel; New York: KTAV, 1980) 41-57, 51-53 claims that it is the intent of the law, i.e. life. For critique see Räisänen, *Law*, 65-6.

he is no longer *hypo nomon*, no longer does he attempt to obey the law in order to be saved; in Christ he has eternal life.[97]

Paul, on the other hand, sees the Jew[98] as living *en nomǭ* (Rom 2:12; Gal 3:11, 21; 5:4; Phil 3:5), *ek nomou* (Rom 4:13; Gal 3:18; Rom 10:5), and *hypo nomon* (1 Cor 9:20), as attempting to gain *dikaiosynē* (= *dikaiosynēn tēn ek nomou*, Rom 10:5; *dikaiosynēn tēn en nomǭ*, Phil 3:6) either *dia nomou* (Gal 3:21; Rom 4:13) or *ex ergōn nomou* (Gal 2:16; 3:2, 5, 10; cf Rom 3:21, 28). That is, in order to be saved he is obeying what he believes God's law (= will, requirement) to be. This undoubtedly would include both the oral and written law.

5.4.4 The Abrogation Of The Cultic Law and The Halakah

Did not Paul believe though that God had abrogated the cultic law and the halakah? He certainly insists that neither of these needed to be observed. He insists that Gentiles must not be circumcised (1 Cor 7:18; Gal 2:13; 5:2, 3; 6:2); he, moreover, has become "all things to all men;" to the Jew he has become a Jew, to those outside the law he has become as one outside the law (1 Cor 9:20-22). But in the "capital epistles" (cf Eph 2:15) Paul does not explicitly thematize what has happened to the cultic law. Christ, however, is our paschal lamb (*to pascha*, 1 Cor 5:7).[99] With regard to the halakah there is no evidence that Paul *as a Christian* believed that it ever was a requirement of God.

Is it not true, then, that Paul when he says that Christ is the end of the law, is referring to the abrogation of the cultic law and the halakah? The answer is no![100] Only the moral law has come within the horizon of the discussion, only it

---

[97] Paul views himself as "*mē echōn ... dikaiosynēn tēn ek nomou*" (Phil 3:9) and as *mē ... hypo nomon* (1 Cor 9:20). He castigates the Galatians who wish to be *hypo nomon* (Gal 4:21) and *en nomǭ dikaiousthe* (Gal 5:3, 4).

[98] The Jew would see one who lives as a Gentile as *anomos* (1 Cor 9:21; cf Rom 2:17) and as *mē nomon echonta* (Rom 2:14).

[99] A statement not at odds with Hebrews which sees Christ as the fulfillment of the OT sacrifices. This, however, is not what Paul is thematizing in Romans and Galatians.

[100] The halakah, however, is probably included in Paul's use of the law when he states that the Jews, from their viewpoint, tried to gain righteousness and life by observing the law: i.e., Rom 3:28; Gal 2:16; 3:2, 5, 10, 11; 4:21; Phil 3:6, 9. But when Paul states their plight from his present Christian viewpoint it is hardly the case that they were enslaved to the halakah or the ceremonial law, or that it was necessary to observe these in order to gain life.

Two other passages where the moral law is not referred to are 1 Cor 9:20 and Eph 2:15. In 1 Cor 9:20 *tois hypo nomon hōs hypo nomon* is similar in meaning to *tois Ioudaios hōs Ioudaios* and means simply that Paul, when among Jews, observed specifically Jewish customs. Eph 2:15 seems to refer to the abolishing of specifically Jewish items of the law, i.e., the ceremonial law and the halakah. In context it must refer to those parts of the law which separate Gentiles from Jews. At any rate in Eph 6:2 the fifth commandment of the decalogue is still valid.

is in mind when Paul raises the hypothetical possibility that a Gentile can by nature do what the law requires (*physei ta tou nomou poiōsin*, Rom 2:14) and an uncircumcised man can keep the precepts of the law (*ta dikaiōmata tou nomou*, Rom 2:26). Keeping the *entolai theou* has nothing to do with such external matters as circumcision or uncircumcision (1 Cor 7:18-19). Nor is it in mind when Paul says that the law is spiritual but "I" (*egō*) am carnal, sold under sin (Rom 7:14). Phil 3:6 ("as to righteousness under the law blameless") indicates that in aspects of the law other than the moral, Paul was able to keep its precepts.

The ceremonial law or the halakah is not abolished in the sense that it is now wrong to observe it, or that it was ever necessary to perform it in order to gain life. Abraham was already justified before he was circumcised (Rom 4:10; cf 3:31; 4:9, 11, 12), and Paul, when he is among Jews, continues to observe the halakah and Jewish customs (1 Cor 9:20-22).[101] He believes, however, that it is a denial of the Gospel to compel Gentiles to do likewise. Paul's polemic against circumcision must be understood in the context of those who insist that it is necessary to submit to it in order to gain righteousness and life. It is neither circumcision nor uncircumcision which counts for anything, but a "new creation" (*kainē ktisis*, Gal 6:15), and "keeping the commandments of God" (*tērēsis entolōn theou*, 1 Cor 7:19). True circumcision is something which is spiritual and inward, and which the believer can possess whether or not he is physically circumcised (cf Rom 2:28, 29; Phil 3:3; Col 2:11).

Only the law as an expression of God's will is in mind when Paul considers the possibility of a Gentile doing by nature what the law requires (*physei ta tou nomou poiōsin*, Rom 2:14) and an uncircumcised man keeping the precepts of the law (*ta dikaiōmata tou nomou*, Rom 2:26). Keeping the commandments of God has nothing to do with such external matters as circumcision or uncircumcision (1 Cor 7:18, 19).

5.4.5 THE LAW IS VALID FOR THE BELIEVER

There are many indications that the "moral" law is valid for the believer in the sense that he is to look to it for moral guidance and empowered by the Spirit should endeavor to obey it. We observed earlier that Paul never cites a ritual law which is valid although he does so cite moral laws.[102] He indicates that the commandments between man and man (the "moral" law) need to be kept but gives no such indication for the commandments between God and man (the "ceremonial" law).[103]

---

[101] According to Acts 21:23-26. Paul purifies himself in the temple.

[102] Schrage, *Einzelgebote*, 231-33.

[103] Sanders, *Fulfilling*, 125.

Paul believes in the moral life and condemns immorality.[104] A Christian is to bear fruit[105] and lead a life characterized by righteousness (*dikaiosynē*)[106] and obedience (*hypakoē*).[107] Romans begins (1:5) and ends (16:26)[108] with the obedience of faith. Paul strongly affirms that neither the *adikoi*, *pornoi*, *eidōlolatrai*, *moichoi*, *malakoi*, *arsenokoitai*, *kleptai*, *methysoi*, *harpages*, (1 Cor 6:9-10) nor those who do the *ta erga tēs sarkos* (Gal 5:19-21) will inherit the kingdom of God.

Since the Christian has died and risen with Christ there has been a change of lordship.[109] He now belongs to God. He is a slave of God (Rom 6:22), is a new creature of God (2 Cor 5:17), and is empowered by the Spirit of God. He is to live to God (Gal 2:19), bear fruit for God (Rom 7:4), and to present himself in holiness to God (Rom 6:11-19). It would be strange indeed if Paul did not think that he should obey the commands of God or look to the law of God for instruction.

On questions of guidance Paul appeals to the law (1 Cor 9:8, 9; 14:34, 35) He is not *anomos theou* but *ennomos Christou* (1 Cor 9:21). For him the law is still "the law of God" (Rom 7:22, 2; 8:7), holy, just, good and spiritual (Rom 7:12; 14). He endeavors (1 Cor 7:19), to fulfill the law (Gal 5:14; Rom 8:4; Rom 13:8-10) and keep the commandments of God. The law we should fulfill explicitly includes the second table of the decalogue - not to commit adultery, kill, steal, or covet - and "any other commandment" (Rom 13:8-10).

For Paul *agapēseis ton plēsion sou hōs seauton* (Lev 19:18 = Rom 13:9; Gal 5:14) is the fulfilling of the law (Rom 13:9; Gal 5:14).[110] It is the summation of the decalogue, not man's relation with God, but man's relation with his fellow man. Christians are indebted (*opheilete*) to love one another (Rom 13:8), and to serve (*douleuete*) one another in love (Gal 5:13). Love does no wrong to a neighbor (Rom 13:10; cf . 14:15). Love heads the list of, and is perhaps the summation of, (a) the fruits of the Spirit in Gal 5:22-23, and (b) the ethical injunctions in Rom 12:9-21.

---

[104] See Rom 1:18-3:20; 6:1-23; 12:1-15:13; 1 Cor 3:10-13; 5:1-6:20; 13:1-13; Gal 5:1-6:10; Phil 2:5-11. Note particularly Paul's virtue lists (1 Cor 13; Gal 5:22-24; cf Col 3:12-17) and vice lists (Rom 1:29-31; Gal 5:19-21; 1 Cor 6:9-10; cf Col 3:5-9; Eph 5:3-5.

[105] See Gal 5:22-23; Phil 1:11; Rom 7:4; 6:21, 22; cf Col 1:10; Eph 5:9.

[106] See Rom 6:13, 16, 18, 19, 20; 14:17; 2 Cor 6:7, 14,; 9:10; Phil 1:11; cf Eph 4:24; 5:9; 6:14; 1 Tim 6:11; 2 Tim 2:22; 3:16.

[107] Rom 6:16; 15:18; 16:19; 2 Cor 7:15; 10:5, 6; Phlm 21.

[108] Should Rom 16:26 turn out to be Pauline.

[109] On our dying and rising with Christ as the basis for ethical action see Tannehill, *Dying and Rising*, 77-83.

[110] See Karl Kertelge, "Gesetz und Freiheit im Galaterbrief," NTS 30 (1985) 382-394, 389-391.

E. P. Sanders notes the remarkable way in which Paul's paraenesis is in accord with the law and Jewish tradition. Gal 5:14 and Rom 13:8-10 are well known ancient Jewish summaries of the law based on Lev 19:18.[111] Paul's vice lists feature idolatry and sexual immorality, the sins most characteristic of the Gentiles as the Jews saw them (e.g., Gal 5:19-22; 1 Cor 5:10-11; 6:9; cf Rom 1:18-32).[112]

By way of conclusion to this section I would like briefly to discuss three texts over which there has been some disagreement but which nonetheless support Paul's view that the law is valid. They are Gal 5:14; Rom 13:8-10; and Rom 8:4.[113]

5.4.5.1 GALATIANS 5:14

At Gal 5:3 Paul warns his converts that if they receive circumcision they are bound to keep the whole law (*holon ton nomon poiēsai*), yet at 5:14 they are to fulfill the whole law. He says, "The whole law is fulfilled in one word (*ho gar pas nomos en heni logǭ*), 'You shall love your neighbor as yourself'" (= Lev 19:18).

Burton notices the paradox; he resolves it by claiming that at 5:3 and previously in Galatians *nomos* is used in a legalistic sense but at 5:14 *nomos* is divine law consisting in an ethical principle. Also at 5:3 the reference is to keeping laws in slavish obedience but at 5:14 fulfilling the law is the result of life by the Spirit.[114]

To overcome the difficulty Betz posits a distinction between "doing the law" (5:3) and "fulfilling the law" (5:14). The prescriptions and prohibitions of the Jewish Torah are demands "to be done," but love is the result of the liberation of the Spirit. The reason Paul connects the Torah with love here is that the Galatians are so preoccupied with the Torah and circumcision. Christians simply need to live a life in accordance with the Spirit, because such a life is *de facto* the fulfillment of the Torah.[115]

In resolving the difficulty between 5:3 and 5:14 Hübner believes that we must take (*ho pas nomos*) seriously. We do not take it seriously if we reduce its content (a) by having the Torah, in all its individual commandments, participating in the love commandment and thereby omitting circumcision, the

[111] Sanders, *Jewish People*, 94.

[112] Sanders, *Jewish People*, 95. For a recent discussion and summary of various ways in which the moral law functions for the believer see Mohrlang, *Matthew and Paul*, 33-42.

[113] Rom 3:31 does not seem to have this point in mind. It rather seems to say that justification by faith is witnessed to in the OT. see Hofius, *Gesetz*, 278-80; cf Rhyne's, *Law*, comments on Rom 3:31 above 62-64.

[114] Burton, *Galatians*, 294.

[115] Betz, *Galatians*, 275-6.

food laws, and the purity laws, or (b) by saying that the Torah as a whole is so directed towards the love commandment that its other stipulations become superfluous.[116] To overcome the dilemma with 5:3 he posits a critical and ironical sense for (*ho pas nomos*).[117] He notes that the phrase is attributive (*ho pas nomos*) not predicative (*pas ho nomos*). The attributive use emphasizes the totality of the law rather than its individual pronouncements;[118] *ho pas nomos* requires a contrasting plural but Paul makes it consist of a single saying (*en heni logǭ*). With this paradox he makes absurd the Jewish ideal of keeping the whole law.[119]

The difficulty between 5:3 and 5:14 is not solved by positing a different kind of law between the two verses (Burton, Hübner),[120] nor by observing the difference between the attributive and predicative use (Hübner), nor by making a distinction between doing the law and fulfilling the law (Betz). Mussner correctly observes that the attributive *ho pas nomos* stresses the entire law as opposed to its individual regulations.[121] Sanders rightly rejects Hübner's distinction between *holos ho nomos* and *ho pas nomos* and argues that both refer to the Mosaic law. Paul as a Jew quotes a passage on which Jews based a summary of the law (Shabbath 31a; Tob 4:15).[122] Furthermore at Rom 13:8-10 the same passage summarizes four of the ten commandments and "any other commandment." According to Sanders Paul flings his opponents terms back at them, and tells them that love is the real way to fulfill the entire law. Paul does not explain how one who does not accept circumcision can fulfill the entire law, but his assertion is made easy by the fact that in Judaism the law was often summarized in a similar way.[123]

The difficulty between 5:3 and 5:14 is, I believe, resolved by observing the reason for which one obeys the law. At 5:3 the Galatians would keep the law in order to be justified (5:4). Having begun their course in the Spirit (*pneumati*) they would complete it in the flesh (*sarki*) (3:3; cf 4:29-31). At 5:14 the Christian does not obey the law in order to be saved. He is justified on the basis of faith in Christ and not on the basis of obedience to the law (Gal 2:16-17; 3:8, 24; cf 5:4). By faith he will receive future salvation (= "the hope of righteousness," 5:5) and by faith he already has present salvation (= the Spirit,

[116] Hübner, *Law*, 36.

[117] Hübner, *Law*, 37; and Hübner *Ganze*.

[118] Hübner, *Law*, 37; *Ganze* 241 n 11.

[119] Hübner, *Law*, 37.

[120] Cf Bruce, Galatians, 243.

[121] Mussner, *Galaterbrief*, 37; cf Lightfoot, *Galatians*, 208; Van Dülmen, *Gesetz*, 60.

[122] See Sanders, *Palestinian Judaism*, 112-114.

[123] Sanders, *Jewish People*, 96-7, 115; cf Wilckens, *Entwicklung*, 174-175.

3:2, 5, 14; 4:6, 29; 5:5; 5:16-26; 6:8). To obey the law in order to be saved is to be enslaved because one needs to obey it perfectly.[124] Van Dülmen notes that the unbeliever is "under the law" and cannot fulfill the law, but the believer has received the gift of the Spirit and is able to fulfill it.[125] It is, then, the same law, but the Christian obeys the law in the power of the Spirit and not in order to be saved.

5.4.5.2 ROMANS 13:8-10

Rom 13:8b reads *ho ... agapōn ton heteron nomon peplērōken*. This sentence could mean (a) "he who loves his neighbor (*ton heteron*) has fulfilled the law" (*nomon*), or (b) "he who loves has fulfilled the other law" (*ton heteron nomon*). A few scholars have opted for (b). For Marxsen followed by Leenhardt it is the Mosaic law as opposed to the civil law of Rome mentioned in 13:1-7,[126] but for Gutbrod it is the twofold love commandment which is identical with the law of Christ (Gal 6:2).[127] A few scholars who adopt (a) do not believe that *nomos* here refers to the OT law. For Sanday and Headlam it is not merely the Jewish law, but law as principle[128] and for Bläser it is Christ as law.[129]

But Wilckens[130] observes that nowhere else does Paul use *agapan* absolutely, that *ho heteros* is frequently a designation for one's neighbor,[131] and that *ho heteros* as one's neighbor corresponds to *tǭ plēsion* in v 10.

The context indicates that Paul is referring to the OT law. 13:9 - "You shall not commit adultery ... kill ... steal ... covet" - refers to the second table of the decalogue.[132] These and "any other commandment" (v 9) are summed up in the commandment "You shall love your neighbor as yourself" (v 9). The summary of the law (*anakephalaioutai*) (v 9) does not mean that the law is to be obeyed only insofar as it meets the criterion of love; it means the reverse, the requirement of love is important because it summarizes the law.[133] There are somewhat similar summaries in Judaism[134] but Paul's summary here seems to be

---

[124] See comments of Gal 5:3 above 88-89.

[125] van Dülmen, *Gesetz*, 60-1.

[126] Willi Marxsen, "Der heteros nomos Röm 13,8," TZ 11 (1955) 230-237; Leenhardt, *Romans*, 337-38.

[127] Gutbrod "nomos," TDNT IV 1071, 1076.

[128] Sanday and Headlam, *Romans* ad. loc; see Ceslaus Spicq, *Agape in the New Testament* (London: Herder & Herder, 1963) 56ff.

[129] Bläser, *Gesetz*, 236, 239.

[130] Wilckens, *Römer* III, 68.

[131] i.e., Rom 2:1, 21; 1 Cor 4:6; 6:1; 10:24, 29; 14:17; Phil 2:4.

[132] see Wilckens, *Römer* III, 69-71; Schlier, *Römerbrief* 395.

[133] See Ridderbos, *Paul*, 282.

[134] See Sanders, *Jewish People*, 95, 115 n 4; Betz, *Galatians*, 274, and Käsemann, *Romans*, 361

taken from the Jesus tradition (cf Matt 22:39; Mark 12:31; Luke 10:27). "Any other commandment" could theoretically allow for cultic legislation but Paul, as elsewhere in Romans (e.g., 2:16-29) seems to have only the ethical part of the law in mind.[135]

Käsemann recognizes that Rom 13:8-10 refers to the Torah, but, as we have seen he holds that Paul does not believe in the validity of the law.[136] He, therefore, sees this text as a problem since there is no polemic against the Torah. To evade this problem he claims that Paul is not presenting his own argument but is pointing the community to a familiar tradition![137] However, even if Käsemann is correct about the tradition aspect, the context indicates that Paul agrees with the tradition.

5.4.5.3 *Romans 8:4*

In Rom 8:4 the just requirement (*dikaiōma* = singular) of the law is to be fulfilled (*plērōthę̄* = passive) in us (*en hymin*). The singular *dikaiōma* indicates the essential unity of the law's requirements;[138] it seems that the love commandment is in view, for according to Gal 5:14 and Rom 13:8-10 love is the fulfillment and summation of the law.[139] The passive "fulfilled" is not a divine passive[140] for the context is one of human responsibility and action, albeit action which is enabled by the Holy Spirit.

En hēmin has been taken in a local sense,[141] an instrumental sense,[142] or as both instrumental and local.[143] The context indicates human obedience and therefore an instrumental sense, but it also indicates the enablement of the Holy Spirit and therefore a local sense.[144]

Käsemann observes that v 4a is similar to Matt 5:17-20 and *dikaiōma tou nomou* means the legal claim as in 1:32 and *plēroun* means the keeping of a

---

against Hübner, *Ganze*, 248-256.

135 See Hübner, *Law*, 83-85, 100; Käsemann, *Romans*, 361; Bultmann, *Theology* I 341; Bläser, *Gesetz* 42-43 et. al.

136 See above 57.

137 Käsemann, *Romans*, 361.

138 See Cranfield, *Romans* I 384.

139 Cf Richard W. Thompson, "How is the Law Fulfilled in Us? An Interpretation of Rom 8:4," Louvain Studies 11 (1986) 31-40, 32-33.

140 Against Brendon Byrne, "Living out the Righteousness of God: The Contribution of Rom 6:1-8:13 to an Understanding of Paul's Ethical Presuppositions," CBQ 43 (1981) 557-581; see Thompson, *Fulfilled*, 34.

141 Käsemann, *Romans*, 219.

142 Schlier, *Römerbrief*, 243.

143 Wilckens, *Römer* II, 128 & n 525; Thompson, *Fulfilled*, 37.

144 See Thompson, *Fulfilled*, 36-40.

norm. As with his explanation of Rom 13:8-10 he evades the force of these observations by claiming that Paul is taking over an existing formula.[145] He does not explain, however, why Paul does not draw attention to his qualified support of the formula or disagreement with the formula; he does not explain why Paul does not simply omit the formula if he does not agree with it.

5.4.6 THE LAW OF CHRIST

We have seen in the previous section that the law is valid for the believer and that the believer is not *anomos theou* but *ennomos Christou* (1 Cor 9:21). At Gal 6:2 Paul further states that Christians should fulfill "the law of Christ" (*ton nomon tou Christou*). C. H. Dodd[146] has argued that Paul is referring to the teaching of the historical Jesus as binding upon the Christian. He notes that the phrase *ton nomon tou Christou*[147] is in the context of a series of moral injunctions in the ethical section of Galatians. The implication is that by obeying these injunctions, the Christian fulfills (*anapleroō*) the law of Christ; by acknowledging the binding character of such injunctions he is *ennomos Christou*. In Gal 6:1-5 the main theme is that of a Christian who falls into sin. The *pneumatikoi* are to restore him in a spirit of *prautēs* (one of the fruits of the Spirit in 5:23). They are to bear one another's *barē* and their own *phortion* (6:5); they are to restore the erring brother. Both of these injunctions have parallels in the Matthean tradition, the latter in Matt 18:15-20 and the former in Matt 23:4. The scribes and Pharisees, as teachers and pastors of the people, are criticized because they lay upon their people *phortia barea* which they will not touch with their finger.

Further support for the authoritative character of the teaching of Jesus is found in 1 Cor 7 and 9. That those who proclaim the gospel should get their living by the gospel, is something which the Lord commanded (*ho kyrios dietaxen*, 1 Cor 9:14). In 1 Cor 7:25 (cf 7:10) Paul denies that he has an *epitagē kyriou* (even though the word used there is *parangellō*). Paul, moreover, contrasts the *epitagē* of Christ with his own *gnōmē* even though he believes that *gnōmē* to be directed by the Spirit (7:25, 40); the *epitagē kyriou* remains uniquely authoritative.

---

145 Käsemann, *Romans*, 217-218. For a survey of other ways in which scholars have tried to evade the import that the law is to be obeyed in this verse see Ridderbos, *Paul*, 279-281.

146 C. H. Dodd, "ENNOMOS CHRISTOU," *Studia Paulina: In honorem Johannis de Zwaan septuagenarii* (eds. J. N. Sevenster and W. C. van Unnik. Haarlem; Erven F. Bohn, 1953), 96-110.

147 With regard to the grammatical considerations, Burton, *Galatians*, ad. loc., 392, observes that just as the law of Moses (Luke 2:23; Acts 13:37) is the law of God enunciated by Moses, here, "the law of Christ," is the law of God enunciated by Christ. By use of the term *tou Christou* in preference to *Iēsou* or even *Christou*, its authoritative character is suggested.

Dodd[148] notes that although the precepts in 1 Cor 7:10-11 and 9:14 are the only ones expressly attributed to "the Lord," there are other references to the sayings of Jesus. In Rom 14:10-23 Paul proceeds from general ethical maxims which he expects his readers to accept, i.e., "that nothing is unclean of itself" (v 14) and "that everything is clean" (v 20). His ground for saying this is *pepeismai en kyriǭ Iēsou.* The saying is reminiscent of Mark 7:18-19. The rhetorical question *sy de ti krineis ton adelphon* (Rom 14:10) is similar to Matt 18:10. In Matthew the maxim is in the context of the danger of scandalizing (*skandalizein*) a little one (18:6). Paul enjoins his readers not to put a *skandalon* in the way of the weak brother (Rom 14:23). In Mark the sequence of the sayings of "scandal" and "little ones" ends with *eirēneuete en allēlois* (9:50); this seems to be echoed in Rom 14:19. Dodd concludes that Rom 14 is full of reminiscences of what is accepted as the teaching of Jesus; the method followed is similar to that used in both 1 Cor 7:10-11 and the rabbinic writings (whereby halakah is based on the precepts cited from the Torah).[149] This thesis is doubtless correct in so far as torah is understood in terms of revelation and instruction.

5.5. CONCLUSION

Telos in Rom 10:4 means "end." Christ is the appointed end of the law in the sense that for the believer he brings the enslaving, condemning, and death-dealing effects of the law to their appointed end. The law remains God's law; the believer both looks to it for instruction and, led by the Spirit, is enabled to fulfill it. It is true that for Paul the halakah and the ceremonial law are not valid; but such questions lie beyond the horizon of the discussion in Rom 10:4.

---

[148] Dodd, ibid., 106-07.

[149] W. D. Davies, *Paul and Rabbinic Judaism* (1948. r.p. New York: Harper & Row, 1967), 138-41 adds numerous other examples. That Paul is dependent on the teaching of the historical Jesus has been given a thorough examination by David L. Dungan, *The Sayings of Jesus in the Churches of Paul* (Philadelphia: Fortress, 1971). Cf G. N. Stanton, *Jesus of Nazareth in New Testament Preaching* (SNTSMS 27; Cambridge: Cambridge University Press, 1974), 86-116. Further supporters of the view that the law of Christ refers to the authoritative words of Christ are A. Feuillet, "Loi de Dieu, loi du Christ et loi de l'Esprit d'après les épîtres pauliniennes. Les rapports de ces trois lois avec la Loi Mosaique," NovT 22 (1980) 29-65, 45-51; Birger Gerhardsson, *Memory and Manuscript: Oral Tradition and Written Transmission in Rabbinic Judaism and Early Christianity* (Lund: C. W. K. Gleerup, 1961), 310, 319; Heinz Schürmann, "'Das Gesetz des Christus' (Gal 6,2): Jesu Verhalten und Wort als letzgültige sittliche Norm nach Paulus," in *Neues Testament und Kirche: Für Rudolf Schnackenburg* (ed. Joachim Gnilka. Freiburg, Basel and Vienna: Herder, 1974) 282-300; and Wilckens, *Entwicklung*, 175-76.

CONCLUSION

The various emphases on the law in Paul's letters can be explained mainly by the situation in which he is writing, but in part by developments in his thinking. The passage of time, and the new and varied problems and situations Paul meanwhile faced among his churches, led him to reflect further on his theology. This does not mean that he has retracted what he said earlier.[1]

Romans develops themes with reference to the law which are absent from Galatians but anticipated in Corinthians.[2] It gives a full exposition of the righteousness of God,[3] relates the problem-solution of the law to the Adam-Christ typology,[4] and spells out the relationship between law, sin, condemnation, and death.[5] Romans also gives a more comprehensive and clear statement of themes which are already in Galatians: e.g., The law provokes sin, and God is directly involved in the process of making mankind disobedient (Rom 5:20; 11:32-36). The law is summed up in the commandment to love one's neighbor as oneself (Gal 5:14; Rom 13:8-10; = Lev 19:18). Salvation is all of God, all the glory belongs to God, and boasting is therefore excluded.[6]

In his letters Paul has faced varied situations. In writing to the Galatians he tends to downplay the law because of their attempt to be saved by means of it. In 1 Corinthians he stresses the law and moral values since he is facing an antinomian front. In Romans he gives a carefully balanced statement and assures his readers that he is not an antinomian.[7]

Paul's view of the law has similarities with Judaism. Both agree that the law originates with God and expresses the will of God, and that the doers of the law will be justified.[8] But Paul rejects the Jewish view that God gave the Mosaic law so that righteousness and life (or salvation) might be attained by means of the law.[9] The law was given so that it might be part of the dilemma of man.[10] The dilemma stems from the moral not cultic aspects of the law. God has consigned all to sin (Gal 3:22), to the law (Gal 3:23), and to disobedience (Rom 11:32). He has imprisoned us in order that He might have mercy on us (Rom 11:32), that we

---

[1] See above 45-55.

[2] See above 53-55.

[3] See above 124-127.

[4] See above 72-74, 121-123.

[5] See above 69-108.

[6] See above 75, 93-96, 124-127.

[7] See above 4-18, 53-55.

[8] See above 90-93.

[9] See above 90-93.

[10] See above 37-39.

might be justified by faith in Christ (Gal 3:22, 23, 24, 25, 26), and that God might receive the glory.

Paul's radical difference from the Jewish view stems from his starting point that salvation comes only through the atoning death and resurrection of Jesus and through the believer's participation in that death and resurrection. To attempt to attain righteousness and life by obedience to the law is to deny the necessity of the death and resurrection of Jesus as a saving event.

God gave the law with the requirement that it be obeyed. But sin as a personified power entices us to disobey. Since we are fallen (or *en sarki*) we are unable to obey the law (Rom 7:5, 7-25), sin gets its base of operations by means of the law, and we are taken captive to sin. In this situation the law can only enslave and condemn to eschatological death (see esp Rom 7:5).[11] The solution is God's saving action in the death and resurrection of Jesus.[12]

Christ died for us (e.g. 1 Cor 15:3-5; Rom 4:25; Gal 3:13), and we died with him. In his death Christ has died to sin and to the law. He defeated sin (Rom 8:3; 6:10), endured the curse of the law (Gal 3:13), and through his sacrificial death has met the requirement of the law. By dying with Christ we have died to sin (Rom 6) and the law (Rom 7:4-6; Gal 2:19); they are no longer master over us and the law can no longer enslave and condemn us.[13] By rising with Christ we have received righteousness and life, the eschatological righteousness and life which the law promised for those who obey the law.[14]

Paul gives a coherent total view of the law.[15] The negative and positive statements on the law stem from the distinction between the law as a means of salvation and as a way of life for the Christian. To those in Christ the law remains God's law; consequently, they look to the law for instruction (cf 1 Cor 9:8, 9; 14:21, 34), and empowered by the Spirit they obey it (Rom 8:4-9). They obey the law not to get saved, or to stay saved, but because they have been saved.[16]

[11] See above 69-108.

[12] See above 109-128.

[13] See above 70-71, 109-118.

[14] See above 118-128.

[15] See above 38-44.

[16] See above 98-99 n. 160; 119-120 n. 54.

BIBLIOGRAPHY

Aland, Kurt. et. al., eds. *The Greek New Testament*. 3rd ed. New York, London, Edinburgh, Amsterdam, Stuttgart: United Bible Societies, 1975.

Badenas, Robert. *Christ the End of the Law: Romans 10:4 in Pauline Perspective*. JSNT Supplement Series 10; Sheffield: JSOT, 1985.

Bammel, E. "Nomos Christou," in *Studia Evangelica* III. ed. F. L. Cross. Berlin; Akademie Verlag, 1964, 120-128.

Bandstra, Andrew John. *The Law and The Elements of The World: An Exegetical Study in Aspects of Paul's Teaching*. Kampen: J. H. Kok, 1964.

Banks, Robert. *Jesus and The Law in The Synoptic Tradition*. SNTSMS 28; Cambridge: Cambridge University Press, 1975.

—"The Eschatological Role of Law in Pre- and Post-Christian Jewish Thought," in *Reconciliation and Hope*. ed. Robert Banks. Grand Rapids: Eerdmans, 1974, 173-185.

Barrett, C. K. *From First Adam to Last: A Study in Pauline Theology*. New York: Scribner's, 1962.

—*The Epistle to the Romans*. HNTC; New York: Harper & Row, 1957.

—*The First Epistle to the Corinthians*. 2nd ed. BNTC; London: Black, 1971.

—*The Second Epistle to the Corinthians*. BNTC; London: Black, 1973.

Barth, Karl. *The Doctrine of God*. Vol. II of his *Church Dogmatics*. trans. G. W. Bromiley, et. al. Edinburgh: T. & T. Clark, 1957.

—*The Epistle to The Romans*. trans. Edwyn C. Hoskins (1933). r.p. New York: Oxford University Press, 1977.

Barth, Markus. "The Faith of the Messiah" HeyJ 10 (1969), 363-370.

—*Ephesians*. 2 Vols. AB; New York: Doubleday, 1974.

—"Die Stelle des Paulus zu Gesetz und Ordnung," EvT 33 (1976), 466-526.

Bauer, Walter. *A Greek-English Lexicon of the New Testament and Other Early Christian Literature*. Translated and adapted by William F. Arndt and F. Wilbur Gingrich. 2nd ed Revised and augmented by F. Wilbur Gingrich and Frederick W. Danker. Chicago: University of Chicago Press, 1979.

Beker, J. Christiaan. *Paul the Apostle: The Triumph of God in Life and Thought*. Philadelphia: Fortress, 1980.

Benoit, Pierre. *Exégèse et théologie* II. *La théologie de Saint Paul*. Paris: Cerf, 1961.

Berger, Klaus. "Abraham in den paulinischen Hauptbriefen," MTZ 17 (1966), 47-89.

Bertram, Georg. "aphormē," TDNT V, 472-474.

Bertram, Georg. "ergon," TDNT II, 635-652.

Betz, Hans Dieter. *Galatians: A Commentary on Paul's Letter to the Churches in Galatia*. Hermeneia. Philadelphia: Fortress, 1979.

Black, Matthew. *Romans*. NCB; London: Oliphants, 1973.

Blank, Josef. "Der Gespaltene Mensch: Zur Exegese vom Rom. 7, 7-25," BibLeb 9 (1968) 10-20.

Bläser, P. Peter. *Das Gesetz bei Paulus*. Münster: Aschendorff, 1941.

Blass, F. and A. Debrunner. *A Greek Grammar of The New Testament and Other Early Christian Literature*. Translated and edited by Robert W. Funk. Chicago: University of Chicago, 1961.

Bonnard, Pierre. *L' épître de Saint Paul aux Galates*. Neuchatel: Delachaux & Niestle S. A., 1953.

Bornkamm, Gunther. "Sin, Law, and Death," in Gunther Bornkamm, *Early Christian Experience*. trans. Paul Hammer. New York: Harper & Row, 1969.

—"Gesetz und Natur (Rom. 2, 14-16)." In *Studien zu Antike und Urchristentum. Gessamelte Aufsätze* II, 93-118. BEvT 28. Munich: Chr. Kaiser, 1963.

—"The Letter to the Romans as Paul's Last Will and Testament," r.p. in *The Romans Debate*. ed. Karl P. Donfried. Minneapolis: Augsburg, 1977, 17-31.

Borse, Udo. *Der Standort des Galaterbriefes*. BBB 41; Cologne: Hanstein, 1972.

Botterweck, G. Johannes; and Ringgren, Helmer. *Theological Dictionary of The Old Testament.* 5 Vols. Grand Rapids: Eerdmans, 1974-1986.

Brandenburger, Egon. *Fleisch und Geist: Paulus und die dualistische Weisheit.* WMANT; Neukirchen-Vluyn: Neukirchener Verlag, 1968.

Branick, Vincent P. "The Sinful Flesh of the Son of God (Rom 8:3): A Key Image of Pauline Theology," CBQ 47 (1985) 246-262.

Bratsiotis, N. P. "Bāśār," TDOT II, 313-332.

Braun, Herbert. "Römer 7,7-25 und das Selbstverständnis des Qumran-Frommen," ZTK 56 (1959), 1-18.

Brauch, Manfred T. "Perspectives on 'God's Righteousness' in Recent German Discussion," in E. P. Sanders, *Paul and Palestinian Judaism.* Philadelphia: Fortress, 1977, 523-42.

Bring, Ragnar. *Commentary on Galatians.* Philadelphia: Muhlenberg, 1961.

—*Christus und das Gesetz: Die Bedeutung des Gesetzes des Alten Testaments nach Paulus und sein Glauben an Christus.* Leiden: E. J. Brill, 1969.

—"Paul and the Old Testament: A Study of Election, Faith and Law in Paul, with Special Reference to Romans 9.30-10:30," ST 25 (1971) 21-60.

Brown, Colin (ed). *The New International Dictionary of New Testament Theology.* 3 Vols. Translated with additions and Corrections, from the German *Theologisches Begriffslexicon zum Neuen Testament.* eds. Lothar Coenen, Erich Beyreuther, and Hans Bietenard. Grand Rapids: Zondervan, 1975, 1976, 1978.

Bruce, F. F. *Commentary on Galatians.* NIGTC: Grand Rapids: Eerdmans, 1982.

—*1 and 2 Corinthians.* NCB; London: Oliphants, 1971.

—"The Curse of The Law," In *Paul and Paulinism: Essays in honour of C. K. Barrett.* ed. Morna D. Hooker and S. G. Wilson, 27-36. London: SPCK, 1982.

—*The Epistle of Paul To The Romans.* TNTC; London: Tyndale, 1963.

—"Paul And The Law of Moses," BJRL 57 (1975), 259-279.

—*Paul: Apostle of The Heart Set Free.* Grand Rapids: Eerdmans, 1977.

—"The Romans Debate-Continued," BJRL 64 (1982) 334-359.

Büchsel, Friedrich. "katakrinō," TDNT III, 951-52.

—"Katara," TDNT I, 449-451.

Buck, C. H. and Taylor, G. *Saint Paul: A Study of The Development of His Thought.* New York: Scribner's, 1969.

Bultmann, Rudolf. "Christ the End of the Law," in Rudolf Bultmann, *Essays Philosophical and Theological.* London: SCM, 1955, 36-66

—*Der Stil der paulinischen Predigt und die Kynischstoische Diatribe.* FRLANT; Göttingen: Vandenhoeck & Ruprecht, 1910.

—"Dikaiosynē Theou," JBL 83 (1964), 212-216.

—"Pisteuō," TDNT VI, 174-82, 197-228.

—*Theology of The New Testament.* 2 Vols. trans. Kendrick Grobel. 2 Vols. New York: Scribner's, 1951, 1955.

Burton, Ernest de Witt. *A Critical and Exegetical Commentary on the Epistle to the Galatians.* ICC; Edinburgh: T. & T. Clark, 1921.

Byrne, Brendon. "Living out the Righteousness of God: The Contribution of Rom 6:1-8:13 to an Understanding of Paul's Ethical Presuppositions," CBQ 43 (1981) 557-581.

Calvin, John. *Institutes of The Christian Religion.* 2 Vols. ed. John T. McNeill; Philadelphia: Westminster, 1960.

—*The Epistles of Paul the Apostle to the Galatians, Ephesians, Philippians and Colossians.* ed. D. W. Torrance and T. F. Torrance; Grand Rapids: Eerdmans, 1965.

Campbell, David. H. "The Identity of *egō* in Romans 7:7-25," *Studia Biblica III: Papers on Paul and Other New Testament Authors.* ed. E. A. Livingstone. JSNT Supplement Series 3; Sheffield: JSOT, 1980, 57-64.

Campbell, W. S. "Christ the End of the Law: Rom 10:4," *Studia Biblica III. Papers on Paul and Other New Testament Authors*. ed. E. A. Livingstone. JSNT Supplement Series 3; Sheffield, JSOT, 1980, 73-81.

—"Why Did Paul Write Romans?" ExpT 85 (1974), 264-269.

Clemen, Carl. *Die Chronologie der paulinischen Briefe aufs neue untersucht*. Halle, 1893.

Conzelmann, Hans. *History of Primitive Christianity*. trans. John E. Steely. Nashville: Abingdon, 1973.

—"Die Rechtfertigungslehre des Paulus: Theologie oder Anthropologie?," EvT 28 (1968), 389-404.

—*An Outline of the Theology of the New Testament*. trans. John Bowden. London: SCM, 1969.

Cosgrove, C. H. "The Mosaic Law Preaches Faith: A Study in Galatians 3," WTJ 41 (1978-79), 146-171.

Cranfield, C. E. B. "Some Notes on Romans 9:30-33," in *Jesus und Paulus: Festschrift für Werner Georg Kümmel zum 70. Geburtstag*. (eds.) E. Earle Ellis and Erich Grässer. Göttingen: Vandenhoeck & Ruprecht, 1975, 35-43

—"St. Paul and the Law," SJT 17 (1964), 42-68.

—*A Critical and Exegetical Commentary on the Epistle to the Romans*. 2 Vols. ICC; 6th ed.; Edinburgh: T. & T. Clark, 1975, 1979.

Dahl, N. A. "Two Notes on Romans 5," ST 5 (1951), 37-48.

Danker, F. W. "Romans V. 12. Sin under Law," NTS 14 (1968), 424-439.

Davies, R. E. "Christ in our Place - The Contribution of the Prepositions," TynBul 21 (1970), 81-90. Davies, W. D. *Paul and Rabbinic Judaism*. 1948. r.p. New York: Harper & Row, 1967.

Davies, W. D. "Paul and The Law: Reflections on Pitfalls in Interpretation," in M. D. Hooker and S. G. Wilson, *Paul and Paulinism, Essays in Honour of C. K. Barrett*. London: SPCK, 1982, 4-16.

—*Torah in The Messianic Age and/or the Age to Come*. JBL Monograph Series. Vol VII; Philadelphia: SBL, 1952.

Delling, Gerhard. "Stoicheion," TDNT VII, 670-87.

—"telos," TDNT VIII, 49-57.

Dodd, C. H. "ENNOMOS CHRISTOU," in J. N. Sevenster and W. C. van Unnik, eds., *Studia Paulina: In honorem Johannis de Zwaan septuagenarii*. ed. J. N. Sevenster and W. C. van Unnik. Haarlem; Erven F. Bohn, 1953,

—*The Epistle of Paul to the Romans*. r.p. London: Fontana Books, 1959.

—*The Bible and the Greeks*. London: Hodder & Stoughton, 1935.

Doeve, J. W. "Some Notes With Reference To TA LOGIA TOU THEOU in Rom III 2," in *Studia Paulina: In honorem Johannis de Zwaan septuagenarii*. eds., J. N. Sevenster and W. C. van Unnik. Haarlem; Erven F. Bohn, 1953, 111-123.

Donaldson, T. L. "The 'Curse of the Law' And the Inclusion of the Gentiles: Galatians 3:13-14," NTS 32 (1986) 94-112.

Donfried, Karl P. "False Presuppositions in the Study of Romans," r.p. in *The Romans Debate*. ed. Karl P. Donfried. Minneapolis: Augsburg, 1977, 120-148.

—"Justification and Last Judgement in Paul," ZNW 67 (1976) 90-110.

—(ed) *The Romans Debate*. Minneapolis: Augsburg, 1977.

Drane, John W. *Paul: Libertine or Legalist? A Study in the Theology of the Major Pauline Epistles*. London: SPCK, 1975.

—"Tradition, Law and Ethics in Pauline Theology," NovT 16 (1974), 167-178.

—"Why did Paul write Romans?" in *Pauline Studies: Essays Presented to F. F. Bruce on his 70th Birthday*. eds. Donald A. Hagner and Murray J. Harris. Grand Rapids: Eerdmans, 1980, 209-227.

Dungan, David L. *The Sayings of Jesus in the Churches of Paul*. Philadelphia: Fortress, 1971.

Dülmen, Andrea van. *Die Theologie Des Gesetzes by Paulus*. Stuttgart: Verlag Katholisches Bibelwerk, 1968.

Dunn, James D. G. *Baptism in The Holy Spirit*. SBT 2nd series 15; London: SCM, 1970.

—*Christology in The Making; A New Testament Inquiry Into the Origins of the Doctrine of the Incarnation*. Philadelphia: Westminster, 1980.

—*Jesus and The Spirit*. London: SCM, 1975.

—"Rom. 7, 14-25 in the Theology of Paul," TZ 31 (1975) 257-273.

Duncan, G. S. *The Epistle of Paul to the Galatians*. London: Hodder and Stoughton, 1934.

Dungan, David L. *The Sayings of Jesus in the Churches of Paul*. Philadelphia: Fortress, 1971.

Eckert, Jost. *Die urchristliche Verkündigung im Streit zwischen Paulus und seinem Gegnern nach dem Galaterbrief*. Biblische Untersuchung 6. Regensburg: Pustet, 1971.

Eichholz, Georg. *Die Theologie des Paulus im Umriss*. Neukirchen, Neukirchener Verlag, 1972.

Enslin, Morton Scott. *The Ethics of Paul*. New York: Harper & Brothers, 1930.

Esser, Hans-Helmut. "Nomos," NIDNTT I, 438-451.

Feuillet, A. "La Citation d'Habacuc II.4 et les huit premier Chapitres de L'épître aux Romains," NTS 6 (1959-60), 52-80.

—"Loi ancienne et Morale chrétienne d'après l'épître aux Romains," NRT 92 (1970), 785-805.

—"Loi de Dieu, loi du Christ et loi de l'Esprit d'après les Epîtres pauliniennes. Les rapports de ces trois lois avec la Loi Mosaique," NovT 22 (1980), 29-65.

Fitzmeyer, J. A. "Saint Paul and the Law," *The Jurist*, 27 (1967), 18-36.

Flückiger, Felix. "Die Werke des Gesetzes bei den Heiden," TZ 8 (1952), 17-42.

—"Christus des Gesetzes *telos*," TZ 11 (1955) 153-157;

Friedrich, G. "Das Gesetz des Glaubens Rom 3.27," TZ 10 (1954), 401-417.

Fuchs, Ernst. *Die Freiheit des Glaubens. Römer 5-8 ausgelegt*. BEvt, Vol. 14. Munich: Chr. Kaiser Verlag, 1949.

Fuller, Daniel P. "Paul and 'the Works of the Law'," WTJ 38 (1975), 28-42.

—*Gospel and Law: Contrast or Continuum?* Grand Rapids: Eerdmans, 1980.

Fung, Ronald Y. K. "The Impotence of the Law," in *Scripture, Tradition, and Interpretation: Essays Presented to Everett F. Harrison by His Students and Colleagues in Honor of His Seventy-fifth Birthday* eds. W. Ward Gasque and William Sanford La Sor. Grand Rapids: Eerdmans, 1978, 34-48.

Furnish, Victor Paul. *The Love Command in the New Testament*. London: SCM, 1972.

—*Theology and Ethics in Paul*. Nashville & New York; Abingdon, 1968.

Gale, H. M. *The Use of Analogy in the Letters of Paul*. Philadelphia: Westminster, 1964.

Gamble, Harry Jr. *The Textual History of the Letter to the Romans*. Grand Rapids: Eerdmans, 1977.

Gaston, Lloyd, "Paul and the Torah," In *Anti-Semitism and the Foundations of Christianity* ed. A. T. Davies, 48-71. New York: Paulist, 1979.

—"Works of Law as a Subjective Genitive," SR 13 (1984) 39-46.

Gerhardsson, Birger. *Memory and Manuscript: Oral Tradition and Written Transmission in Rabbinic Judaism and Early Christianity*. Lund: C. W. K. Gleerup, 1961.

Gifford, E. H. *The Epistle of Paul to The Romans*. London: Murray, 1886.

Grafe, Eduard. *Die Paulinische Lehre von Gesetz nach den vier Hauptbriefen*. Leipzig: Mohr (Siebeck), 1893.

Green, W. S. (ed.). *Approaches to Ancient Judaism* Vol. 2. Missoula, MT: Scholars Press, 1980.

Greidanus, Sidney. "The Universal Dimension of Law in the Hebrew Scriptures," SR (1985) 39-51.

Gundry, Robert H. "Grace, Works, and Staying Saved in Paul," Bib 66 (1985) 1-38.

—"Moral Frustration of Paul Before His Conversion: Sexual Lust in Romans 7:7-25" in *Pauline Studies: Essays Presented to F. F. Bruce on His 70th Birthday*. ed Donald A. Hagner and Murray J. Harris. Grand Rapids: Eerdmans, 1980, 228-245.

——*Sōma in Biblical Theology with Emphasis on Pauline Anthropology*. SNTSMS 29; Cambridge: Cambridge University Press, 1976.
Gutbrod, Walter, "nomos," TDNT IV, 1036-1085.
Guthrie, Donald. *Galatians*. NCB; London, Oliphants, 1969.
——*The Pastoral Epistles*. London: Tyndale, 1957.
——*New Testament Introduction: The Pauline Epistles*. Chicago: Inter-Varsity, 1963.
Hahn, Ferdinand. "Gesetzesverständnis im Römer- und Galaterbrief," ZNW 67 (1976) 29-63.
Harrisville, Roy, A. *Romans*. Minneapolis: Augsburg, 1980.
Haufe, Christoph. "Die Stellung des Paulus zum Gesetz," TLZ 91 (1966) 171-178.
——*Die Sittliche Rechtfertigungslehre des Paulus*. Halle (Salle), 1957.
Hayes, Richard B. *The Faith of Jesus Christ*. Chico, California: Scholars Press, 1983.
Hellbardt, Hans. "Christus, das *telos* des Gesetzes," EvT 3 (1936) 331-346.
Hofius, Otfried. "Das Gesetz des Mose und das Gesetz Christi," ZTK (1983) 262-283
Hooker, Morna D. "Paul and 'Covenantal Nomism'," In *Paul and Paulinism: Essays in Honour of C. K. Barrett* ed. Morna D. Hooker and S. G. Wilson, 57-66. London: SPCK, 1982.
Howard, George E. "Christ the End of the Law. The Meaning of Romans 10:4ff.," JBL 88 (1969), 331-337.
——"On the 'Faith of Christ'," HTR 60 (1967), 459-465.
——*Paul: Crisis in Galatia. A Study in Early Christian Theology*. SNTSMS 35; Cambridge: Cambridge University Press, 1979.
Hübner, Hans. "Das ganze und das eine Gesetz," KD 21 (1975), 239-256.
——"Das Gesetz als elementares Thema einer Biblischen Theologie," KD 22 (1976) 250-76.
——*Law in Paul's Thought*. trans. James C. G. Greig; ed. John Riches. Edinburgh: T. & T. Clark, 1984.
——"Gal 3,10 und die Herkunft des Paulus," KD 19 (1973), 215-231.
Huby, J. *Saint Paul, épître aux Romains*. ed. S. Lyonnet: Paris; Beuchesne, 1957.
Hultgren, Arland J. "The *Pistis Christou* Formulation in Paul," NovT 22 (1980) 249-263.
Jeremias, Joachim. "Pais Theou," TDNT V, 678-717.
Jervell, Jacob. "Die offenbarte und die verborgene Tora," ST 25 (1971) 90-108.
——"The Letter to Jerusalem," in *The Romans Debate*. ed. K. P. Donfried; Minneapolis: Augsburg, 1977, 61-74.
Jewett, Robert. "The Agitators and the Galatian Congregation," NTS 17 (1970-71), 198-212.
——*Paul's Anthropological Terms: A Study of Their Use in Conflict Settings*. Leiden: Brill, 1971.
Johnson, Luke Timothy. "Romans 3:21-26 and the Faith of Jesus," CBQ 44 (1982) 77-90.
Johnson, S. Lewis Jr. "Romans 5:12 - An Exercise in Exegesis and Theology," in *New Dimensions in New Testament Study*. eds Richard N. Longenecker and Merrill C. Tenney. Grand Rapids: Zondervan, 1974, 298-316.
Jüngel, Eberhard. "Das Gesetz zwischen Adam und Christus," ZTK 60 (1963), 42-74.
——*Paulus und Jesus. Eine Untersuchung zur Präzisierung der Frage nach dem Ursprung der Christologie*. Hermeneutische Untersuchungen zur Theologie; Tübingen: J. C. B. Mohr, 1962.
Kaiser, Walter C. Jr., "Leviticus 18:5 and Paul: Do this And You Shall Live (Eternally?)," JETS 14 (1971) 19-28.
Karris, Robert J. "Romans 14:1-15:13 and the Occasion of Romans," r.p. in in *The Romans Debate*. ed. K. P. Donfried; Minneapolis: Augsburg, 1977, 75-99.
Käsemann, Ernst. "'The Righteousness of God' in Paul," in Ernst Käsemann, *New Testament Questions of Today*. trans. W. J. Montague. London: SCM, 1969, 168-182.
——*Commentary On Romans*. Grand Rapids: Eerdmans, 1980.
Keck, Leander. *Paul and His Letters*. Philadelphia: Fortress, 1979.
——"The Law and 'The Law of Sin and Death' (Rom. 8:1-4): Reflections on the Spirit and Ethics in Paul," In *The Divine Helmsman: Studies on God's Control of Human Events. Presented to Lou H. Silbermann*, ed. J. L. Crenshaw and S. Sandmel, 41-57. New York: KTAV, 1980.

Kelly, J. N. D. *A Commentary on The Pastoral Epistles*. BNTC; London: A & C Black, 1963.

Kertelge, Karl. "Exegetische überlegungen zum Verständnis der paulinischen Anthropologie nach Römer 7," ZNW 62 (1971), 105-114.

—"Gesetz und Freiheit im Galaterbrief," NTS 30 (1985) 382-394.

—*Rechtfertigung bei Paulus. Studien zur Struktur und zum Bedeutungsgehalt des paulinischen Rechtfertigungsbegriffs*. Münster: Aschendorff, 1967.

Keuck, Werner. "Das 'Geistliche Gesetz': im Röm: 7, 14a in der Auslegung der griechischen Väter," in Helmut Feld and Josef Nolte (eds.) *Wort Gottes in der Zeit*. FS Karl Herman Schelkle. Düsseldorf: Patmos, 1973), 215-235.

—"Dienst des Geistes und des Fleisches", TQ 141 (1961), 257-280.

Kim, Seyoom, *The Origin of Paul's Gospel*. Grand Rapids: Eerdmans, 1982.

Kittel, Gerhard, and Friedrich, Gerhard, eds. *Theological Dictionary of the New Testament*. trans. Geoffrey W. Bromiley 10 vols. Grand Rapids: Eerdmans, 1964-1976.

—"Dogma," TDNT II, 230-32.

Klein, Günter. *Rekonstruktion und Interpretation. Gesammelte Aufsätze zum Neuen Testament*. BEvT; München: Chr. Kaiser Verlag, 1969.

—"Paul's Purpose in Writing The Epistle To The Romans," r.p. in *The Romans Debate*. ed. Karl P. Donfried. Minneapolis: Augsburg, 1977, 32-49.

Kleinknecht, H. "Nomos," TDNT IV, 1022-1035.

Knox, John. *The Ethic of Jesus in the Teaching of the Church. Its Authority and Its Relevance*. New York: Abingdon, 1961.

—*The Epistle To The Romans*. IB; New York: Abingdon, 1954.

Knox, W. L. *St. Paul and the Church of the Gentiles*. Cambridge: Cambridge University Press, 1939.

Kuhn, Karl Georg. "*Peirasmos - hamartia - sarx* im Neuen Testament und die damit zusammenhangenden Vorstellungen," ZTK 49 (1952), 200-222.

Kümmel, Werner Georg. *Römer 7 und die Bekehrung des Paulus*. Leipzig: J. C. Hinrichs, 1929.

—*Introduction to the New Testament*. trans. A. J. Mattil, Jr. London: SCM, 1966.

Kurzinger, Josef. "Der Schlüssel zum Verständnis von Rom 7," BZ 7 (1963), 270-274.

Kuss, Otto. "Nomos bei Paulus," MTZ 17 (1966), 173-227.

—*Der Römerbrief*. 3 Vols; Regensburg: Pustet, 1957-78.

Ladd, George Eldon. "Paul and the Law," in J. McDowell Richards, ed., *Soli Deo Gloria*. Festschrift: William Childs Robinson. Richmond: John Knox, 1968, 50-67.

Lagrange, M. J. *Saint Paul épître aux Galates*. Paris: J. Gabalda, 1950.

Lambrecht, Jan "Man before and without Christ: Romans 7 and Pauline Anthropology," *Louvain Studies* 5 (1974) 18-33.

Lang, Friedrich. "Gesetz und Bund Bei Paulus," in *Rechtfertigung: Festschrift für Ernst Käsemann zum 70 Geburtstag*. eds. Johannes Friedrich, Wolfgang Pohlmann, and Peter Stuhlmacher. Tübingen: Mohr (Siebeck), and Göttingen: Vandenhoeck & Ruprecht, 1976, 305-320.

Leenhardt, Franz J. *The Epistle to the Romans: A Commentary*. trans. Harold Knight. London: Lutterworth, 1961.

Liddell, H. G. and Scott, R. *A Greek-English Lexicon*. Revised and augmented by H. Stuart-Jones and R. McKenzie. 9th ed. Oxford: Clarendon, 1940.

Lietzmann, Hans. *An Die Römer*. HNT; 4th ed. Tübingen: Mohr (Siebeck), 1933.

Lightfoot, J. B. *The Epistle of Saint Paul to the Galatians*. 1865. Reprint. Grand Rapids: Zondervan, 1957.

Lindemann, Andreas. "Die Gerechtigkeit aus dem Gesetz: Ewägungen zur Auslegung und zur Textgeschichte von Römer 10 5," ZNW 73 (1982) 231-250.

Little, Joyce A. "Paul's Use of Analogy: A Structural Analysis of Romans 7:1-6," CBQ 46 (1984) 82-90.

Lohmeyer, Ernst. "Gesetzeswerke," ZNW 28 (1929), 177-209 r.p. in *Probleme paulinischer Theologie*. Darmstadt: Wissenschaftliche Buchgesellshaft, 1954, 33-74.

Lohse, Eduard. *Colossians and Philemon*. trans. William Poehlmann and Robert J. Karris. Hermeneia; Philadelphia: Fortress, 1971.

—"'Ho nomos tou pneumatos tēs zōēs', Exegetische Anmerkungen zu Röm 8,2." *Neues Testament und Christliche Existenz*. FS Herbert Braun. ed Hans Dieter Betz and Luise Schottroff; Tübingen: Mohr (Siebeck), 1973, 279-287.

Loisy, Alfred. *The Birth of the Christian Religion*. trans. L.P. Jacks; New Hyde Park, NY: University Books, 1962.

—*The Origins of The New Testament*, trans. L. P. Jacks. New Hyde Park, NY: University Books, 1962.

Lonergan, Bernard J. F. *Method in Theology*. New York: Herder and Herder, 1972.

Longenecker, Richard N. *Paul: Apostle of Liberty*. New York: Harper & Row, 1964.

—"The Obedience of Christ in The Theology of the Early Church," in *Reconciliation and Hope: New Testament Essays on Atonement and Eschatology Presented to L. L. Morris on his 60th Birthday*. ed. Robert Banks. Grand Rapids: Eerdmans, 1974, 142-152.

—"The Pedagogical Nature of the Law in Galatians 3:19-4:7," JETS 25 (1982) 53-61.

Lull, David J. *The Spirit in Galatia. Paul's Interpretation of Pneuma as a Divine Power*. Chico, Ca: SBL, 1980.

—"'The Law was our Pedagogue': A Study in Galatians 3:19-25," JBL 105 (1986), 481-498.

Luz, Ulrich. *Das Geschichtsverständnis Des Paulus*. BEvT; Munich: Chr. Kaiser Verlag, 1968.

—"Zum Aufbau von Röm. 1-8," TZ 25 (1969), 161-181.

Lyonnet, Stanislas, "L'Histoire du salut selon le chapitre vii de l'épître aux Romains," Bib 43 (1962) 117-151.

—"'Tu ne convoitera pas' (Rom.7)," in *Neutestamentica et Patristica: Eine Freundesgabe, Herrn Professor Dr. Oscar Cullmann zu seinem 60. Geburtstag überreicht*. NovT Sup 6; Leiden: Brill, 1962, 157-165.

—"Pauline Soteriology," in A. Robert and A. Feuillet, eds., *Introduction to the New Testament*. New York: Tournai, 1965, 820-865.

—"Questiones ad Rom. 7,7-13," VD 40 (1962), 163-183.

—"St Paul: Liberty and Law," *The Bridge*, 4 (1962), 229-251.

Manson, T. W. "St. Paul's Letter to the Romans - And Others," r.p. in *The Romans Debate*. ed. K. P. Donfried; Minneapolis: Augsburg, 1977, 1-16.

Martin, Brice L. Matthew and Paul on Christ and the Law: Compatible or Incompatible Theologies? Unpublished Ph. D. Dissertation. Hamilton, Ontario: McMaster University, 1977.

—"Paul on Christ and the Law," JETS 26 (1983) 271-282.

—"Some Reflections on the Identity of *egō* in Rom 7:14-25," SJT 34 (1981), 39-47.

—"Some Reflections on the Unity of the New Testament," SR 8 (1979) 143-152.

Marxsen, Willi "Der heteros nomos Röm 13,8," TZ 11 (1955) 230-237.

Maurer, Christian. *Die Gesetzeslehre des Paulus nach ihrem Ursprung und in ihrer Entfaltung dargelegt*. Zollikon-Zurich: Evangelischer Verlag, 1941.

MacGorman, H. W. "Problem Passages in Galatians," SWJT 15 (1972), 35-51.

McEleney, Neil J. "Conversion, Circumcision, and the Law," NTS 20 (1974), 319-41.

Metzger, Bruce M. *A Textual Commentary on The Greek New Testament*. London: United Bible Societies, 1971.

Meyer, Paul. "Roman 10:4 and the End of the Law," in *The Divine Helmsman: Studies on God's Control of Human Events*, ed. J. L. Crenshaw and S. Sandmel. New York: KTAV, 1980, 59-78.

Meyer, Rudolf. "Sarx," TDNT VII, 110-119.

Michel, Otto. *Der Brief an Die Römer*. KEK; 4th ed. Göttingen: Vandenhoeck & Ruprecht, 1966.

van der Minde, Hans-Jürgen. *Schrift und Tradition bei Paulus: Ihre Bedeutung und Funktion im Römerbrief.* Paderborner Theologische Studien, Bd. 3 Munich: Verlag Ferdinand Schöningh, 1976.

Minear, Paul S. *The Obedience of Faith*. SBT; London: SCM, 1971.

Mitton, C. L. "Romans vii Reconsidered," ExpT 65 (1954) 132-35.

Mohrlang, Roger, *Matthew and Paul: A Comparison of Ethical Perspectives*. SNTSMS 48; Cambridge: Cambridge University Press, 1984.

Moo, Douglas J. "Israel and Paul in Romans 7. 7-12," NTS 32 (1986) 122-135.

Moore, George Foot. *Judaism in The First Centuries of The Christian Era: The Age of the Tannaim*. 3 Vols. Cambridge: Harvard University Press. 1927, 1930.

Morris, Leon. "The Theme of Romans," in *Apostolic History and The Gospel: Biblical and Historical Essays presented to F. F. Bruce on His 60th Birthday*. eds. W. W. Gasque and Ralph P. Martin. Exeter: Paternoster, 1970, 249-263.

Moule, C. F. D. *The Epistles of Paul The Apostle to the Colossians and to Philemon*. CGTC; Cambridge: Cambridge University, 1957.

Moulton, J. H. and Milligan, G. *The Vocabulary of the Greek New Testament*. London: Hodder and Stoughton, 1930.

Müller, Christian. *Gottes Gerechtigkeit und Gottes Volk*. FRLANT 86; Göttingen, Vandenhoeck & Ruprecht, 1964.

Murray, John. *The Epistle to the Romans*. 2 Vols. NICNT; Grand Rapids: Eerdmans, 1958, 1965.

Mussner, Franz. "'Christus (ist) des Gesetzes Ende zur Gerechtigkeit fur jeden, der glaubt' (Rom. 10:4)," in *Paulus - Apostat oder Apostel*, ed. M. Barth, J. Blank, J. Bloch, F. Mussner, and R. J. Zwi Werblowsky. Regensburg: Pustet, 1977, 31-44.

—*Der Galaterbrief.* 3rd ed. Freiburg: Herder, 1977.

Nestle, Eberhard and Erwin, Kurt Aland et. al. (eds.), *Novum Testamentum Graece*. 26th ed.; Stuttgart: Deutsche Bibelstiftung, 1979.

Nygren, Anders. *Commentary on Romans*. trans. C. G. Rasmussen; Philadelphia: Fortress, 1949.

Oepke, Albrecht. *Der Brief des Paulus an die Galater*. THKNT; 3rd ed. Berlin: Evangelische, 1957.

—"mesitēs, mesiteuō," TDNT IV, 598-624.

O'Neil, J. C. *Paul's Letter to The Romans*. Baltimore: Penguin, 1975.

Ortkemper, Franz-Josef. *Das Kreuz in der Verkündigung des Apostles Paulus*. Stuttgart: Katholisches Bibelwerk, 1967.

Ostborn, Gunnar. *Tōrā in the Old Testament: A Systematic Study*. Lund: Hakan Ohlssons Botryckeri, 1945.

Osten-Sacken, Peter von der. "Die paulinische Verständnis des Gesetzes im Spannungsfeld von Eschatologie und Geschichte," EvT 37 (1977), 549-87.

—*Römer 8 als Beispiel paulinischer Soteriologie*. FRLANT 112; Göttingen, Vandenhoeck & Ruprecht, 1975.

Packer, James I. "The 'Wretched Man' of Romans 7," SE II, 1964, 621-627.

Percy, E. *Die Probleme der Kolosser und Epheserbriefe*. Lund: C. W. K. Gleerup, 1946.

Räisänen, Heikki. "Das 'Gesetz des Glaubens' (Rom. 3.27) und das 'Gesetz des Geistes' (Rom. 8.2)." NTS 26 (1980), 101-17.

—"Legalism and Salvation by the Law," in *Die paulinische Literatur und Theologie*, ed. S. Pederson, 63-83. Scandinavische Beitrage. Aarhus: Forlaget Aros, 1980.

—*Paul and the Law*. WUNT 29; Tübingen: Mohr (Siebeck), 1983.

—"Paul's Theological Difficulties with the Law," *Studia Biblica III: Papers on Paul and Other New Testament Authors*. ed. E. A. Livingstone. JSNT Supplement Series 3; Sheffield: JSOT, 1980, 301-320.

Reicke Bo. "Caesarea, Rome, and the Captivity Epistles," in *Apostolic History and the Gospel*. FS F. F. Bruce. eds. W. W. Gasque and Ralph P. Martin. Exeter: Paternoster, 1970, 277-286.

Reinhartz, Adele, "The Meaning of *nomos* in Philo's *Exposition of The Law*," SR 15 (1986), 337-345.

Rhyne, C. Thomas. *Faith Establishes The Law*. Chico, CA; Scholars Press, 1981.

—"Nomos dikaiosynēs and the meaning of Romans 10:4," CBQ 47 (1985) 486-499.

Ridderbos, Herman. *Paul: An Outline of His Theology*. trans. John Richard De Witt. Grand Rapids: Eerdmans, 1975.

—*The Epistle of Paul to the Churches of Galatia: The English Text with Introduction Exposition and Notes*. Grand Rapids: Eerdmans, 1953.

Riesenfeld, Harald "Peri," TDNT VI, 53-56.

Ritschl, Albrecht. *Die Entstehung der altkatholischen Kirche: Eine kirchen- und dogmengeschichte Monographie*, Bonn, 1850.

Robertson, A. T. *A Grammar of the Greek New Testament in the Light of Historical Research*. New York: George H. Doran, 1914.

Robinson, D. W. B. "Faith of Jesus Christ - A New Testament Debate," *The Reformed Theological Review*, 29 (1970), 71-81.

Robinson, John A. T. *The Body*. London: SCM, 1952.

—*Redating The New Testament*. London: SCM, 1976.

Roloff, Jürgen. *Das Neue Testament*. Neukirchener Arbeitsbücher; Neukirchen-Vluyn, 1977.

Sand, Alexander. *Der Begriff "Fleisch" in den paulinischen Hauptbriefen*. Regensburg: Pustet, 1967.

—"Gesetz und Freiheit. Vom Sinn des Pauluswortes: Christus, des Gesetzes Ende," TGl 61 (1971) 1-14.

Sanday, William, and Headlam, Arthur C. *A Critical and Exegetical Commentary on the Epistle to the Romans*. ICC; 5th ed. Edinburgh: T. & T. Clark, 1902.

Sanders, E. P. "On the Question of Fulfilling the Law in Paul and Rabbinic Judaism," in *Donum Gentilicium: New Testament Studies in Honour of David Daube*. eds. E. Bammel, C. K. Barrett, and W. D. Davies, 103-26. Oxford: Clarendon, 1978.

—"Patterns of Religion in Paul and Rabbinic Judaism: A Holistic Method of Comparison," HTR 66 (1973), 458-476.

—*Paul and Palestinian Judaism: A Comparison of Patterns of Religion*. Philadelphia: Fortress, 1977.

—*Paul, the Law, and the Jewish People*. Philadelphia: Fortress, 1983.

Sanders, J. A. "Torah and Christ," Int 20 (1975), 372-90.

Sandmel, Samuel. *The Genius of Paul: A Study in History*. r.p. Philadelphia: Fortress, 1979.

Schlier, Heinrich. *Der Brief an Die Galater*. KEK; Göttingen: Vandenhoeck & Ruprecht, 1965.

—*Der Römerbrief*. HTKNT; Freiburg: Herder, 1977.

Schmidt, Hans Wilhelm. *Der Brief des Paulus an die Römer*. THKNT; Berlin: Evangelische, 1963.

Schneider, E. E. "Finis Legis Christus," TZ 20 (1964) 410-422

Schoeps, H. J. *Paul: The Theology of the Apostle in the Light of Jewish History*. London: Lutterworth, 1961.

Schrage, Wolfgang. *Die konkreten Einzelgebote in der paulinischen Paränese: Ein Beitrag zur neutestamentlichen Ethik*. Gutersloh: Mohn, 1961.

—*Ethik des Neuen Testament*. Göttingen: Vandenhoeck & Ruprecht, 1982.

Schreiner, Thomas R. "Is Perfect Obedience To The Law Possible? A Re-examination of Galatians 3:10," JETS 27 (1984) 151-160.

Schrenk, Gottlob. "dikaiōma," TDNT II, 219-22.

—"dikaiōsis," TDNT II, 223-4.

—"Entolē," TDNT II, 545-556

Schürmann, Heinz. "'Das Gesetz des Christus' (Gal 6,2): Jesu Verhalten und Wort als letzgültige sittliche Norm nach Paulus," in *Neues Testament und Kirche: Für Rudolf Schnackenburg*. ed. Joachim Gnilka. Freiburg, Basel and Vienna: Herder, 1974, 282-300.

Schweitzer, Albert. *The Mysticism of Paul The Apostle*. trans. W. Montgomery. New York: Holt, 1931.

Schweizer, Eduard "Dying and Rising with Christ," NTS 14 (1967) 1-14.

—"Sarx," TDNT VII, 98-105, 108-110, 119-151.

—"Zur Herkunft der Präexistenzvorstellung bei Paulus," EvT 19 (1959), 65-70.

Segal, Alan F. "Covenant in Rabbinic Writings," SR 14 (1985) 53-62.

—"Torah and *nomos* in Recent Scholarly Discussion," SR 13 (1984), 19-27.

Sieffert, Friedrich. "Bemerkungen zum paulinischen Lehrbegriff, namentlich über das Verhaltnis des Galaterbriefs zum Römerbrief," JDTh, 14 (1869), 250-275.

—"Die Entwicklungslinie der paulinischen Gesetzeslehre nach der vier Hauptschriften des Apostels," *Theologische Studien*, Göttingen, 1897.

Snodgrass, Klyne R. "Justification by Grace - To The Doers: An Analysis of Romans 2 in the Theology of Paul," NTS 32 (1986) 72-93.

Spicq, Ceslaus *Agape in the New Testament*. trans. Sister Marie Aquinas McNamara : London: Herder & Herder, 1963.

Stalder, Kurt *Das Werk des Geistes in der Heiligung bei Paulus*. Zurich: EVZ-Verlag, 1962.

Stanton, G. N. *Jesus of Nazareth in New Testament Preaching*. SNTSMS 27; Cambridge: Cambridge University Press, 1974.

Stauffer, Ethelbert "Egō," TDNT II, 343-362.

Stendahl, Krister. "The Apostle Paul and the Introspective Conscience of the West," HTR 56 (1963), 199-215.

Stowers, Stanley Kent. *The Diatribe and Paul's Letter to the Romans*. Chico. CA: Scholars Press, 1981.

Strack, Hermann L. and Billerbeck, Paul. *Kommentar zum Neuen Testament aus Talmud und Midrash*. 6 Vols; Munich: Beck, 1922-1961.

Stuhlmacher, Peter. "'Das Ende des Gesetzes' über Ursprung und Ansatz der paulinische Theologie," ZTK 67 (1970), 14-39.

—"Das Gesetz als Thema biblischer Theologie," ZTK 75 (1978), 251-80.

Stuhlmacher, Peter. *Gerechtigkeit Gottes bei Paulus*. Göttingen: Vandenhoeck & Ruprecht, 1966.

—*Versohnung, Gesetz und Gerechtigkeit: Aufsätze zur biblischen Theologie*. Göttingen: Vandenhoeck & Ruprecht, 1981.

Suggs, M. Jack. "The Word is Near You: Romans 10:6-10 within the Purpose of the Letter," in W. R. Farmer, C. F. D. Moule, and R. R. Neibuhr, eds., *Christian History and Interpretation: Studies Presented to John Knox*. Cambridge: Cambridge University Press, 1967, 289-319.

Tannehill, Robert C. *Dying and Rising with Christ: A Study in Pauline Theology*. BZNW 32; Berlin: Töplemann, 1967.

Teeple, Howard M. *The Mosaic Eschatological Prophet*, Philadelphia: SBL, 1957.

Thisleton, Anthony C. "Flesh," NIDNTT I, 671-682.

Thompson, Richard W. "How is the Law Fulfilled in Us? An Interpretation of Rom 8:4," Louvain Studies 11 (1986) 31-40.

Traub, Helmut. "ouranos," TDNT V, 497-502, 509-536.

Turner, Nigel. *Syntax*. Vol III of James Hope Moulton, *A Grammar of New Testament Greek*. 4 Vols. Edinburgh: T. & T. Clark, 1963.

Tyson, Joseph B. "'Works of Law' in Galatians," JBL 92 (1973), 423-431.

Urbach, Ephraim E. *The Sages: Their Concepts and Beliefs*. 2 Vols. trans. Israel Abrahams. Jerusalem: Magnes, 1975.

Vanhoye, A. "Un médiateur des anges en Ga 3, 19-20," Bib 59 (1978), 403-11.

Wedderburn, A. J. M. "Adam in Paul's Letter to the Romans," in *Studia Biblica III: Papers on Paul and Other New Testament Authors*. ed. E. A. Livingstone. JSNT Supplement Series 3; Sheffield: JSOT, 1980, 413-430.

—"The Theological Structure of Romans V. 12," NTS 19 (1973), 339-354.

Weiser, Artur. "pisteuō," TDNT VI, 182-196.

Weiss, Herold. "The Law in the Epistle to the Colossians," CBQ 34 (1972), 294-314.

Westerholm, Stephen, "Torah, *nomos*, and law: A question of 'Meaning'," SR 15 (1986), 327-336.

Whiteley, D. E. H. *The Theology of St. Paul*. Philadelphia: Fortress, 1964.

Wilckens, Ulrich. "Die Bekehrung des Paulus als religionsgeschichtliches Problem," ZTK 56 (1959), 273-293.

—*Der Brief an die Römer*. 3 vols. EKKNT; Zurich: Benziger Verlag, 1978, 1980, 1982.

—*Rechtfertigung als Freiheit: Paulusstudien*. Neukirchen-Vluyn: Neukirchener Verlag, 1974.

—"Statements on the development of Paul's View of the Law," in M. D. Hooker and S. G. Wilson [eds.], *Paul and Paulinism: Essays in Honour of C. K. Barrett*. London: SPCK: 1982, 17-26.

—"Zur Entwicklung des paulinischen Gesetzesverständnises," NTS 28 (1982), 154-190.

Williams, Sam K. "The Righteousness of God in Romans," JBL 99 (1980) 241-290.

Wrede, W. *Paulus*. Halle, 1904. ET *Paul*. trans. E. Lumminis. London: Green, 1907.

Wright, N. T. "The Meaning of *peri hamartias* in Romans 8:3," in *Studia Biblica III: Papers on Paul and Other New Testament Authors*. ed. E. A. Livingstone. JSNT Supplement Series 3; Sheffield: JSOT, 1980, 453-459.

Wuellner, Wilhelm. "Toposforschung und Torahinterpretation bei Paulus und Jesus," NTS 24 (1978), 463-483.

Zahn, Theodor. *Der Brief des Paulus an die Galater*. Leipzig: Deichert, 1907.

—*Der Brief des Paulus an die Römer*. Leipzig: Deichert, 1910.

Ziesler, J. A. *The Meaning of Righteousness in Paul*. SNTSMS 20; Cambridge: Cambridge University Press, 1972.

INDEX OF AUTHORS

INDEX OF REFERENCES

I. THE OLD TESTAMENT

II. THE NEW TESTAMENT

III. JEWISH LITERATURE

INDEX OF SELECTED TOPICS